The Life, Times
and Treacherous Death of
JESSE JAMES

The Life, Times
and Treacherous Death of
JESSE JAMES

by FRANK TRIPLETT

With an Introduction and Notes by Joseph Snell

SAID TO BE AN AUTHENTIC
REPRINT OF THE LONG
SUPPRESSED, 1882
EDITION

TRUTH IS MORE INTERESTING THAN FICTION

LONGMEADOW
P R E S S

Copyright © 1970, by The Swallow Press Inc.

This 1992 edition published by Longmeadow Press,
201 High Ridge Road, Stamford, CT 06904. All
rights reserved. No part of this book may be reproduced
or utilized in any form or by any means, electronic
or mechanical, including photocopying, recording
or by any information storage and retrieval system,
without permission in writing from the Publisher.

This edition published by special arrangement
with William S. Konecky Associates

Jacket design by Irving Freeman

Library of Congress Cataloging-in-Publication Data

Triplett, Frank.
    The life, times, and treacherous death of Jesse James / by Frank
  Triplett : with an introduction and notes by Joseph Snell.
        p.   cm.
    Originally published: St. Louis : J.H. Chambers, 1882.
    Includes bibliographical references and index.
    ISBN 0-681-41649-1 : $7.98
    1. James. Jesse, 1847-1882.   2. Outlaws—West (U.S)—Biography.
  -History—1848-1950.   I. Title.
    [F594.J27T76   1992]
    354.'552'092—dc20
    [B]   92-9867
                                                               CIP

ISBN 0-681-41649-1

Printed in the U.S.A.

0 9 8 7 6 5 4 3 2 1

TABLE OF CONTENTS

———————

TABLE OF ILLUSTRATIONS

PHOTOGRAPHS

EDITOR'S INTRODUCTION

Jesse James is one of the best known badmen in America. It would be safe to say that more has been written about him than any other desperado, gunfighter, or outlaw in all the United States. His life has been the subject of more than half a hundred books, countless articles, several motion pictures, and at least one television series.

Almost from the very first he and his brother Frank have been pictured as good boys gone bad because of northern Missouri's refusal to accept them after their Civil War careers as Southern guerrillas and bushwhackers. Blame, too, was laid at the doorsteps of the railroads which were supposedly bleeding Missouri farmers dry. Jesse was the poor man's champion and fought the good fight by robbing, wrecking, and pillaging railroad property. The Pinkertons were at fault too, for, after all, they threw the bomb which killed Jesse's half brother, Archie Samuel, and maimed his mother Zerelda, though admittedly nearly a decade after the War had ended.

So there was nothing for poor Jesse to do but take the owl hoot trail and steal and kill and corrupt while wearing the mantle of America's Robin Hood. It didn't matter that thousands of other Confederates returned peacefully to Missouri, and other states, and lived successful, long lives with their former enemies. But it was the War that turned Jesse into an outlaw in spite of himself.

The canonization of Jesse and Frank James began in 1876 with the publication of the first book about their careers. Ground work had been laid for several years previously by their friend, John N. Edwards, who had been at one time editor of the Kansas City *Times* and had allowed the boys considerable column space to defend themselves against charges of corruption. From time to time Edwards championed their cause in the paper, picturing them as innocents who were wrongly blamed or who had been driven to a life of crime.

Nearly all the early biographies of the Jameses support the thesis of a Civil-War-engendered career of crime by citing robberies directly following that conflict. Perhaps Jesse and Frank did commit robberies in those early post-War years, but if they did they kept themselves pretty well disguised. Through research in local Missouri newspapers, the earliest date historians have been able to assign to the James boys as possible criminal suspects is 1869, shortly after the robbery of the Gallatin bank on December 7. From the tone of the Gallatin *North Missourian*, December 16, and Liberty *Tribune*, December 17, the James boys were not well known. The *North Missourian* merely stated that the suspects were "two brothers by the name of James." The *Tribune*, which was near the Jameses' home ground, cited them as "noted bushwhackers during the war . . . [who] were regarded as desperate men." No mention of any previous suspicions was made. At any rate the War was nearly five years ended before we can be sure the Jameses turned outlaws.

If no one knew Jesse James then, they did by the next summer; for in spite of the fact that he and Frank had fired at Clay county Deputy Sheriff John S. Thomason, who was attempting to arrest them for the Gallatin robbery, Jesse vehemently denied his guilt in letters to the editor of the Kansas City *Times;* these were republished in the Liberty *Tribune* on July 15 and 22, 1870.

From then on the James brothers were fair game for all crimes committed in western Missouri. In no time their names were household words and by the middle of the decade they were the partial subjects of Augustus C. Appler's *The Guerrillas of the West; or the Life, Character, and Daring Exploits of the Younger Brothers* (St. Louis, Eureka Publishing Co., 1876). Next year John N. Edwards published his *Noted Guerrillas, or the Warfare of the Border* (St. Louis, Bryan, Brand & Co., 1877) in which the James boys were gently caressed.

Before Jesse's death in April, 1882, at least two more James brothers books were written. Both books continued the mythmaking and spawned many fictitious episodes which have since been handed down from generation to generation of biographers. One of these books, written by Joseph A. Dacus, was copyrighted in 1879 but bears the publication date of 1880. It was called *Life and Adventures of Frank and Jesse James and the Younger Brothers, the Noted Western Outlaws* and was published in St. Louis by N. D. Thompson & Co. The other was J. W. Buel's *The Border Outlaws*, published in 1881 by the St. Louis firm of Dan. Linahan & Co.; the version I have seen also contains Buel's *The Border Bandits* and carries the story up through Jesse's assassination. The dual-volume edition is dated 1882; published by Linahan & Co., it contains the two titles by Buel bound as one volume with continuous pagination.

By the time of Jesse's murder, therefore, the James boys were already well on their way to becoming legendary characters and their "stature" was such that Bob Ford's shooting served as a starting gun in a race among publishers to become the earliest out with authentic lives of the notorious Missouri outlaws.

Perhaps the first of these was Jacob Spencer's *The Life and Career of Frank and Jesse James* which was written by the editor of the St. Joseph *News* in less than a week after Jesse's death. A little slower in production, but fast nevertheless, was Frank Triplett's *The Life, Times and Treacherous Death of Jesse James*. Seven weeks after the slaying, the Triplett book was on the market. It boasted one advantage over the other biographies which were assailing the market—official sanction from both Jesse's wife and his mother.

As the reader of this present volume will see, the original publisher included copies of letters signed by Mrs. James, authorizing the edition and acknowledging assistance in its preparation; and a copy of a "receipt for royalty advanced" signed by Mrs. James and Mrs. Samuel.[1]

---

[1] Photoengraving was not in use as early as 1882; therefore, Chambers & Co. could not reproduce any signed documents in precise facsimile. Obviously they did not even attempt a close facsimile, except in the signatures. The present reprint edition does reproduce the original publisher's "Authority to Publish" pages in facsimile. It can be seen that the format of all four documents is the same, whereas the format of each of the original documents (letters, likely handwritten; and a receipt, possibly handwritten, at least in part) must have been different. Also, note that Mrs. Jesse James' four signatures, for example, appear to be identical. This could only be one work of an engraver used four times; actual signatures written four separate times would differ slightly.

However, the path toward publication did not run smoothly. Before the book was in print, Mrs. James and Mrs. Samuel denied emphatically that they were a party to such authorization and assistance.

> My very soul revolts at the suggestion of lending my name or sanction to any publication of Jesse James' career, yet I have been represented as dictating such a book, and coming to St. Louis [the place of publication] to revise such matter as had already been prepared for the publication.
>
> Though I have frequently and publicly declared that I know absolutely nothing concerning any and all crimes charged to the commission of my husband, and that under no circumstances would I lend my name to any publication descriptive of his career, yet I am again required to reassert all that I have previously said, and to also particularize the cause for this repetition. A publisher in St. Louis, named J. H. Chambers, has circulated broadcast an assertion that he was having prepared by a writer named Frank Triplett a book on the lives and career of Frank and Jesse James, and that all the matter it would contain would be furnished by me. This statement is absolutely false, as I am not, never have been, and never will—because I cannot —furnish any facts criminating either Frank or Jesse James.[2]

The publisher was not to be defeated, however, and in the same issue of the St. Louis *Post-Dispatch* which carried the statement by Jesse's wife, Chambers & Co. declared that "persons entertaining any doubt as to the sources of our information or its full and reliable character can have all doubts removed by calling at our office, corner Third and Locust streets, and inspecting the contract, letters, receipts, etc., signed by Mrs. James and Mrs. Samuel."

Ramon Adams, one of the West's foremost bibliographers, states that Triplett's book was issued in "two editions, one thought to have been issued in the summer of 1882, the second in early November." The second was printed after Frank James surrendered and it contained an additional chapter on him. Both editions were suppressed, according to Adams. "Apparently [Missouri Governor Thomas T.] Crittenden did not become aware of the book for several months after its publication," he states, "but when he did, he caused all copies he could lay his hand on to be destroyed."[3]

---

[2] From a statement made by Mrs. James and printed in the St. Louis *Post-Dispatch*, May 1, 1882, and reprinted in Ramon F. Adams, *Burs Under the Saddle* (Norman, University of Oklahoma Press, 1964), p. 511.

[3] *Ibid.*, pp. 510-512.

Wright Howes states that Triplett's book was issued in three editions, the first in May of 1882, the second between June and November, and the third in November. Howes also says: "It is alleged that efforts were made to suppress this biography. The scarcity of all issues tends to confirm this."[4]

In spite of Mrs. James' and Mrs. Samuel's declaration that they had nothing to do with the book, they sued Chambers & Co. in 1884 for royalties, claiming that they were due $2,150 on a sale of 20,000 copies. The jury, however, found that only 4,500 copies had been sold and awarded the two ladies $942.[5]

Of the author, Frank Triplett, little is known. For a few years in the late 1870's and early 1880's he wrote several books with such titles as *Sketches of Western Adventure; Prospecting, Assaying and Mining; The Enchanted Isle; Bebe, A Norman Idyl; The Doctor's Daughter; Conquering the Wilderness; History . . . of Great American Crimes;* and *The Authorized Pictorial Lives of Stephen Grover Cleveland and Thomas Andrew Hendricks.* There is some suggestion that he had been a military man, for his title pages sometimes listed him as "Colonel" Frank Triplett. Perhaps the colonelcy was honorary, however, for a search of all rosters of Union and Confederate regular and volunteer officers failed to reveal his name. The *Army Register* for years before and after the Civil War likewise does not list him.

Triplett was a resident of St. Louis at least as early as 1879 where he and Albert P. Hall operated the firm of Triplett & Co., manufacturers' agents. By 1881 Triplett was general superintendent of the Silver Crescent Mining, Milling and Smelting Co. of St. Louis. In 1883 he listed himself in the city directory as an author, the only time he did so. In years after that, to 1891, he was listed as a mining engineer. But when and where Mr. Triplett was born, whom he married, when he died, and what he did with the major portion of his life is not known.

[4] Wright Howes, *U.S. Iana* (New York, R. R. Bowker, 1962), p. 591. Howes notes that the first edition has a frontispiece illustration of Jesse returning from a raid; the verso title page carries an illustration of Jesse fleeing after wrecking a train. The frontispiece illustration in the second edition is a bust of Jesse. The third edition has the added chapter on Frank. Howes' listing is correct.

[5] William A. Settle, Jr., *Jesse James Was His Name* (Columbia, University of Missouri Press, 1966), p. 194.

We are compelled to assume that for the most part writing was his avocation, and the mining industry his vocation. He was, however, a reasonably literate man and the biography of Jesse James abounds with quotations from Dickens and Shakespeare, none of which is attributed by name, but always by epithet (e.g., "Sam Weller's creator" or "the greatest mind of them all").

As an author, Triplett usually wrote massive volumes devoted principally to exciting subjects. He is not noted for his accuracy when it came to writing biography and one should keep that in mind when reading his *Jesse James*. Triplett must have been a diligent worker, for the production of the manuscript in only three weeks would be no small feat.[6] There is indication, however, that much of it was not original nor dictated by the two Zereldas. He "borrowed" a considerable portion of his manuscript from newspapers and other authors. This is particularly noticeable in that portion of the book which deals with Jesse's death and the period immediately afterwards. Triplett apparently clipped articles from the Kansas City *Times* and perhaps other newspapers, edited the stories slightly, and inserted them into his manuscript. With careful comparison one can find page after page of text which agrees completely, except for minor word and punctuation changes, with news stories from the *Times* of April, 1882.

Both mechanical and editorial flaws are common in the finished product and Triplett apologizes for them briefly in his Compiler's Epilogue:

> For more than a week from thirty to sixty pages of manuscript (making from twenty to forty printed pages) were furnished daily to the compositors. In this haste no time was given for any attempt at fine writing.

The most direct evidence of this hasty method of preparation comes in Chapter 46 when, under the appropriate heading of "An Error," Triplett corrects and amplifies his earlier description of the seige of Dr. Samuel's house.

---

[6] Some stories in Missouri during 1882 claimed that Governor Crittenden helped arrange Jesse's assassination and that knowledge of the arrangement had leaked out prior to Ford's deed. If there is any truth in these stories and if Triplett were aware of them before Jesse's death, one is tempted to wonder if perhaps he began his manuscript earlier and in fact devoted more than three weeks to its preparation.

Much of the motivation for the hasty preparation of the volume was commercial. The method of preparation bears a striking analogy to the quickly prepared biographies of national figures that have appeared in paperback editions shortly after their deaths over the past few years, or, again, the books on the Apollo 11 moonshot that appeared in July, 1969.

One problematic point is defining Triplett's exact relation to the book. Although I have referred to him as author, he calls himself "a compiler;" it is difficult to say how much work he actually did himself. His use of the title compiler may be a cover-up, used in order to sustain the fiction of Mrs. James' and Mrs. Samuel's supposed contribution. Or their contribution may have been genuine and Triplett legitimately considered himself a compiler. Or Triplett may have served as the senior member of a staff of writers and newspaper clippers hastily gathered together by the publisher for the purpose of expediting production. We just do not know.

There should, however, be no confusion as to the value of the Triplett book. While not primarily a source book of data, it does have a significant historical place in the Jesse James corpus. Furthermore, it is a masterpiece of the style that reached an even greater height *because* of its method of production. Triplett's complaint is worth quoting:

> A great deal of time, too, was lost, owing to the necessity that existed for making the notes from the dictation of parties, who had but little idea of literary composition, and who detailed the occurring events, not in regular chronological order, but as they happened to think of them. The Mosaic artist is said to use dozens of shades in his delicate art, but these shades are arranged in classes and in so orderly a manner that he knows just where to find any shade desired at any time.

With less orderly material, Triplett did what he could with it. The reader will be struck by the disorganization that comes over the book after the death of Jesse. What happened was quite simple, of course; Triplett had to use filler and a lot of it. But it shows just as clearly the power of James' personality and of Triplett's talent to order the book in its earlier portions. This book, no matter how flawed stylistically, can be read seriously and profitably by any student of literature.

Perhaps the governing feature of the Triplett biography is its subjectivity. This is one of the most, if not *the* most, pro-James books ever written, even outstripping efforts of John N. Edwards. Triplett castigates Governor Thomas T. Crittenden, Police Commissioner Henry H. Craig, Sheriff James H. Timberlake, the Pinkertons, and all who were on the side of the fence opposite Jesse and Frank James. On the other hand, he goes to great lengths to exonerate Jesse from certain robberies and gilds his pages with exotic passages to polish the armor of his tarnished knight.

Many times he includes whole chapters detailing certain robberies only to say later they were not committed by the Jameses and they had nothing to do with them. Perhaps he had a sincere intention to remove guilt from Jesse but one also has the feeling that much of his verbiage is merely padding, for if all the non-Jesse material were removed the book would be small indeed.

Just why Triplett was so vicious when writing about Crittenden is not known. By and large, for his role in the removal of Jesse, the governor was not condemned by the newspapers, though public opinion treated him less kindly. But Triplett libels the governor with nearly every mention, not only in relation to Jesse but in other facets of the governor's career, particularly his alleged murder of two persons during the Civil War. It is nearly impossible to keep from thinking that there was a prior, direct, and unpleasant relationship between the author and the governor which influenced the James narrative.

Today original copies of Frank Triplett's biography are extremely rare. Only nine copies are known to exist; this reprint was made from a copy of the first issue (according to Howes' classification). If Governor Crittenden and Frank James did join forces to destroy the books they were very successful. The fact remains, however, that the Missouri court ruled that at least 4,500 copies of the book were sold. Where are they now?

The original volume was well printed and bound for its day. It was printed letterpress on a flat natural vellum sheet and the engravings "made specially for this edition" were set at the facing pages of chapters with only three exceptions. The book was duodecimo with sixteen introductory pages and 416 pages of text. The most striking feature of the volume is the pictorial cloth covers. We have reproduced on this edition the cover illustration, which gives a different title from the title page and shows a gunfighter, presumably Jesse himself, with his pistols drawn. The original book spine, which is not herein reproduced, shows two six-shooters crossed over a rifle with black banner unfurling down. The cover was originally stamped in both gold and black on green cloth.

This version of *The Life, Times and Treacherous Death of Jesse James* is a reprint, not a facsimile. However, every effort has been made to preserve the mechanical errors that characterize the hasty typesetting of the original, and to follow the several versions of the book's title used. In the interest of precision, these various titles are here listed. The title page title is the longest; it is reprinted in facsimile elsewhere in this volume and runs as follows: *The Life, Times and Treacherous Death of Jesse James: The Only Correct and Authorized Edition. Giving Full Particulars of Each and Every Dark and Desperate Deed in the Career of This Most Noted Outlaw of Any Time or Nation. The Facts and Incidents contained in this Volume, were Dictated to Frank Triplett, by Mrs. Jesse James, Wife of the Bandit, and Mrs. Zerelda Samuel, His Mother.* The front cover of the volume bears the legend *Life and Times of Jesse & Frank James* [:] *Revenge.* The book spine offers the third version, *Life of Jesse & Frank James,* and includes the word *Triplett.* Also, we have the running heads throughout the book itself: *Life and Times of Jesse and Frank James.* Finally, there is the title, *The Life and Times of Jesse and Frank James, and Their Bands of Highwaymen,* which the publishers used in their salesmen's prospectus; while the prospectus was not a part of the book itself and is therefore not herein reproduced, it seemed appropriate to note this additional variation in the title.[7]

---

[7] The prospectus was a formidable volume in itself: approximately 120 pages in length, with cloth cover, stamped on the front as described above for the book. The prospectus contained the following from the complete book: title page, table of contents, publisher's preface, the opening page of each chapter plus one or more other pages from each chapter, some illustrations. Inside the front cover were pasted samples of the spines for the two editions. The last ten pages of the book were lined, blank pages for the salesman to write the names of subscribers. Preceding this was the sales page describing the book and announcing the two "editions"—cloth, $2.00; leather, $2.50.

Bracketed items in the text are editorial interpolations; on the two occasions when Triplett uses brackets (both times quoting a court reporting from Coroner's Inquest), we have altered them to parentheses, to prevent confusion. My footnotes are distinguished from Triplett's by the use of superior figures; they are intended to amplify rather than correct in most cases, for no one today can truthfully say that this is fact while this is fiction about the Jameses. No doubt some well-informed James gang buff will call me to task where I have erred. More power to him if his efforts unearth one more ray of honest light. I apologize in advance for errors contained in my editorial matter. They were committed in honest, if ill-informed, innocence.

In order to guide the serious student of the text we should provide some notions as to the original mechanical style of the book. Variations in the spelling of proper names are common. The noticeable case is the spelling of Dick Liddil's name. Depending on Triplett's original and borrowed sources, the spelling may be Little, Liddil, Liddel, or what have you. Even a final "s" appears on Mrs. Samuel's name occasionally.

Triplett employed the comma freely. I have only once clarified the punctuation of the original by the insertion of a semicolon. Triplett often uses spellings which today have lost their currency; for example, he spells stayed *staid*, scurrying *skurrying*, the noun canvas *canvass*, Dakota *Dacotah*. There is, of course, a certain point at which it becomes impossible to distinguish between the typographer's errors and Triplett's affectations of style; consider the word *corse,* which could either be an error for corpse or a genuine use of the archaic word for corpse. Similarly, Triplett refers to *Cerbeus;* this could be his mistake for Cerberus or the typesetter's. The expression *coign of vintage* is probably coign of vantage, good vantage point.

He lapses into newspaper style often, commonly abbreviating first names, as with *Ol.* for Oliver, *Arch.* for Archibald, and so on. Several of these abbreviations are, however, inscrutable today; any reader who can puzzle out *Peyt.* deserves to be congratulated. Triplett's unfamiliarity with Spanish is obvious in his references to *Paso Robles*, a city Jesse visits in California. He alternately uses lower case and upper case letters for directions of the compass and place designations (north-western, but North; Troth avenue, but Troost Street).

For general help in editing this book I have relied heavily on William A. Settle's *Jesse James Was His Name*, the finest biography of James yet published. In fact I would suggest that readers of this Triplett volume simultaneously peruse a copy of Dr. Settle's book. *Jesse James Was His Name* gives the most accurate description of James events available and the reader can check Settle against Triplett episode for episode and derive considerably more satisfaction from the 1882 book than he would otherwise.

I would like to express my appreciation to Edward Knowles, a Topeka journalist who happens to be, I believe, one of our most knowledgeable persons on the subject of Jesse James. He has helped me immeasurably, offering information, guidance, and an overall control that made my task much easier than it would have been otherwise. It is his plan, too, to someday publish a biography of Jesse James; perhaps this effort will give him the incentive to pursue his research.

JOSEPH W. SNELL
Kansas State Historical Society

THE LIFE, TIMES

AND TREACHEROUS DEATH

—OF—

JESSE JAMES.

THE ONLY CORRECT AND AUTHORIZED EDITION.

GIVING FULL PARTICULARS OF EACH AND EVERY DARK AND
DESPERATE DEED IN THE CAREER OF THIS
MOST NOTED OUTLAW OF ANY
TIME OR NATION.

The Facts and Incidents contained in this Volume, were Dictated

—TO—

FRANK TRIPLETT,

—BY—

MRS. JESSE JAMES, AND MRS. ZERELDA SAMUEL,

Wife of the Bandit. *His Mother.*

CONSEQUENTLY EVERY SECRET ACT — EVERY HITHERTO
UNKNOWN INCIDENT — EVERY CRIME AND
EVERY MOTIVE IS HEREIN
TRUTHFULLY
DISCLOSED.

TRUTH IS MORE INTERESTING THAN FICTION.

1882.
J. H. CHAMBERS & CO.,
CHICAGO, ILL. ST. LOUIS, MO. ATLANTA, GA.

PUBLISHERS'[1] PREFACE.

When we concluded to issue a "Life" of the most remarkable
outlaw that the world has ever seen, it was our intention to
produce the best work of the kind extant — all of the matter we
intended to be not only fresh, but well written, and in lieu of the
"blood and thunder" stories, usually found in works of this class,
we determined to give only the facts. The illustrations were made
expressly for this work, and are fresh, apposite, and in the highest
style of the engraver's art, many of them taken from photographs from life accessible only to ourselves.[2]

In order to arrive at inside facts we made arrangements to secure
them from the wife and mother of Jesse James, who, of course,
know more of his life than every other person on earth. These
we perfected and obtained a letter authorizing us to publish a Life
at their dictation, and this authorization was closed by a full
contract, by which Mrs. James and Mrs. Samuel were to receive
a royalty on each and every copy sold, in return for their having
furnished facts for this Life and for giving it their aid and sanction.

Unprincipled parties, seeing in our book the annihilation of
the sales of their so-called "Lives" of Jesse James, have not
scrupled to endeavor to delude the public mind in regard to our

[1]That is, the original publisher, J. H. Chambers & Co., 1882.

[2]The illustrations in this present reprinting were also made expressly for
this work, and are taken almost entirely from the original engravings. The
paintings are acrylic on boards and are reproduced in a duo-tone.

authority to issue this work; hence, we have given, on this and page sixteen,[3] letters, receipts, etc., with *fac simile* signatures of Mrs. James and Mrs. Samuel, the wife and mother of Jesse James, who have furnished the facts and accounts to us, thus enabling us to present wonderful incidents, strange episodes, and startling facts never before disclosed, and which were absolutely unattainable from any other sources. "Truth is stranger than fiction," and vastly more interesting; hence, the intelligent reader cannot but prefer this *true history* to the distorted myths and fables of the various meretricious, re-hashed publications purporting to be lives of the outlaw.

The public may rest assured that in this work they are receiving the facts as dictated by Mrs. James and Mrs. Samuel, and the electrotype proofs have been submitted to Mrs. James and by her approved.

J. H. CHAMBERS & CO.

AUTHORITY TO PUBLISH.

NEAR KEARNEY, MO., April 7.—We, the undersigned, Mrs. Zerelda Samuel, mother of Jesse W. James, and Mrs. Jesse James, his wife, hereby certify that the work entitled "The Life, Times and Treacherous Death of Jesse James," to be published by J. H. Chambers & Co., of St. Louis, is the only correct and authorized edition of his life.

We have furnished the facts from Jesse James' private memoranda and from our own knowledge of the occurrences, and we know them to be authentic.

Said work is compiled by Frank Triplett, at our dictation.

Zerelda Samuel

Mrs. Jesse James

---

[3]The material originally on "page sixteen" has been moved to this section in order to maintain continuity.

KANSAS CITY, April 15, 1882.—J. H. CHAMBERS & Co., St. Louis, Mo.: I have seen Mr. Frank Triplett, and have explained to him that the statement (in the Kansas City *Journal* of late date) that I would furnish no facts in regard to the life of my husband, Jesse James, was meant to indicate that I would not furnish them to the press for publication.

It was not meant to apply to my book, dictated to Mr. Triplett, and to be published by you.

In it I give all facts! Any further statements to the contrary, whether oral or written, should be regarded as the falsehoods of interested parties, who, by such a course, desire to make capital for the sale of their own so-called "Lives of Jesse James." I never authorized a single item for any other work than for the one to be published by you, nor do I intend to.

Respectfully,

Mrs. Jesse James

KANSAS CITY, April 21, 1882.—J. H. CHAMBERS & Co.: I received your letter to-day, and contents noted. I do *certainly* want a *written contract* for royalty, and it *must* be *done* before the books are *put on sale.* * * * All articles that may appear in newspapers, so-called *interviews* with me, are *false*, for I have not had an interview with any *newspaper reporter*, and furthermore I *do not intend* to have any. Hoping to hear from you soon, I am yours truly,

Mrs. Jesse James

The receipt for royalty advanced reads thus:

KEARNEY, MO., April 15.—Received of J. H. Chambers & Co. $50 (fifty dollars), being an advance on our royalty on "The Life and Times of Jesse James," which they are preparing for publication at our dictation.

Zerelda Samuel
Mrs. Jesse James

CONTENTS.

CONTENTS

"Come on, if You Mean Fight!"—Rush of the Guerrillas—Johnson's Death and Defeat—Panic-Stricken Flight—Deadly Pursuit—No Quarter—Five Chase Sixty—Number Killed—Anderson's Loss—Part of Jesse James in this Battle—A Practical Retort to Gen. Fiske's General Order: "No Quarter to Guerrillas."

CONTENTS

Contents

CONTENTS

CONTENTS

CONTENTS

CONTENTS

CONTENTS

Massacre—Oath of Allegiance—Dick Little's Anecdote—Cowardly Attack on a Steamer—Jesse's Musical Talent—The Escort—What Major Edwards Says—The Spoils Found—The Auction—John T. Samuel—An Error—Names for His Pets—Wild Bill Bluffed—Providential Interference—Jesse's Present to Ford—What Mrs. James Says—A Brother-in-Law—Cole Younger Talks—Was Frank James There?—The James Brothers Contrasted.

INTRODUCTION.

———

DURING the long and vindictive war between the States, there developed, on the side of the South, small bands of light cavalry, or, as they were almost universally called, guerrillas, or bushwhackers, such as the vicissitudes of warfare had never before produced. Fiercer than the Bedouin Arabs, confident as the Mamelukes, they united the infinite physical endurance of the Western Indian and the indomitable soul and mental qualities of the Anglo-Norman. Mounted on the finest steeds that money, or enterprise, could obtain, they swooped down upon their enemies with the eager velocity of the eagle, reckless of numbers, despising danger and death. Encumbered with no useless sabres or rifles, but belted round with revolvers, they struck the foe full in the front, and "fought it out" at close quarters. Riding like demons, a revolver in each hand, the bridle reins between their teeth, their onset was like the broadside of a seventy-four: the two first revolvers emptied were thrust back into the belt, and two more were drawn, and so on until the foe had fled, or the charges were all exhausted. Once I asked Bill Anderson this question: "But suppose you strike an enemy who will stand even until all of your revolvers are emptied, what then?" Said he, in his rather feminine voice: "It would be about time to think of running ourselves; but, by G——! they don't stand;" and he rode off humming "When This Cruel War Is Over."

That such cavalry as this is the most effective ever known, we have but to recall the battle at Centralia, Missouri, miscalled a massacre. Here Anderson, aided by the Jameses, Youngers, Todds, and other noted guerillas, overthrew a greatly superior force, commanded by an undoubtedly brave man, killing a larger number of men than they had in their own ranks; their numbers being two hundred and sixty-two, the enemy's dead two hundred and eighty-two. In this fight, each party marching under the sombre emblem of "no quarter," the guerrillas had three men killed, one mortally and two slightly wounded. Five of these men, whom war and circumstance had turned to human tigers, thirsting for blood, pursued sixty of their defeated enemies for six miles, leaving along their pathway fifty-two of this number, that, stricken by the angel of death, would never rise again until the sounding of the final trump.[1] Amongst these five pursuers were Jesse and Frank James.

This is but an instance of the guerrilla mode of fighting: first they sighted the enemy, and then, regardless of numbers or position, rushed upon him, terrible as the storm — resistless as the angel of death. From this school of rough riders graduated these men, who, denied a share in the general amnesty, hunted like wolves, a price upon their heads, and forced from the laws' protection, turned upon the society that had made them outlaws, and bitterly avenged themselves. The pupils of this school had not learned the meek lesson of returning good for evil, but were masters of the art of retaliation. Their ethics were not to turn the cheek for the second blow, but, in their wrath, to rend the smiter.

Growing to manhood, in martial camps, where he was best man who was best fighter; where the chief pre-eminence was the brain to plot revenge, and the quick eye and steady hand to carry it out, can we blame them that they would not deliver themselves into the hands of cruel and relentless enemies for a trial they knew would be but a mockery of justice? The men who had robbed their

---

[1]According to official Union army reports, which were undoubtedly biased, the guerrilla force numbered in excess of 600 men while that of the Union commander was only 150 to 200. There were 126 Union dead, seventeen of whom had been scalped. *The War of the Rebellion: A Compilation of the Official Records of the Union and Confederate Armies* (Washington, Government Printing Office, 1893), Series I, vol. 41, pt. 1, Reports, pp. 417, 440, 442.

families, burned their homes, and hung their relatives, they well knew would mix but little equity with stern justice (or, rather, cruelty!) in dealing with them. Some of them tried it; notably Jim Jackson. His fate was murder, after surrender, by a band of Home Guards.

With these examples before their eyes, the Jameses did not meekly deliver themselves "like lambs to the slaughter;" but since the law could not, or would not, protect them, why, they would defy it. Who can blame them? Would not you, reader, with the God-given instinct of self-preservation strong upon you, despise the truckling justice (or want of it, rather!) that oppressed the weak; and pandered to the strong? They had not found, as noble old Richelieu puts it—

> "For justice
> "All place a temple, and all season summer."

For them there was no safety under the broad aegis of their country's laws; for them, though peace had once again, like a gentle dove, brooded over the land, there was no peace; for them there waited only the hangman's halter and the felon's grave; or if, by any miracle, cleared from the perjured witness and the prejudiced judge, they might hourly expect the assassin's bullet from any hidden covert.

Under such circumstances, who of us all, with the manhood to defend himself, would hesitate a moment which course to pursue; resistance or submission? And what did resistance mean but a defiance of the authorities who constitute law, but alas! not always justice.

CHAPTER I.

OUTBREAK OF THE WAR.

Kearney—Dr. Reuben Samuel—Home of the James Brothers—Its Location—Their Childhood—Character—Their Father—His Ministry—Education—Culture—His Death in California—Their Mother—Her Marriage to Dr. Samuel—Civil War—The Home Guard—His Mode of Warfare—Who Was His Enemy—His Style of Argument—Recreation—Industry—His Treatment of Women and Children—Hanging of Dr. Samuel—His Wife's Devotion—Torture of Jesse James—Frank Forced from Home—Parting Threats.

SOME thirty miles out of Kansas City, on the Hannibal and St. Joseph Railroad, lies the quiet little hamlet of Kearney. Inhabited by a half rural population, it is the last spot upon which prescience would cast as the termination to some great tragedy, and no one who should pass it upon the railroad would be apt to predict of it, as Rousseau is said to have done of the almost equally unpretentious Island of Corsica: "I cannot but think that this place is destined to make a mighty stir in the world."

Three miles from Kearney, lying in a north-easterly direction and reached by a somewhat rough country road winding over hill and dale, now bending abruptly to the right or left, now following the gentle meanderings of some rippling stream, lies a sheltered and secluded farm house. A well-kept yard, surrounded by a neat plank fence, encloses the house, and everywhere there is a sense of neatness and unpretentious comfort. In front of the house is a stile, over which the footman can walk, or at which the horseman can dismount, and its companion, a long horse-rack, to which a dozen horses can be tied, showing that hospitality is the rule, and not the exception here. Trees and flowers adorn the yard, and the scent of roses and the song of birds mingle in its atmosphere. This is the home of Dr. Reuben Samuel, the step-father of the noted James boys, Jesse and Frank. Small in stature, kindly of face, no man has seen greater trouble, nor has a more affectionate, gentle disposition. But our story is of other members of this household. An old family Bible, whose somewhat worn and time-stained pages show that it is not only for ornament that it is kept, tells us that Robert James and Zerelda Cole were married December 28th, 1841, and that of this union there sprung Alexander F. James (Frank), who was born January 10th, 1843 (an erasure and substitution make it read 1844!); Jesse Woodson James, born September 5th, 1847; Susan Lavinia James, born November 25th, 1849; and Robert James, who lived but five days.[1] Robert James, at the time of his marriage, was a Baptist preacher, licensed in May, 1839. After settling in Clay county he visited California, and died there August 18th, 1850. Mrs. James, after remaining a widow for five years, married Dr. Reuben Samuel on the 25th September, 1855. From this marriage there resulted Sarah L. Samuel, born 26th December, 1858; John T. Samuel (now lying dangerously wounded at home!), born May 25th, 1861; Fannie Quantrell Samuel, born October 18th, 1863, and Archie Peyton Samuel, born July 26th, 1866, and murdered by Pinkerton's men with a bombshell on the night of January 26th, 1875. Besides the death of Robert and Archie, the Bible also records that of Jesse W. James, April 3d, 1882. The lives of the various members of the family flowed on in an even, quiet manner until the breaking out of the great civil war. Had this not occurred, who knows but that the subject of this sketch, following in the footsteps of his noble and talented father, might have made his mark in the pulpit? Genial, affectionate and lively, there was nothing in his childhood or early youth to foreshadow his adventurous career that was destined to become

[1] Robert R. James was born July 19 and died August 21, 1845. Homer Croy, *Jesse James Was My Neighbor* (New York, Duell, Sloan and Pearce, 1949), p. xi.; Settle, *Jesse James*, p. 7.

more thrilling than any romance, or that would point to an ending certainly as tragical as could well have been devised. Dr. Fitzgerald, a well known citizen of Clay county, a deeply read scholar and a refined gentleman, denies that Jesse's father was an ignorant, itinerant preacher, as the authors of some of his so-called lives have declared, but gives him the character not only of a sincere Christian, but also of a cultivated scholar. Who can say but that Jesse, too, under happier auspices and more smiling stars, might not have achieved a name that would have resounded in the annals of his country. Butler says:

"Fate steers—we do but row;"

and that grand master mind of all expresses the same idea in different words:

"There's a divinity doth shape our ends,
Rough-hew them how we may."

But it is useless to speculate on what might have been. The fierce cauldron of civil war had begun to boil, throwing, as do all violent convulsions, the scum and dregs of society to the surface of affairs. Especially was this the case in the Border States, when that class usually denominated by the negro "poor white trash," saw in this ebullition a chance to avenge the many fancied insults of their wealthier neighbors. The formation of Home Guards and Enrolled Militia enabled them to do this in a certain manner, and one not very dangerous; as these bands, unlike the true soldiers in the Federal armies, made the bulk of their war upon their neighbors' hog-pens and corn-cribs, with an occasional deviation against a helpless male non-combatant or women and children. Unlike the gallant soldiers who, beneath the stars and stripes, waged honorable warfare for principles they deemed essential to the preservation of a union loved of their forefathers and fought for by themselves, seeing in sectional disturbance only the chance for rapine and plunder, not the sad spectacle of a nation almost in its death agony, they were brutal and intolerant to the last degree. He who differed with them was "a d—d rebel;" he who dared to assert his right to think for himself must be silenced.

Murder was their usual mode of argument; arson their recreation, and robbery their industry.

Their mode of warfare was unique. Ascertaining that all the combatants of some defenceless home were away, they would charge down upon the house, surround it, and begin a search for arms and the munitions of war. Woe unto the decrepid male, or, in his absence, the women and children, if some old, worn-out gun or pistol could be found. True it might be dangerous only to the one who would be venturesome enough to fire it off, and might have been preserved only as an heirloom, or merely from oversight. It makes no difference to them; here is the justification for pillage, arson or even worse.

To these gentry he who had wealth or culture was a rebel or disloyal; he who had accumulated property had committed the unpardonable sin; hence an early persecution of Dr. Samuel and his family began, which forced Frank, the elder of the boys, first into the "brush" for safety, next into the guerrilla band for revenge. In 1861 Jesse, slight in figure, young in years, and almost girlish in face, remained at home attending to his duties on the farm, peaceable and desiring peace. He hoped that those who had forced Frank into the war might overlook one who was a mere child, but subsequent events showed that he had greatly over-rated their magnanimity. One day, soon after the Plattsburg raid, the house of Dr. Samuel was surrounded by seventy-five "home guards," under command of Lieutenants Culver and Younger. They burst into the house, seized Dr. Samuel, and after trying to extort money and information from him, took him to the woods, hung him twice, letting him down after each time; but this *heroic* treatment failing to accomplish the desired purpose, they hung him once more, this time allowing him to remain suspended. At the time the doctor was being thus treated, one of these *brave soldiers* (?) was employed in brutally insulting his wife. Catching her by her sleeve, he tore it from her dress; then taking her by the shoulder he threw her across the room, tearing her dress almost off, and causing her to strike violently against the wall, and all of this when she was soon to become a mother. Still others of these "home guards" had gone to the field after Jesse. Taking him from the plow, they drove him before them, he on foot, they on horses, lashing him with his plow lines and beating him with their bayonets. His mother begged on bended knees to spare her boy; but not until they had exhausted their strength, as well as their malice, did they cease. Then they left, threatening still worse treatment on their next visit. Mrs. Samuel hastened to the wood, cut down her husband, and by tender and unremitting nursing fanned the feeble, lingering spirit of vitality back to life again.

On the next visit they had threatened what they would do. To Jesse their next visit was harmless: they had waked into full life and furious passion the sleeping lion in his nature, and he had gone forth to join with Frank in the search for vengeance. Emerson says that:

"Nothing is given; everything is sold. The arrows given by Achilles to Paris caused the former's death, and that by the belt that Hector had given to Achilles was his body dragged around the walls of Troy."

These may not be the exact words, but they convey the idea, and so each stroke of the plow lines upon the delicate body of the boy, still scarce more than a child, might have represented the number of the hecatomb of victims that fell beneath his shots. These strokes found him a boy; they left him a man—no, not a man, but a tiger with a fiercer thirst for human gore than the mad man-slayer of the Indian jungles. Foremost in every battle, in which the swift riding bands of the guerrillas participated, was Jesse James. Riding like a centaur, a dead shot with either hand, he excited the admiration and critical comment even of Bill Anderson, who might truly be called a connoisseur in human slaughter. Always singling out the most prominent enemy, he rode against him like an avenging Nemesis, and as the tide of battle swept along, he was ever seen upon its foremost crest. The avalanche bore not more surely death and destruction in its thundering crash, than did the mad, resistless charge of the guerrilla. It paused for no consideration, it was wise in its madness, for no enemy ever stood before the desperation of its onward whirl. It struck alike the iron veteran and the trembling, skulking militiaman, and their lines melted like snow beneath a summer sun. It was reckless, desperate bravery gone mad; and it excelled the ordinary bravery of the trained soldier, as much as bravery itself excels cold cowardice. The man whose nerves were not of triple steel left the guerrilla band for the quiet and comparative safety of the regular armies. He who could not

"Look on death with smiling lips"

tarried not long with these Anglo-Norman Comanches. To Jesse James there was something congenial in this wild life of blood and battle. He courted danger as most youths do their mistresses, and toyed with the Delilah of ambush and attack. In a few days after joining Quantrell,[2] he and Frank fought in that desperate fray against the Ninth Kansas Cavalry at Kansas City, seventy against hundreds. The guerrillas almost annihilated their foe. After this there were skirmishes innumerable, in all of which, though greatly outnumbered, Quantrell was ever victorious. It was a "war to the knife, the knife to the hilt." The federal commanders of departments, despairing of ever whipping or capturing these jungle tigers, who carried death in both hands, early in 1862 began to issue their proclamations of "No quarter to guerrillas." But this was a game that two could play at, as witness Bill Anderson's practical reply (in deeds not words) to Sunday-school Gen'l Fiske's blood-thirsty edict when he met Johnson at Centralia.

[2]Triplett uses a spelling common for the times. Actually the name was William Clarke Quantrill.

CHAPTER II.

THE SACK OF LAWRENCE.

Quantrell—Todd—The Youngers—Gathering of Guerrillas—The Midnight
Council—The Vote—Quantrell's Decision—General Deliberation—Onward
March—They Enter Kansas—Their Guides—Lawrence in Sight—The Guer-
rilla Charge—War to the Knife—Flight of Jim Lane—Sack of the City—
Given to the Flames—Gathering of the Militia—The Retreat—Its Horrors
—Surrounded—Battle at the Barn—Stand at Lone Jack—Cut off—The
Charge—Its Success—The Last Stand—Final Charge—Disbandment—
Safety.

IT had been determined amongst Quantrell, the Youngers, Todd,
and other leaders that Lawrence, Kansas, the home of Jim
Lane; Lawrence, the rendezvous of "red-leg" and "jay-hawker"
who brought here the plunder wrung from the women and children
of Missouri, should suffer next in turn. This expedition was not
lightly undertaken nor its dangers underestimated. Quantrell well
knew that his every move was watched by the Federal soldiery and
spies, and he realized that even though he might make his spring
like a mad lion upon the doomed town, yet his retreat would
be through the gathering hosts of red-legs, jay-hawkers, militia and
U.S. soldiers. None of these dangers were hidden from his followers, but at the council held 'neath the summer skies all were called
on to give their votes and opinions pro and con in regard to the
attack. When the Jameses, Youngers, and other leaders had voted
unanimously for the attack, the rank and file were called up and
their opinions solicited. They were given in one word, "Forward!"

On the 19th day of August, 1863, they commenced their march, not a man having refused to accompany the band on its desperate mission. Crossing into Kansas at or near an insignificant town called Aubrey, in Johnson country, he secured guides and marched between Olathe and Spring Hill, thence through Franklin county. Camping on Cole creek about eight miles from Lawrence over night, they came in sight of that doomed city early on the morning of August 21st, 1863. It was just after sunrise when the inhabitants heard what was new to ears in Kansas, the guerrilla yell. Charging upon the town like the resistless waves of the sea, his two hundred followers struck Lawrence with fire, steel and shot. Woe to the jayhawkers who lay dreaming of easy victories over helpless women and children! woe to those who, though foes, were honorable foes, fighting only men in a manly way! Woe to town and men! The tiger is upon you and none may curb his fury. The close of that day saw Lawrence a smoking ruin, filled with dead men and homeless women and children. Jim Lane, the chief object of this attack, which was to retaliate for his pillage and burning of Osceola, Mo., escaped. Crawling on hands and knees through the mud and slop of ditches; he hid in a corn-field, and was thus saved, to die by his own hand at last. In this attack Jesse James is said to have killed thirty men, thus running his score up to this time about one hundred; Frank killed thirty-five.

Now began the retreat. Harassed on every side, Quantrell fled as flies the lion, turning often to rend and slay. At Black Jack, some fifteen miles from Lawrence, the guerrillas took shelter in a large barn and made a stand. This was done more to recruit their worn-out horses than to cover themselves from the foe that swarmed on every side. The Kansans made a number of bold assaults, but it was child's play for the guerrilla to repel them; still they were losing heavily in horses, and Quantrell realized that it was necessary to make some bold move to brush his enemies from his front, so that he might escape. What should it be? The old heroic remedy; one of their resistless charges, that shall incline the militia to fight, if fight they would, at a respectful distance. It was made, and in a single dash thirty-two of the militia are left lying dead, their comrades scattered in a panic.[1] It is no time, however, to follow up a flying foe, for thousands of others are gathering on flank, in rear and front. Every avenue of escape seems closed. Five thousand men encompass them, but still they turn and rend the pursuer. At Spring Hill they see their path completely blocked; three hundred fresh Kansans barricade their way. Caught at last! No, not quite. One wild, fierce yell and the enemy wait for no further parley, but break like a flock of sheep in disgraceful panic, scattered like chaff by a breath of air. This is but a reprieve, however, for bolder foes assail them on every side. At last they reach Shawnee in Johnson county, and here their last fierce stand is made. If they can but break through the line, they can disband, and safety lies before them in Missouri. Quantrell was a man of but few words; no mock heroic or sentimental speeches for him: "Boys," said he, "if we break that line, we will separate and thus baffle pursuit; if we don't, this is as good a place to die as another." A wild, fierce yell, a rush as of a gathering storm, and the line is broken. The men now disband, and all except twenty-one, left upon the tangled grass of Kansas prairies as food for the wolf and vulture, find safety in their old haunts.

[1] Quantrill had a brief skirmish with pursuing civilian recruits and federal soldiers at the farm of Josiah Fletcher about fifteen miles south of Lawrence. There was no loss of life as stated here. Mary P. Clark Collection, manuscript division, Kansas State Historical Society; William Elsey Connelley, *Quantrill and the Border Wars* (Cedar Rapids, Iowa, The Torch Press, 1910), p. 400; Albert Castel, *A Frontier State at War: Kansas, 1861-1865* (Ithaca, Cornell University Press, 1958), p. 134.

One of the earliest known photographs of Jesse James, at age 17, in 1864.

CHAPTER III.

PROMOTED.

The Rest—Guerrillas Re-assemble—Divided into Squads—Quantrell's Judgement of Jesse James—He is Given a Command—His Maiden Effort as a Commander—His Plans—The Foe Surprised—An Utter Rout—Terrific Slaughter—The Foe Annihilated—His Further Career.

AFTER a few weeks' rest Quantrell divided out his band into squads of twenty-five or thirty, and to Jesse James, who had been tried as by fire, was given command of one of these. His maiden effort as a commander was made near Blue Springs. Captain Ramsom, with about one hundred Federal Cavalry, was on the march to Pleasant Hill, when Jesse ambushed him with his little squad of twenty-five guerrillas. The ambush was a perfect success; a storm of bullets poured into the Federal line, causing them to break in confusion, then came the whirlwind rush, accompanied by the death-shots dealt by either hand. Some idea may be formed of the terrible nature of the contest when it is known that not over twenty-five or thirty of the Federals escaped. On James' side one man was killed and three wounded, all slightly.

Uniting forces with his brother Frank, some six or eight days later, the two, with about fifty men, struck the command of Captain Blunt and his company of about eighty men. There were the usual accompaniments of the attack of this invincible light Cavalry; the rush, the yell, death shots at close quarters from revolvers in ambidextrous hands, and a fleeing foe. Blunt flew with a loss of half of his command.

Next came Lieutenant Nash's defeat near Warrensburg; then the annihilation of the garrison of Camden.

The next engagement in which Jesse participated was one in which the guerrillas met foemen worthy of their steel. The guerrillas under Todd struck a company of the 2d Colorado Cavalry under Captain Wagner. The 2d, as well as the 3rd Colorado, was composed of plainsmen, hunters, trappers, freighters and gamblers; men who had lived the life of the border until their nerves were like steel. They had the Indian's ferocity and the bull-dog pluck of the Anglo—Norman. These men were familiar with danger, scorned death and handled a revolver as a boy would a top. The sudden broil was to them no novelty, and a hand to hand encounter with pistol or knife was a matter of daily occurrence. Their resistance was desperate, and they stood like men, until Jesse James, raging in the fray like a demon of destruction, rushed at their Captain and sent a ball from his unerring pistol through his heart. This act caused a panic to spread through the hitherto firm ranks of the Colorado Cavalrymen, and breaking they, like all their predecessors, fled in the utmost consternation.

Jesse's next fight (at Harrisonville) was not so successful, the guerrillas being forced to retire, and at Flat Rock Ford on Grand River, shortly after, he was shot through the breast, a minnie ball tearing through his right lung. From this terrible injury, so great was his vitality and iron nerve, he recovered sufficiently in four weeks to again mount his horse, and in less than six weeks he reported for active service. But why enumerate here the deeds that in the palmy days of Greece would have made Jesse James a demigod? Is not the tale already told by abler pens? A few more incidents, and we are done with his adventures during the war, not one-half of which have we attempted to relate.

In the fall of 1864, Jesse determined to pay a visit to his home, although he well knew the dangers that beset every inch of his path. But "fortune favors the brave," and only one incident occurred to break the monotony of his journey. Coming one day suddenly upon three of the militia, he was commanded to halt; but not considering three militiamen any odds against one guerrilla, he drew his pistols, and in much less time than it has taken to recount it the three men lay weltering in their blood. No other adventure happening, he was soon safely at his home, warmly welcomed by a loving mother and kind friends. Two days' rest here was all he permitted himself, and again he rode away to join the gathering force for the grandest stroke the guerrillas ever made, save the sack and burning of Lawrence.

CHAPTER IV.

The Battle At Centralia.

Anderson Visits Centralia—The West-Bound Train—The Futile Struggle—
Twenty-four Soldiers Slain—Train Fired—Deport Burned—Construction
Train Destroyed—Guerrillas Retire—Singleton's Barn—Arrival of Major
Johnson—Vain, Glorious Boasts—Seeks the Enemy—The Advance Guard—
Ominous Signs—The Skirmish—Todd and Anderson—Johnson's Halt—
"Come On, if You Mean Fight!"—Rush of the Guerrillas—Johnson's Death
and Defeat—Panic-Stricken Flight—Deadly Pursuit—No Quarter—Five
Chase Sixty—Number Killed—Anderson's Loss—Part of Jesse James in
this Battle—A Practical Retort to Gen. Fiske's General Order: "No Quarter
to Guerrillas."

CENTRALIA lies in a high level prairie in Boone county, Missouri, and is the junction of the Boone county Branch of the
old North Mo. R.R. with the main line. On the 27th day of September, 1864, Bill Anderson moved into Centralia from his camp
at Singleton's, four miles to the south-east. He, as well as all of the
guerrillas, had been forced in self defense to adopt the black flag,
as none of their followers were ever spared when captured. Waiting in Centralia until eleven o'clock, he surprised a train westward
bound carrying, amongst other passengers, some Federal soldiers.
As the train halted, Anderson charged it, and was met by a wild
fire from those of the Federals who had muskets. It is a matter of
doubt whether Anderson would have spared any of these men,
but after their firing every one knew but too well what their fate
would be. A rapid fusilade from their revolvers, and in less than a
minute from the first shot Anderson was in undisputed possession of

the train. Ordering all of the passengers on to the platform, he separated the Federal soldiers from the citizens, classing with the former one unlucky civilian, who had taken a fancy to a Federal blouse. This work of separation completed, the work of death began, and soon twenty-four corpses dressed in blue were staring blankly at the autumn sky. The train was then fired, the engine's levers pulled wide open, and under a full head of steam she dashed away towards Sturgeon, eight miles distant. Next a construction train and the depot were given to the flames, and Anderson, having completed the work of destruction, warned the citizens not to bury the corpses, and returned to his rendezvous at Singleton's.[1]

Word was in some way conveyed to Mayor [Major] Johnson, a fighting man, in command of a battalion of over three hundred militia.[2] Johnson was at the time hunting Anderson. At the head of his column he, too, carried the sombre ensign, that neither asks nor renders quarter. There is no doubt that Maj. Johnson was a brave man, but there is also not the least doubt that he greatly underrated the fighting qualities of Anderson and his men. Upon the citizens requesting him to detail men to inter the corpses they had been forbidden to bury, he is said to have broken out: "Bury them, the d—d cowards! No—if they had fought like men they would not need burial!"

Again, when warned by the citizens not to risk a battle with Anderson when their numbers were so nearly equal (Major Johnson had three hundred or over, Anderson exactly two hundred and sixty-two), "Do you dare warn me against fighting equal num-

[1]Triplett's account of the Centralia massacre and its aftermath is at wide variance with available contemporary sources. The sole survivor of the massacre, Sgt. Thomas Goodman, First Regiment Engineers, Missouri Volunteers, wrote that the federal troops, twenty-seven in number, were all unarmed soldiers going home on discharge or furlough. "A True Narrative by Sergeant Thomas M. Goodman," manuscript division, Kansas State Historical Society.

[2]Maj. Albert V. E. Johnston, 39th Infantry, Missouri Volunteers. The unit was a regularly constituted regiment called to federal service just days before the fight. There is no basis for Triplett's later assertion that it was a guerrilla force.

bers," said the Major, "why I can give them three to one and whip them." Seeing how useless it was to remonstrate, the citizens desisted from further parley and saw the doomed men ride off to defeat and death. As the lion in his lair, or the tiger in his jungle, Todd and Anderson lay in ambush waiting for the gallant Major. Their only fear was that his heart might misgive him, and that he might turn from the fray and within the shelter of the block houses at Sturgeon balk them of their prey. Vain fear! Riding gaily on to the masked demon of death that silently awaited them, they talked loudly of what they intended doing to the "d—d Secesh" when they returned to Centralia. One and all seemed to have forgotten the quaint text in the "Book of books:" "Let him that putteth on his armor boast as he that taketh it off." The merry jest and echoing laugh went round, and the cavalcade looked and acted like a party going to a bridal, rather than men doomed by Atè to a fearful destruction. A small guard, thrown out in advance, had returned to the main body, reporting that Anderson had been to the barn, staying there long enough to rest and feed his men and horses. From the barn, so they reported, a broad trail had been made, leading to the woods beyond. Had Major Johnson been a frontiersman or one skilled in guerrilla warfare, this would have been ominous news; it would have shown him that they wanted to be followed. Riding on toward the wood, ten men suddenly showed themselves upon the crest of a long ridge about a mile distant. This line trotted slowly toward Johnson's command in open skirmishing order. Following some distance behind came Todd and Anderson in battle array. Johnson, too, was steadily advancing, no kind angel having suggested to him to turn and flee the wrath so soon to burst upon him. Here the Federal skirmishers opened fire with their muskets, doing no harm, and soon they and the advanced guard of the guerrillas were briskly engaged. As previously instructed, Thrailkill,[3] who commanded the guerrilla advance, ever foremost amongst whom were Jesse and Frank James, fell slowly back to the main column. Johnson's men, too easily elated, interpreted this

[3]Maj. John Thrailkill, regular unit unknown.

as a signal victory and dashed forward, anxious to exterminate the flying foe. When Thrailkill reached the main body, the guerrillas again formed into a line of men two deep, with double intervals between the files for the freer handling of arms and horses. Major Johnson also re-formed his disordered troops and called out to the advancing destroyers: "Come on, now, if you mean to fight."

It was a bold challenge, and boldly was it accepted. The September sun, golden and glorious, hung low in the west, and the cool hush of the evening pervaded all nature. It was like some soft sylvan idyl about to be transformed into the harsh burst of martial music.

The men of Todd and Anderson had looked well to bridle, girth and revolver; arms and accoutrements were perfect. For a moment all was still as death; song, jest and laugh were hushed to ominous silence, as they drew in their breath as one man—the next moment the very heavens seemed rent with a yell, as much more terrible than the Redman's as the vices and virtues of the Anglo-Norman exceed those of the Indian. Simultaneously there was a bound forward of every horse, and then began one of those mad, terrific rushes of the guerrilla, that can only be compared to the fury of the tempest, or the mad fall of the mountain torrent. The Federals fired one volley, then turned in panic stricken flight. In the lines where these terrible riders first struck them, there were seventy-five dead men, and twenty-five dead horses. Of the guerrillas three were killed, one was mortally and two were slightly wounded. This and two horses killed was the extent of their loss.

Some sixty of the Federals, prudent men, had in their foresight mounted their horses, the more swiftly to follow the foe they intended to annihilate. These sixty, in their flight, were followed by five of Anderson's men, prominent amongst them Frank and Jesse James. Of these sixty, fifty fell before they reached Sturgeon. Out of Johnson's three hundred men, only eighteen escaped, making the number killed just two hundred and eighty-two, or twenty men more than Todd and Anderson commanded in all.[4]

This fight has been called a massacre, though way so any fair minded man is puzzled to tell. Both parties were marching under the black flag, and the fate that the militiamen met would have been that of the guerrilla had the conditions of the fight been reversed. That this is true is proven by the fact that, long before Todd, Anderson and others were forced into this species of retaliation, every captured guerrilla was shot whenever and wherever taken. If necessary, numerous instances could be cited to prove this fact.

[4]Both Goodman's narrative and official reports state Johnston's force numbered less than 200 men while Anderson was estimated to have between 600 and 700 men. The official returns of the battle list two officers and 114 enlisted men killed, with two enlisted men wounded and six missing. Parts of Cos. A, G and H, 39th Infantry totaling 125 men engaged Anderson. Thirty-three men had been left at Centralia and of these fifteen were killed. The War of the Rebellion, Series I, vol. 41, pt. 1, pp. 417, 440-443.

CHAPTER V.

THE WAR CLOSES.

Further Adventures—Ambuscades—Surprises—Long Marches—Various Adventures—Fall of 1864—An Ambush—A Fight—Wounded—Crushed by his Horse—Rescued by Todd—Again in the Field—Jesse and Frank Separate—Jesse Goes to Texas—Returns to Missouri—Reach Lexington—Meet Major Rodgers—Fired Upon While Carrying Flag of Truce—Charge into a Regiment—Desperately Wounded—Recovers—Goes to Nebraska—Quantrell's Death—End of Jesse's War Record.

A FTER this combat, where tigers met men, we shall enter into no detailed account of Jesse's battles and adventures, but shall hasten on to his career after the close of the war. True his days were days of almost continuous battles, and his nights were filled with long marches and short bivouacs. His adventures exceeded those of the heroes of romance. In the fall of 1864 fortune seemed again to tire of guarding her favorite, and in an ambush and subsequent fight of a few against hundreds he again fell, wounded in the left side and arm. The fight surged desperately around him, but with an undaunted soul he fought on, lying crushed beneath his horse. A swooping charge of Todd's rescued him. A little rest, less nursing and this youth of iron nerves was again able to ride.

In November of 1864 he, his brother Frank and others of the guerrillas, seeing that their mission was about finished in Missouri, started for Texas, and here he and Frank separated; Frank going with his old leader, Quantrell, to Kentucky. On the route to Texas there was ambush after ambush; no time for the splendid pistol practice to grow rusty either by day or night; but at last they reached Sherman December 2nd. Here the guerrillas split into two detachments; some going into Western Texas; others under Arch. Clements returning to Missouri, Jesse James being one of the latter. Again begins the routine of marching and battling. Against skirmishes innumerable and ambushment everywhere, they fight their way back until they reach Lexington. Here Jesse and others, under a flag of truce, meet brave, liberal old Major J. B. Rogers, a U.S. regular army officer,[1] in order to surrender those who had determined on surrender. All of the regular armies of the South had already (1865) laid down their arms.

Returning to their camp, still carrying a white flag, they were fired upon by eight soldiers of the 2d Wisconsin cavalry, who were riding in advance of their regiment. Charging through and over these men, they empty four saddles and wound two others; but their charge precipitated them upon the main body of the enemy. Turning to retreat, they were hotly pursued, and in this fight, after killing two of his pursuers, Jesse is shot through the right lung with a revolver ball. Still fighting and flying, his horse is shot under him, and the enemy pass over him in chase of his comrades. Extricating himself from his fallen horse, he takes to the woods with five men in eager pursuit. Hunted like a wounded tiger, he still showed that like the tiger, though grievously wounded, he could still slay. Turning when the chase grew too hot, he killed one of his foes and shattered the pistol arm of another. Still three to one they track him until, making one more stand, weak with the terrible loss of blood, reeling in his tracks, he levels his revolver and another goes down never to rise again.

Had the remaining two pursuers been of the blood that sent men into the Federal army instead of into the Home Guards, the

---

[1]Neither the *Official Army Register for 1865* (Washington, 1865), nor Thomas H. S. Hamersly, *Complete Army and Navy Register . . .* (New York, 1888), nor Francis B. Heitman, *Historical Register and Dictionary of the United States Army . . .* (Washington, 1903) lists a Maj. J. B. Rodgers (or Rogers) as a regular or volunteer officer.

career of the most noted outlaw of this or any age had ended here. A bold rush, two steady shots and a bleeding, shattered corpse would have been the result; but they were only Johnson county militia, so they very promptly turned and took to their heels. James, bleeding profusely, had but strength enough to stagger a few hundred yards further into the woods, and faint from loss of blood he fell upon the edge of a narrow stream. Here he lay for two days and a night and gained strength enough to crawl to a field, where he found a friend who, placing him upon a horse, conveyed him to the house of a Mr. Bowman, distant fifteen miles. A few days after he was kindly sent by Major Rodgers to his mother in Nebraska, "to die at home," as the brave old gentleman thought. That his wounds *were* terrible and his condition critical is proven by the fact that it was three years before this man of unparalleled constitution and vitality recovered sufficiently to ride a horse.

Here ends the war record of one of the most famous of those world-wide noted light cavalrymen, or guerrillas, who, like Napoleon, seem to have arisen for the purpose of showing that the art of war was still in its infancy and that the science of tactics was yet in a state of evolution. These men and modes of arming and fighting could only have originated amongst those who almost from infancy had been used to the handling of arms and horses; and who, by a free, out-of-door life, had gained constitutions of iron and nerves of steel. Quantrell, whose stormy life poured out through many gaping wounds in the Military Hospital at Louisville, Kentucky, was doubtless the originator of the Missouri style of guerrilla, but that his pupils were as apt as their teacher, witness the Andersons, Jameses, Youngers and Todds. They were all giants in battle, making ruthless but heroic war.

Of the part Jesse James took in these desperate encounters, we have given but a slight account, not having mentioned more than half of them in which he engaged; but, as is well known, his record is the same in all; that of a hero ever foremost in the fray, striking his foe full in the front and never declining combat on account of the superiority of the foe in position or numbers.

L to R, Charles Fletcher Taylor, Frank James, and Jesse James.
(c. 1864)

CHAPTER VI.

AFTER THE WAR.

The Guerrilla Accepts Defeat—Jesse Longs for Peace—Returns with his
Mother from Nebraska to Clay County—Harassed by Enemies—Cowardly
Bullies—The Reign of the Mob—Fate of Andy McGuire—Jim Jackson—
Rage of his Enemies Culminates—The Night Attack—The Result—Two
Dead—Two Wounded—Jesse Leaves Home—His Illness—A Noble Physi-
cian—Jesse's Convalescence—Leaves for New York—By Sea to San Fran-
cisco—Regains his Health—The Call of Duty—Returns Home.

THE war, prolonged by the guerrillas to its utmost limit, had long
been over. One side had buried its hopes and fears, its loves
and animosities, and hoped that the other had done likewise. They
had accepted the inevitable, defeat, in good faith, as the brave
men on the other side had in good faith tendered amnesty. Defeated,
despoiled, and worn with marching and with battle, they needed
rest and they desired it, but for some of them this rest was to be
denied.

Among these were the Jameses and Youngers. Jesse James, still
worn with wounds, a hacking cough a constant attendant, an
occasional hemorrhage sapping at his life, had returned with his
mother to their home in Clay County. He had by the early part of
1866 fought so plucky a fight against death that he was again able
to ride. In this condition it would be thought that he would be
permitted to settle down to the peaceful avocations of civil life,
but such was not the case. With soldiers, the battle over, the foe
is like a brother, but the militiamen never forgives. A coward in

war, he is naturally a bully in peace, and the enemies of Jesse James proved no exception to this rule. He soon found, from dark looks and ominous threats, that if he would ride in safety he must pay for life, what the bold must ever pay for freedom, the price of eternal vigilance—the eye always ready for the ambush, the pistol ever ready for the foe.

Even had he not heard of the bitter threats and seen the lowering frowns of secret, as well as of avowed enemies, he could read in passing events the fate that awaited him if he relaxed his watch-fulness, or trusting to a magnanimity that they did not possess, he surrendered to the foe.

Richard Burns did so; murdered in Jackson county.

George Roberson fancied security and found a halter at Lexington.

Jim Jackson surrendered to Home Guards in Montgomery county and was murdered in cold blood.

But why prolong the list? Educated in a school that had made him strong and self-reliant, Jesse James did not intend to surrender to man, while he could defend it, a life given by God, and so when, on the night of the 18th of February, 1867, seven of his old enemies, the militia, surrounded the house, although in bed parched with fever, he determined to sell the remnant of his life as dearly as possible. It was bitterly cold weather and the ground was covered with snow. Rapidly dressing he staggered wearily to the window and looked out. Seven horses were hitched near the house, *all with cavalry saddles on.* Their riders stealing, as they fancied, noiselessly toward the house, a small dog raises the alarm, and the two boys (for, contrary to the expectations of the besiegers, Frank was also at home), raising the window, called out fiercely:

"Come on, you sneaking cowards! We are both here and are ready for you."

A hasty skurrying of flying feet toward their horses, a mounting in hot haste, and a flight as eager as that of Tam O'Shanter, and the famous siege of the James boys by the militia is raised. Frightened by mere "empty sound," as the old Latin poet calls words, they fly into the darkness of the night and are shelterd by its friendly shadows.

This is the affair that the "blood-and-thunder" fabrications of other *so-called* lives magnify into a battle, resulting in the loss of three or four lives, and the exit, for a time, amidst thunder, smoke and blood, of Jesse James *solus*.[1]

One work, the most notoriously incorrect, gives a cut of hideous phantasms in red and brown falling on every hand before another in gray with a smoking pistol in each hand. This cut is entitled: "Jesse James' reception."[2]

His enemies were conquered, but, like the seed of the sown dragon's teeth, others would spring up in their stead. His enemies were an army, this band but the advance guard. What was to be done? He was too sick to ride, but ride he must, if he would save the life he had so nobly defended; and so out into the cold and cruel night he drags his weak, emaciated and fever-stricken form. But fortune had not entirely deserted him; it was not written in his fate that he should die by open enemies, but by a false friend, and so he found a refuge. Here he obtained the needed rest and the attention of a surgeon, who was one of nature's noblemen. Brought back from the dim and shadowy confines of the hidden mysteries of the life beyond, he is sent to New York, and there takes ship for the city by the Golden Gate. The sea air on the voyage and the splendid climate of California did wonders for the invalid, and in six months he was again restored to perfect health. During all these six months spent upon the Pacific Slope, that land profile of sudden broil and fierce encounter, not even so much as a harsh word or evil deed had ever been heard from

---

[1]There is no record in contemporary newspapers that such a fight ever occurred. The origin for this tale appears in John N. Edwards, *Noted Guerrillas, or the Warfare of the Border* (St. Louis, Bryan, Brand & Co., 1877), pp 449, 450, and has been repeatedly quoted since. A thorough search of the Liberty (Mo.) *Tribune* and other area newspapers revealed no report of this incident.

[2]The cut to which Triplett is referring appeared in J. W. Buel's *The Border Bandits* (St. Louis, Dan. Linahan & Co., 1882), p. 313.

or done by this man, whom his enemies delight to represent as a murderer by nature and a robber by profession. His life had passed like a summer idyl, all peace and hope and happiness. Enchanting as was this life by the "peaceful seas," he realized that he had something else to do than to dream idle dreams and enjoy the *dolce far niente* of a balmy climate. There were duties in Missouri to attend to. There was a beloved mother from whom he had never been before so long separated, even when a visit to his home was an adventure that few men would have attempted.

CHAPTER VII.

BANK ROBBERY AT LIBERTY, MO.

Liberty—An Unwelcome Visit—A Novel Criminal Industry—Bank Robbery by Daylight—How it was Done—Numbers Engaged—The Jameses and Youngers Accused—Who was Really There—Amount of Money Obtained— Pursuit of the Robbers—Their Escape—Final Belief in Innocence of Jameses.

BUT we have, in order to follow out events continuously, somewhat anticipated. On the 14th day of February, 1866, just four days before the night siege of Dr. Samuel's house, the Liberty bank, or, as it was termed, the "Clay County Savings Association," was robbed of a large sum, probably as much as $70,000. The number of men engaged in the robbery were twelve, the time was early morning. Riding into town at a moderate gait, three of the robbers were posted at advantageous positions, from which alarms might be given or diversions might be made in favor of their comrades. The remainder rode directly to the bank, then two dismounted and entered with drawn revolvers. Mr. [Greenup] Bird, the cashier, and a young son, [William Bird, clerk] were the only occupants, the institution having been just opened. The operation was a brief one; with pistols cocked and pointed at his head, the cashier was made to open the safe and the entire funds were taken, thrust into a large pair of old-fashioned saddle-bags, and mounting their horses, the robbers dashed down the street firing their revolvers and yelling to intimidate the citizens and prevent pursuit. A broad trail was followed to Mount Gilead church, where the spoils were divided and the gang separated to elude pursuit. During the firing in the street a boy named Wymer, who had been instructed by Mr. Bird to raise the alarm, was fired upon and killed, five balls having been said to have pierced his body.[1]

The accomplished writer of Western fiction, Maj. J. W. Buell, has given, amongst other indisputable (?) evidences of the presence of the James brothers at a bank or train robbery, the following: *An unhesitating readiness to take life; a sack always provided for the spoils; yelling and firing of pistols up and down the streets to intimidate their victims and delay pursuit,* or words to this effect.[2]

Now all of these indications were present at this robbery, and yet Frank James was undoubtedly still in Kentucky and Jesse James at home in bed sick.

Of course there were numbers who were ready to lay this robbery to the charge of the Jameses and Youngers. There were undoubtedly present, so most well-posted men will admit, Jim White and J. F. Edmunson, Bill Chiles, Ol. Shepherd, Monkers, Bud Pence; in addition three brothers from Saline county (never suspected!); Bud McDaniel, one of Anderson's lieutenants, and Dave Means, of Howard county, a new man to all. Knowing the reckless bravery of Jesse James, and forgetting that the same nursery of camp and battle had turned out others fully as bold and reckless, the citizens were prone to charge with this, as with

---

[1]The Clay County Savings Association bank was robbed in the afternoon of February 13, 1866, by two of the twelve gang members. Loot taken amounted to $60,000 in gold, currency, and U. S. Bonds. The boy killed was seventeen-year-old George Wymore, "one of the most peaceable and promising young men in the county." Liberty *Tribune,* February 16, 1866.

[2]Though Triplett complains of Buel's accuracy, he obviously relied heavily on his description of the Liberty robbery and repeated many of Buel's errors. See Buel, *The Border Outlaws* (St. Louis, Dan. Linahan & Co., 1882), pp. 115-119. Note also that Triplett states (p. 27) that the robbery occurred "just four days before the night siege of Dr. Samuel's house," which he avers, (p. 24) occurred on February 18, 1867.

all other crimes requiring able planning and bold execution, a man whom this very readiness of accusation was apt to turn into an outlaw. How many others has such a course forced into crime, since every one is apt to think that, as the homely old proverb has it, he might as well

"Have the game as the name."

Thus began and terminated the initial operation of a new criminal industry, open daylight BANK ROBBERY.

CHAPTER VIII.

TWIN ROBBERIES.

THE LEXINGTON BANK ROBBERY.

Robbery of the Banking House at Lexington, Mo.—How and When it Occurred
—Number Engaged—Its Success—Amount Stolen—The Alarm—Pursuit—
Its Futility and Abandonment—Disappearance of the Bandits—Attempted
Robbery of McLain's Bank at Savannah—A Brave Old Judge—His Ready
Comprehension—Poor Firing—Is Seriously Wounded—The Safe Door
Closed—The Robbery Balked—The Citizens Aroused—Flight of the Rob-
bers—A Hot Pursuit—Nothing Accomplished—Who Were Present—Their
Names—Capture of Two Later—A Strong Alibi.

THE next bank robbery was an unimportant one, so far as the
spoil secured is regarded. It occurred on the 30th day of
October, 1866. Five marauding riders quietly entered this little
city and hitched their horses near the bank of Mitchell & Col It
was nearly twelve o'clock in the day, and that business was dull
with the bank seems proved, not only by the small amount of
booty secured, but also by the fact that not a soul save the cashier,
Mr. [J. L.] Thomas, was in the bank, and he standing in the door.
Two of the robbers quietly entering with a fifty-dollar-bill to
change, Mr. Thomas walked behind the counter, and, while opening the cash drawer, two more of the robbers entered, drew their
pistols and covered him. Of course, being a prudent man, Mr.
Thomas promptly honored the demand for the bank moneys, and
the entire amount, $2,000, was thrust into a sack, Mr. Thomas

was threatened with death, if he made any outcry, and walking out leisurely, they joined their companion, who had been left to watch the horses.

Mounting their steeds, they rode rapidly out of town, and easily eluded a two-days' pursuit that was made after them, although the pursuers, twelve in number, were on their trail in less than two hours after the robbery.

This was at first laid to the ubiquitous James brothers, but afterward every one disbelieved their connection with it.

BANK ROBBERY AT SAVANNAH, MO.

On the second day of March, 1867, five men, *doubtless the same five who had robbed the Lexington bank,* entered Savannah, Mo., the county seat of Andrew county. The town is a small one and at that time contained but thirteen to fifteen hundred inhabitants. In addition to the usual business houses all such towns have, it contained a private banking house of moderate capital. Its proprietor was a man of undoubted nerve, named [John] McLain. The usual tactics of this gang were pursued. The five men entered the town, and, leaving one of their number to guard the horses, the other four entered the bank. The hour was about twelve, and the only persons in the bank were Judge McLain and his son. When the robbers entered, McLain seemed by intuition to divine their object, and, hastily closing his safe door, he secured his revolver, which lay under the counter, and began firing at the robbers, who returned his fire from pistols already drawn. McLain's firing proved defective, as not one of the four robbers were touched, while he, himself, sank to the floor, shot through the breast with a ball from a navy revolver. His son, escaping into the street, alarmed the citizens; and, hastening to join their companion, the robbers mounted and fled, pursued in hot haste by a large number of the enraged citizens. They were trailed for several days, but pursuit was eventually given over without apprehending any of them.[1]

This band consisted of Bill Chiles, Jim White, Bud McDaniel, J. F. Edmunson and Sam Pope; two of them—Pope and McDaniel —were afterwards arrested about the middle of March, but proved an alibi (somewhat too strong!) and thus escaped.

This robbery, too, for a while, was laid to Jesse James and his gang.[2]

Judge McLain, though desperately wounded, eventually recovered, and after a few weeks the occurrence seemed to be entirely forgotten.

[1]The Savannah bank was robbed by six men at 2:30 p.m. March 2, 1867. On McLane's refusal to deliver the keys of the vault, one of the robbers drew a revolver and shot him. McLane returned the fire and the bandits fled, pursued by the city marshal and two persons. This small posse soon returned and a larger group, of forty to fifty persons, took up the chase. Pursuit was unsuccessful, however. Liberty *Tribune*, March 8, 1867.

[2]The local newspapers, at least, did not lay this crime on the James brothers.

CHAPTER IX.

Bank Robbery at Richmond, Mo.

A Daring and Desperate Attack—A Mad Dash—A Determined Mayor—His
Death—Attack on the Jail—A Brave Jailer—His Death—His Son Also
Killed—Mistaken Identities—Proof—Warrants Issued—Peyton Johnes Sur-
rounded—Breaks Through the Line—Man Killed—Little Girl Mortally
Wounded—The Battle—Escape of Johnes—Murder of Andy McGuire—
Also of Dick Burns—Hulse and Hines Flee the Country—Tom Little Hung
by a Mob—Youngers and Jameses Not Guilty.

COMING next in chronological order was the most desperate of
the many attacks made on banking institutions, with the exception of the last bank robbery, or rather attempt at bank robbery,
at Northfield, Minn.

Learning that the firm of Hughes & Co., bankers at Richmond,
Mo., were the recipients of heavy deposits, the marauders to the
number of fifteen, pursuing their ordinary tactics, dashed madly
through the town, yelling like demons, and firing their pistols recklessly up and down the streets. Five or, as some accounts say, six
of the robbers burst into the bank, and secured between four and
five thousand dollars.

By this time the citizens had begun to gather to make some
resistance, and the mayor of the town, named Shaw, in crossing
the street was fired at and killed, he having fired several times
without effect.

An attack was then begun upon the jail, in order to release some
prisoners confined there, as the robbers claimed, unjustly. During
this attack the jailor, named Griffin, and his son, a young man,
were both killed. The citizens having again rallied were firing rapidly,

but ineffectually, upon the robbers, who at last turned in retreat.[1]

The assertion made by many that they had recognized most, if not all, of the parties engaged in this outrage must be taken with some hesitation, for warrants were issued for Allen Parmer in common with others, when it was well known that Parmer was employed in business in Kansas City at the time. Again were the Jameses and Youngers accused of taking part in a heinous crime, though Cole Younger was known to be in Texas, and those who were coolest in judgment thought the proof of the presence of the Jameses so weak that warrants were never issued for them.

Peyt. Johnes, one of the parties for whom warrants were issued, was surrounded a few days afterwards in Jackson county by a squad of about twenty men. Making their attack at night Johnes broke through their line, Killing B. H. Wilson, of Kansas City, and wounding (accidentally) a little girl, who was acting as guide for the party, so dangerously that she died. Passing through the line of pursuers, he dashed away into the darkness untouched by the wild fire of the posse, and escaped.

Andy McGuire was not heard from for some time, but being found in the vicinity of Warrensburg, in Johnson county, he was hung by a mob.

Dick Burns, another party accused of complicity in this robbery, was caught by a mob and also hung.

Bill Hulse and a man named Hines fell under the ban of suspicion, and finding that they, too, would be dealt with by the mob, fled the country.

Tom Little, another supposed member of the gang, was captured at St. Louis weeks afterwards, and being brought back through Johnson county was taken by a mob and hung.

Who of these men, if any, were guilty will most likely never be known, but it seems that eventually all settled down to the belief that the Jameses and Youngers were not concerned in it, though at first almost universally suspected.

[1]The Richmond bank was robbed by twenty men at 2:00 p. m. May 23, 1867. Mayor John B. Shaw, Jailor Berry G. A. Griffin, and his son, Frank, were killed. Loot amounted to about $4,000. Liberty *Tribune*, May 31, 1867, quoting the Lexington *Express*, May 23.

CHAPTER X.

RUSSELLVILLE, KY. BANK ROBBERY.

A Wealthy Kentucky Town—Its Usual Repose Disturbed—Raided by Robbers
—The Usual Accompaniments—Oaths—Yells—Pistol Shots—Panic Stricken
Citizens—Deserted Streets—The Rush to the Bank—Demand for Money—
Sensational Incidents—Who did the Deed—Yankee Bligh's Story—Where were
the Jameses?—Desperate Flight of the Robbers—The Long Pursuit—George
Shepherd—His Capture—Trail—Serves Three Years in Penitentiary—Ol.
Shepherd—His Whereabouts Discovered—A Mob of Vigilantes Undertake
his Arrest—No Surrender—"Well, then, let it be Death."

RUSSELLVILLE, Kentucky, is a beautiful town in Logan county,
lying in the midst of bowering trees and roses, and seeming,
in its quiet and opulence, secure from all want and sorrow. The
people generally were genial, well cultured, and with a sufficiency
of this world's goods to insure them against the annoying cares of
poverty. The town was the seat of educational institutions, and these
were well patronized. The bazars of her tradesmen were full of rich
stocks of goods of every description, and her merchants formed an
aristocracy of wealth and culture. To one who might have dropped
into the town on some early summer day, when the scent of roses
and violets commingled with that of the honeysuckle and the new
mown hay, and dreamy quiet had lulled the senses into security,
the little city would almost have seemed a portion of "Arcadia the
blest," longed for by poets, but alas! as all experience shows, not
attainable on earth.

On this day, on which we call attention to this lovely place, the streets were filled with their usual loungers. Young girls intent on shopping; old ladies bound on the same mission; business men with every thought bent on groceries, grain, or other goods; the lawyer pondering deeply over "learned precedents;" the doctor oracular and grave; all were passing and repassing, when, sudden as a clap of thunder from a clear sky, a shout is heard. Next a loud oath rings out upon the air, and then it is rent with the explosion of revolvers, sharp, quick, ominous. A band of heavily armed and finely mounted men were coming down the street on the wings of the wind. A panic seizes the hurrying, scheming crowd; all thoughts of business and varying interests cease, and the sole desire to get safely under cover is now paramount. Into stores, shops and offices all fly, "staying not upon the order of their going." The experience was a novel one; what did it all mean? The war was over — the armies had dispersed — and yet this had much the seeming of an old war-time sortie.

Innocent Arcadians, it meant that the bank robber was upon you, to despoil and, if need be, to murder in order to carry out his purpose.

It meant reckless firing to clear the streets; it meant a desperate rush upon the bank, a hurried draft, not with pen and paper, but with powder and ball, upon the entire assets of the institution; it meant a hurried retreat before the armed majesty of the law could realize what had transpired; it meant tireless riders on swift steeds, defying dangers and eluding pursuit.

In Missouri it had ceased to be a novelty, but here it startled the entire community as it had never been startled before. But to the details.

It was on March 20th, 1868, when the affair occurred. Five men rode rapidly into the town with the usual accompaniments of yells and curses, driving the citizens into their houses and shops. Three of the bandits posted themselves advantageously in the street, while two rushed into the bank with drawn revolvers, presented them at the cashier and forced him to deliver over every dollar in the bank. The amount was very nearly $15,000.

Having secured this booty in a sack the two robbers joined their friends outside, mounted their horses and left the town at a sweeping gallop. Fear had so completely paralyzed the citizens that it was some time before pursuit was organized, and thus the outlaws gained valuable time on their pursuers. When the latter got on the trail they found that it led away toward the river, and that part of the brigands had crossed over into Missouri. Two of the three had dropped out of the line somewhere between Russellville and the Mississippi, presumably soon after crossing Cumberland river. These two were supposed to be George Shepherd, who on the strength of the evidence was arrested at his home at Chaplin, tried and sentenced to three years in the penitentiary. Some people have doubted if George Shepherd was really guilty; wondering why, if he was, he would stay quietly at home and tamely submit to arrest. Those who argue thus seem to have forgotten that George Shepherd had, whether wisely or unwisely, "given hostages to fortune" by taking to wife Dick Maddux's widow, who had followed her husband from Missouri to Kentucky, where he was killed, while bravely fighting under his old chief, Quantrell.

They lived in Chaplin, where George had brought property and was in a measure tied down.

"But who were with George Shepherd?" will be the next question. The parties were Ol. Shepherd, Cole Younger, Jim White and a fellow named Saunders. Some say Dick Little instead of Jim White, and probably this is correct, as the description of one of them tallies with his precisely.

The fate of these men was as follows: Saunders, who was a great drunkard and whose constitution was wrecked, finding that he could not keep up with the terrible pace of the Missouri outlaws, fell out of the line and made for a hiding place in the mountain spurs between the Cumberland and Tennessee rivers. From here he ventured out in search of whisky, and was killed at a drug store at a cross roads. Desperately wounded, he was threatened with all manner of evil if he would not name his comrades; but, game to the last, he died without making any sign.

Ol. Shepherd, fleeing through the swamps and forests of Southern Missouri with his two companions, first eluded and then dis-

tanced pursuit, and Shepherd went to his home near Lee's Summit.
The officers of the law fearing to attempt his arrest delegated the
job to a company of vigilantes. Surrounding Shepherd in the woods,
they called upon him to surrender. "Not to any of you d—d militia
sneaks," he replied, and began to reply with his revolvers to the
fire of their carbines. Standing off some two or three hundred yards,
they riddled him with balls and at last he sank, seven terrible wounds
upon his person, but fighting to the end. He had lived a guerrilla
of the guerrillas; he had died in combat with the usual odds against
him. The other two escaped.

Of course the James brothers were accused of this crime, but
they were able to prove that it was an utter impossibility that they
could have been there. Frank had a wound still so disabling as not
to permit of his riding; and Jesse, even if his health had not been
so delicate at that time that he could never have accomplished the
terrible ride through Tennessee and on into and through Missouri,
would have been able to have proved, by other means, his innocence
of the charge. Yankee [D.G.] Bligh, by far the shrewdest and most
talented of Western detectives, after looking critically over the whole
field and carefully summing up the evidence pro and con, decided
that the Jameses were not connected with this robbery.[1] It is neither
here denied or affirmed that Jesse was presented by one of the
participators a sum sufficient to go to New York and from thence
to San Francisco.

[1]Settle cites evidence that Bligh was certain Frank and Jesse James committed the robbery. *Jesse James,* pp. 37, 38.

CHAPTER XI.

THE GALLATIN BANK ROBBERY.

An Established Industry—Another Daylight Raid—Vengeance Mixed With Avarice—The Murder of the Cashier—"You'll Make No More Boasts"—Jim Anderson's Purchase—"I Know She's a Good One"—The Mare Escapes —Circumstantial Evidence—An Offer to Surrender—No Guarantee Against Mob Law—The Alibi that Could Have Been Proved—Were the James Boys Present?—The Question Honestly Answered.

IT was in the month of December in the year 1869 that Jim Anderson and an old guerrilla comrade, certain of a warm welcome, rode up to the hospitable door of Dr. Samuel. Dismounting, they found Jesse at home, and the hours sped rapidly away in talking over the war and other topics of interest. At last the conversation turned to considerations of the present.

"What do you intend doing next, Jim!" said Jesse; "will you stay in Missouri?"

"No," said Jim Anderson, "I am not 'stuck' on Missouri, and I think I can find safer places to live in, the way things look. I am going to finish up a little piece of business, however, before going, and would like to have your help. It will pay, I tell you, and you don't seem any too flush of money any way."

"Well, what line of business is it?" said Jesse, "I'd like to make a few dollars if it ain't too much out of the way."

"Well," said Anderson, "I'll tell you." "We," pointing to his comrade, "intend to fix that s— of a b—, Cox, before we leave.

He has been boasting that he killed Bill Anderson, and by G—! I'll have his scalp before I leave the State, or he'll have mine."

"But, Jim," said Jesse, laughingly, "I don't see how I'm to make any money out of Cox's scalp—they don't sell very high in this market."

"No," said Anderson, "but I'm going to kill two birds with one stone: he's cashier of the Gallatin bank, and we'll just take in his money as well as his scalp. If you want to join us, we'd like d—d well to have you."

"Much obliged, Jim," said Jesse, "but so far I've kept out of that business and don't think I'll take hold now. I know Frank and I have been accused of having a hand in everything of that kind that goes; but you know that we are innocent of it, if no one else does."

"Yes," said Anderson, "and I know you are d—d fools to let 'em give you the name and not have the game."

"That may be so, Jim!" said Jesse; "but you see we can prove ourselves not guilty of the others, if we can only be assured of protection against mob violence."

"Assured h—l!" shouted Anderson with a laugh. "Why, what will the assurance amount to? they want to kill you—they intend to play for even, and, by the jumping J— C—! they'll do it. Come along, make a raise, and we'll go to Texas and have a h—l of a time."

"Can't do it, Jim;" said Jesse, "we intend to make a proposition to the governor, that we will give ourselves up and stand trial, if he will give us his word we shall be tried in court and not by a mob."

"Yes, and you'll get it, too," said Anderson, "oh, yes, you'll get it—just like Jim Jackson did, and Burns and Shep and the rest of the boys! they most generally hang guerrillas first and try 'em afterwards—better come with us."

Not this time, Jim," said Jess, and with this the solicitation ceased.

Anderson and his comrade sat a little longer, Anderson meditating, and at last he spoke:

"Jesse," said he, "what did you ever do with the mare you got from Bill?"

"She's out in the stable," said Jesse, "do you want to see her?"

"Yes," said Jim, "I'd like to do so."

Going out to the stable they look the mare over, canvassed her points, and then Jim offered to buy her, saying his horse was about played out, and he wanted something to run on, if he had to run. Telling Anderson that he had presented the mare to his sister, he said he thought she would sell her, but it would take big money to buy her, "for you know," said he, "just what she is."

"I know she's a good one," said Anderson, and proceeding to the house he made a bargain for the mare, paid for her, and rode off with her. The Jameses saw nothing more of the mare, but they heard of her under the following cricumstances:

In the early part of December, 1869, a band of heavily armed and superbly mounted men rode into Gallatin at a sweeping gallop, yelling and frightening the citizens off of the streets and into their houses. The usual bank robbery tactics were followed; some of the men stationed themselves advantageously, while two of them made directly for the bank and entered it. The cashier was covered by a revolver in the hands of one robber, while the other filled a convenient sack with what money he could find. This done, he walked up to the cashier, put a pistol to his head and fired. The cashier, Captain John W. Sheets, fell dead, and returning his pistol to its scabbard, Anderson walked coolly out, saying: "I guess, Mr. Cox, you won't brag any more of killing Bill Anderson,"[1] He had, by mistake, murdered Captain Sheets for Mr. Cox, the former having taken the place of the latter in the bank.

This deed done, the robbers mounted their horses and rode swiftly out of town, going, it is supposed, for the purpose of causing suspicion to fall upon the James boys, towards Clay county.

---

[1]Major S. P. Cox had been in command of the troops which killed Bill Anderson. For an interesting discussion of the theories surrounding the murder of Sheets, see Settle, *ibid.*, p. 40.

Penetrating a few miles into that county, they separated to meet at a rendezvous south of the Missouri river in Jackson county, and after lying there until all excitement was over, made their way into Texas.[2]

The enemies of the Jameses immediately set up the cry that they were the guilty parties; but they were able, by Judge [James M.] Gow and other respectable parties, to prove *alibis,* and rode into Kearney for the purpose of delivering themselves up to be tried. Some of their friends, however, knowing the infuriated state of the Davis county militia, advised them against this move, and so they merely entered their protest against being condemned unheard, and rode out of town, saying that they would come in and surrender for trial at any time they were assured against mob violence.

This, as is well known, was never done, and still another obstacle was placed in the way of doing justice to these men, who had certainly offered fairly: willing to surrender, and only stipulating that they should be guaranteed protection against the mob.

[2]The raid on the Gallatin bank occurred December 7, 1869. The "band" of desperados consisted of two men. A black mare left at the scene by one of the bandits was later traced to Clay county and found to be the property of Jesse James. He issued alibi cards saying that the mare was sold to a man from Topeka, Kansas, for $500 on December 5, two days before the holdup. The alibi cards never fully established Jesse's innocence. St. Joseph (Mo.) *Daily Gazette,* December 9, 1869 and Liberty *Tribune,* July 22, 1870.

CHAPTER XII.

Proposal of Surrender.

Jesse James' Letter—Proposes to Surrender—The Facts—Governor McClurg's Opinion—Captain Thomason—His Character—His Services—Attempts to Arrest the Jameses—Unconditional Surrender Demanded—Failure to Arrest Them—A Dead Horse—A Defeated Posse—St. Louis and Chicago Detectives in the Field—No Results.

AFTER this robbery Jesse James collected all of the facts in the case, pointed out all he knew of it, gave names of parties by whom he could prove *alibis,* and again offered to submit to the law, if he and his brother could be assured of protection against the violence of mobs and of lynch law. Governor [Joseph W.] Mc-Clurg himself looked thoroughly into the merits of the case, and although no one could accuse that sturdy Republican of looking with favor upon any man who had fought under Quantrell or Anderson, still he had the honesty to avow a disbelief in their guilt.[1]

This should have quieted suspicion and allayed animosity; and had it done so at that time, who can say how much it might have saved the State, both in reputation and money.

But this was not to be; their enemies were determined to hunt them, and they did. Amongst others who believed in their guilt was John Thomason, who had been Sheriff of Clay county. He

---

[1]There is no evidence that Jesse James ever offered to surrender and stand trial for the Gallatin robbery. Governor McClurg showed "disbelief in their guilt" in a strange way. On Christmas Day, 1869, he ordered George W. Belt, sheriff of Platte county, to raise a company of men and apprehend the robbers. He offered a $3,000 reward for the capture of Jesse and Frank James.

THE WESTERN UNION TELEGRAPH COMPANY.

The rules of this Company require that all messages received for transmission, shall be written on the message blanks of the Company, under and subject to the conditions printed thereon, which conditions have been agreed to by the sender of the following message.

O. H. PALMER, Sec'y.   WM. ORTON, Pres't.

Dated *Jefferson City Mo Dec 24th* 186*7*

Received at *Independence Mo Dec*

To *Sheriff of Jackson Co*
                    Independence

You will at once organize arm
and equip as Militia thirty (30) or
more men and aid Tomlison Dep
uty Sheriff of Clay county if
called on in capturing or Killing Frank James and Jesse
James or hold such force in
readyness to aid you in such
capture or Killing if they be found
in your county. The State will P
ay expense of force for actual ser
vice. and five hundred (500) Dollars
for the capture of or Killing of e
ach. I write by mail
80 Paid 4.25   J W McClurg

Telegram from Governor J. W. McClurg authorizing reward for Jesse
and Frank James, early in their outlaw career.

is believed to have been a brave, conscientious man; had served in the Confederate army during the war, and returning settled down to a quiet farm life. He was a man who was willing to fight for his beliefs, and believing the James boys to be guilty (no matter how erroneous such a belief), he determined to try and effect their capture.

Gathering a body of armed men, he mounted them on fine horses and set out in pursuit of the two brothers.

As fate would have it he met them in the road near Dr. Samuel's. Calling to them to surrender, they merely refused until satisfied that they could be properly protected by the law. An interchange of shots now took place, and Jesse, having no desire to kill the brave old soldier, who had ventured all and lost all on the same side with himself, fired wild and wide. Finding that, unlike the militia, Captain Thomason didn't, as he expressed it, "scare worth a cent," and thinking that the pursuit wouldn't cease until the leader of it was in some way disabled, Jesse took deliberate aim and shot Thomason's horse dead.[2]

Could Jesse have killed Thomason if he had desired? some may ask. Any one, who knew the quick unerring aim of the man, knows that inside of one hundred yards he never missed his man with a revolver.

When Captain Thomason's horse was killed the pursuit ended, as none of the others cared to press upon these daring men.

After this attempt several Chicago and St. Louis detectives appeared on the scene; Pinkerton's men boasting that they would "have the Jameses dead or alive inside of ten days." How well they predicted has since been made evident.

[2]The Liberty *Tribune*, December 17, 1869, stated that as Thomason's party neared the Samuel house the "two James' rushed out, mounted their horses and brandished their pistols and told them [the posse] to 'come ahead.' Capt. Thomason and party immediately followed after them, and in the chase some 25 to 30 shots were fired, one taking effect in the hand of one of the James'. Sheriff Thomason's horse was also killed, he having previously dismounted." The Gallatin *North Missourian*, December 16, stated that "about dusk the murderers were in Kearney... [and] told the citizens that they had killed the Sheriff and defied everybody. They are two brothers by the name of James."

Jesse James in 1870, at age 23. *Courtesy State Historical Society of Missouri.*

CHAPTER XIII.

STARTS FOR CALIFORNIA.

VERY soon after the Russellville robbery it was that Jesse started
for California. He had in some measure recruited his health
and strength through the care and kind nursing of his Kentucky
friends, but still had a terrible cough accompanied by hectic fever.
Journeying to New York by easy stages so as not to overtax his
strength, he reached there with every probability of safely making
the voyage to the golden shores of the Pacific Slope.

Resting a few days before taking passage, he took in the
principal objects of interest in the great city; and it speaks well
for the natural character of the man that his visits were oftener to
the libraries, art museums, etc., than to the abodes of gilded vice
and sin. Temperate by nature, easy, self-possessed and gentlemanly
in his demeanor, his dress was as modest as the man himself, and
he would never have been selected, so far as any outward indication went, as a bandit and desperado. In one thing only did he

give way to temptation. Like most men of generous impulses, he was a born gambler. His nerve and judgment were both excellent, and in all games of chance he played with great skill. In New York, finding time to hang heavily on his hands, he visited the palatial rooms of John Chamberlain and made several large winnings.

At one of his sittings against faro he seemed to play with unusual recklessness, still fortune favored him. His gains had run up to thousands, but still he played on. At last one of those creatures who hang around such places started to pick up a stack of his "chips" lying on one of the cards. Jesse turned in his seat slightly, and mildly requested him to put the checks back.

"They are mine," said he; "I had not overlooked them; I only left them to see how often they would double before losing."

"I can't help that," said the crab, as these fellows are called in sporting parlance, "the card was 'dead,' and any body has a right to take up a 'sleeper.'"

"Put those checks down this instant," said Jesse, a hard, cold light stealing into his eyes, and the lines around his mouth becoming more firmly set.

The "crab," seeing that this was not a man to be imposed upon, regretfully placed the stack back upon the table.

"Now," said Jesse, turning to the dealer, "is it customary in your house for any stacks that may be overlooked to become the property of any person noticing this state of things?"

"Yes," said the dealer, "such is the custom in all of the houses in New York."

"Then," said Jesse, "I'll submit to custom," and he turned over the checks to the "crab," cashed his own, and left the house with between $4,000 and $5,000.

The next day he was aboard of the steamer bound for the Isthmus of Panama. Here he relaxed his vigilance and gave way thoroughly to social pleasures. He was the life of that little world, and never seemed to tire in his attempts to contribute to the amusement of the rest. At last they reach the Isthmus, cross over to the milder waters of the Pacific, first seen of Balboa, and everywhere his wonder is excited by the rich growth of the tropical trees, fruits and flowers.

At last their new ocean house reaches the Golden Gate and is safely moored to her pier at San Francisco. Amazed at the strangely cosmopolitan crowd of the city, he lingers here a few days, and at last regretfully takes his leave for the health-giving springs at Paso Robles. Here dwelt his uncle, a gentleman of wealth, culture and refinement, and with him Jesse made his home during his sojourn in California.[1] Here, too, he was joined by Frank, as soon as the wound of the latter, received from a mob at Brandenburg, Ky., had healed sufficiently for him to make the trip. Together the two brothers, who, despite all tales to the contrary, were always loving and affectionate towards each other, enjoyed for the first time in years the sense of perfect peace and security.

As elsewhere stated, the climate worked wonders for their health, and in six months, finding no avocations open in the already densely over-crowded marts of the Golden State, they turned back towards Missouri. They concluded to return on horse-back, partly through curiosity, partly that they hoped to find in their long ride something to which they could turn as a business.

Seeing many of that adventurous, hardy class called "prospectors," making their way into the mountains, their "burros" loaded with blankets, tools and supplies, they concluded to try their luck. Purchasing an outfit, they pushed on to Battle Mountain, just then the new excitement amongst miners. Here they went into camp and began work in earnest, for it was always one of their characteristics that whatever they took hold of they did with great energy. Rapidly posting themselves as to the best mode of "prospecting," or searching out the hidden treasures of nature, they soon became proficient, and might have settled down into hard-handed, honest miners, or become mighty millionaires, but for an unlucky incident. The new mining camp had already received the somewhat more

[1]The uncle's name was Drury Woodson James, younger brother of Jesse's father.

than doubtful blessing of a "dance house." This is a peculiarly Western institution; a large barn-like shanty is fitted with a floor, a space railed off for several sets of dancers, and the rest of the room filled with gambling tables and a bar. Every imaginable species of banking game is dealt in these houses, amongst others Spanish Monte. The Jameses frequently visited this place and risked their money freely, but were invariably lucky; Jesse on one occasion "tapping" the bank of "Curley" Sam, the dealer. This so incensed Sam that he formed a clique of the other gamblers and determined to fleece the strangers. The occasion soon came. One night while the Jameses were in the hall listening to the somewhat dolorous strains of the orchestra and amusedly watching the evolutions of the painted prostitutes and their drunken partners, "Curley" came up to Jesse, and touching him on the shoulder, said: "I want my revenge."

"All right," said Jesse, "you can have it; what shall it be?"

"Draw-poker," said Curley, and soon he and his partner were engaged with Frank and Jesse. The gamblers lost steadily, and began to see that in a straight game they were no match for their opponents. Tipping his partner a wink, "Curley" ran over the cards lightly and "palmed out" two aces. Jesse noticed this, but said nothing until they began to bet on their hands. Then watching "Curley" so closely as to give him no chance to "wring in" his stolen cards, he raised him bet after bet until at last Curley weakened, and threw down his hand. Jesse took up the money, looked at Curley's hand, and said: "Seven cards; can't you play like a white man without trying to swindle?"

"It's a lie," said Curley; "I never tried to swindle."

Slapping him in the face with his open hand, Jesse arose from the table, saying to Frank, "See to the door."

Whirling back to back, Frank faces the door while Jesse, not a moment too soon, straightens out his arm, his revolver is heard, and Curley drops upon the floor with his right arm crushed by a pistol bullet. The knife in his upraised hand fell upon the table, its point piercing the stolen hand of the gambler. "Make for the door," said Jesse; and through the crowd that was fast gathering to cut off their access to the open air they fought their way gallantly. The numbers of their enemies did not appal them, and in fact it gave them additional safety, for they feared for a while to fire at the Jameses for fear of hitting each other, so they hacked at them with their Bowie knives. It was a desperate strait; and for awhile it looked as if these men, who had boldly faced all odds upon the field of battle, were destined to be cooped up in a den, like rats in a cage. "Shoot to kill, Frank!" said Jesse, who up to this time had been content to fire only with the purpose of disabling his antagonists. The battle now began in earnest, and the thinning ranks of the gamblers gradually gave way until, by a bold rush, the boys make for the open door, turn, fire a parting volley, and are off.

Nothing was done that night by the gamblers beyond counting up their costs and losses. Curley Sam and two others with broken right arms, one man shot through the forehead and instantly killed, and two others shot by their own party in the affray and dangerously wounded. The Jameses were cut in several places by the knives of their opponents, and two or three bullets had cut their hats and clothing. Their wounds, however, were mere scratches.

In cities where cowards desire revenge they raise a mob; in the mountains they do the same, only they call their mob a "vigilance committee," or *vigilantes*. Such a mob was duly organized the next day by the gamblers, and they were in high glee. But they had reckoned without their host, for, as the gamblers would have expressed it, Frank and Jesse had properly "sized them up," and knew that they would receive a call. Sending Frank to the mountain meadow for their horses, Jesse prepared to hold their cabin against the enemy until his brother's return. Frank arrived about sunset, with the horses fresh and in good condition

"What shall we do?" said Frank.

"Stay and fight it out," said Jesse; "d—d if I'll run from the dirty cowards."

But the cooler counsel of Frank prevailed, and Jesse agreed to go, only stipulating that they should wait until the gamblers appeared and treat them to one of their old guerrilla rushes, and then leave the mountains forever.

The sun had sunk behind "the misty mountain tops," and the winds, chill from their contact with the everlasting summit snows, brought renewed vigor to both men and steeds. Soon the advance of the vigilantes is heard, their ribald oaths making strange contrast with the sighing of the gigantic pines. Nearer they come, and shouts and jeers ring upon the air. At last they are within a hundred and fifty yards of the two men sitting like statues upon their steeds, under the shade of beetling crags. "Now," said Jesse, and with a touch to their noble horses they bounded at once into a full racing gallop straight at the mob. Now goes up the old guerrilla yell, and some of the mob who had heard it in combat in Missouri prudently turned from the road into the dense woods and sought safety in flight. "Them's some of Quantrell's d—d guerrillas," said a Kansan, who had fought them on their retreat from Lawrence; "I know that yell."

Small time was there for interchange of shots: the Jameses are upon them, over them and gone. A few are ridden down and badly bruised, two receive wounds requiring amputation of their arms, and one or two more only slightly wounded, while the boys got off with a slight scratch on Jesse's shoulder, and a trifling wound on Frank's horse. Knowing that they could not return to Battle Mountain they rode to the southward, and after several adventures passed into Arizona. Here they had a brush with a small band of Mescalero Apaches, who were out on a horse-stealing mission, but not averse to a murder if a small party of white men fell in their way. Amazed at the temerity of men who could dare to pass in couples through their country, they made an attack upon them. This was met rather more than half way by Frank and Jesse, who with defiant yells answered the savage war whoop of their enemies, and bursting in full career upon their line killed one savage and mortally wounded another. Turning in swift flight from these daring brothers, the Indians fled in dismay, and the boys, content to "let well enough alone," resumed their journey without pursuing the flying enemy. As far as they could see, looking back over miles of blooming cactus and intervening plain, the Apaches still formed an admiring but respectful group upon a slight eminence.

Could these bronzed savages and their lithe steeds have been transfixed on canvas by a Wimar, it would have presented the finest picture ever seen of Indian admiration. In the Western part of New Mexico, not far from the line of Old Mexico, lived a wealthy ranchero named Armijo. Of near kin to the Armijos of Spain, this old gentleman belonged to the blue blooded families of Castile. His wife, long since dead, had left him a beautiful daughter, Juana, or, as the old gentleman always affectionately called her, Juanita. At two o'clock of the morning of the visit of the Jameses to the hacienda of Don Miguel Armijo the Apaches, under the lead of one of the noted Victorio's warriors, had struck the hacienda, driving off large herds of stock, and having found Juana Armijo out riding with one of her maids, had captured them and ridden off to hold them for ransom or worse fate.

Everybody at the hacienda was in tears. Frank, who is an accomplished linguist, soon ascertained the state of affairs.

"Have you made any pursuit?" said he to Don Miguel. "None," said the old gentleman, "there is no one here to lead them, and of themselves the vacqueros are too cowardly to pursue the Indians.

"Did they get your horses?" asked Frank.

"No; they were being driven in to be branded, so they missed them."

"How many Indians were there?" again asked Frank.

Ascertaining that there were about eight or ten Indians, and that he could get five or six cow-boys, who for Mexicans could fight rather well, he and Jesse got fresh horses, and started in rapid pursuit, the old gentleman showering blessings upon them, but muttering at the same time, *"Pero ellos son Apaches—ellos son Apaches!* ("But they are Apaches—they are Apaches.") No doubt thinking that any other men might be overcome, but the Apaches never.

One of the Mexican vacqueros knew of a trail leading to a pass where the Indians might be intercepted, as they were incumbered with a large drove of cattle and must keep to the broader valley trails. Arriving at the pass at four o'clock in the afternoon they formed an ambush, and waited for the Indians to come up. About six o'clock, unsuspicious of danger, they entered the pass, driving the cattle in advance, and some distance in the rear an old Indian was guarding the captives.

"Now," said Jesse to Frank, "as I'm the best shot I'll take care of the old fellow in the rear, while you and your Mexicans give it to those in front. If I miss the old devil, up go the girls to a certainty.

"Ready," said Jesse, who had leveled on the old Indian, distant a hundred yards; while the rest of the band were in the pass just abreast of the ambush.

"Son Vds. listo," whispered Frank to his men.

"Fuego, hombres!" he shouted.

At that sound the volley roared out. Jesse looked at his man, saw him fumble at his gun, then fall from his saddle, and then turned his attention to the others. Taken completely by surprise, and retreat cut off up the pass by the dense masses of cattle and in the rear by their enemies, every Indian was killed in the narrow canyon, and left for the beasts of prey and carrion birds.

The Signorita Juana welcomed them as angels of deliverance, and the next afternoon she, her maid and his herds were delivered into the hands of the old Don. His gratitude knew no bounds, and it is said that a somewhat warmer feeling than that of gratitude had already taken possession of his daughter toward the man whose deadly aim and dauntless courage had saved her from a fate a thousand times worse than death; but Jesse, sighing only for a pair of blue eyes that he knew were ready to smile upon him in Missouri, insisted on getting back home once more. Refusing princely offers of remuneration, the old Don at last prevailed upon them to accept the sum of $5,000, and they rode off, never again to see the face of the kindly old Don and his lovely daughter. To them the knowledge may never come of his fate; but should it ever reach them, could they be blamed if their hearts and eyes were filled with tears for the brave, even if guilty, man, who came to them as an angel of light, even though by others painted in colors of the blackest shade?[2]

[2]Just where Triplett got his information about the western adventures of the James brothers is not known. No contemporary evidence is available. Perhaps some inspiration came from Dr. J. A. Dacus who described similar adventures between pages 93 and 102 of his *Life and Adventures of Frank and Jesse James* (St. Louis, N. D. Thompson & Co., 1880).

CHAPTER XIV.

BANK ROBBERY AT CORYDON, IOWA.

The Philosphy of Honesty—A Cynical View—Speculations—Jameses Still
Hunted—Forced to the Bad—A Stroke Planned—The Bloodshed Stipulated
For—A Quiet Ride—The Town Reached—The Streets Cleared—The Bank
Entered—It Vaults Rifled—The Amount Realized—The Flight—Pursuit—
Discontinued at Cameron—Incidents of the Robbery—Number Engaged—
Who Were the Men? A Hard Question—Estrangement of Friends.

IT was the turn of Iowa to next submit to a daylight bank robbery.
Kentucky and Missouri had already seen the spectacle, and the
stroke was destined to fall next upon the thrifty commonwealth of
a more Northern sister. Corydon is a small town in Wayne county,
situated in the midst of a fertile district, and doing an excellent
business with the surrounding yeomanry. It contained a bank in a
flourishing condition, and was as quiet a community as could have
been found in the land.

The ordinary condition of affairs, however, was greatly disturbed one lovely June day[1] by a party of Missouri raiders, variously stated as containing five and seven members. No matter what
their numbers; they were sufficient to completely cow all of the
inabitants and cause them to keep a healthy distance from the
bank, whose cashier they intended to interview and relieve of the

[1]According to Settle, *loc. cit.*, p. 43 the date was June 3, 1871. The Liberty
Tribune, June 16, 1871, gives the date as June 8. The victim was the bank
of the Ocobock Brothers.

burden of caring for his surplus funds. We will first ask, and try to answer, the question: "Who were the raiders?" Some cynical old philosopher has said that no man is more than ninety-five per cent. honest. Many others have also doubted that honesty was an absolute quality, and putting the case in this wise they almost seem to carry out their argument. "A millionaire," say they, "may not give way to the temptation of stealing another million; still place him in absolute want, unable to obtain food and shelter for a suffering family, and the man who was superior to the temptation of a million dollars will stoop to the petty theft of a loaf of bread."

It is easy to carry out the parallel between the starving man and the James brothers, and show that never, until forced by the utmost necessity, did they rob an individual or a corporation. After the surrender of the Rebel armies, as almost any man now grown can well remember, the entire machinery and control of the government, laws, courts, etc., were in the hands of the enemies of those who fought in the armies of the South. No southern man could vote, hold office, or *sit on a jury*. In some sections of this State, from the very close of the war, those who had fought "in the ranks of the blue" showed a most commendable generosity and magnanimity. A rebel neighbor could not be oppressed merely because he was a rebel, and he was sure of a fair, square trial, even if his political enemies did fill the jury box to the exclusion of his friends. This however was not the case in other counties— notably Ray, Clay, Johnson, etc. In these counties a vindictive animosity was cherished by those who, in the militia, had perchance been worsted in combats with the bodies of irregular light-cavalry under Quantrell, Anderson and others. Their victims might surrender for trial, conscious of innocence, but their certain doom was an already prepared halter and a gaping grave. The judge might be a fair-minded man, the jury true to their oaths, but what they were disposed to spare the hyenas of the mob were sure to rend. At least three several times did the Jameses offer to surrender, if only they could be assured a fair trial. They were conscious of their innocence, and knew that they could establish it by overwhelming evidence. They feared no man, but they did not intend to submit their necks to the mob; nor did they, for they well knew that in that court they had already been tried and found guilty. Governor McClurg came nearer to doing them justice than any subsequent Governor. He was convinced of their innocence, but did not think a trial necessary, consequently the boys never received a public vindication and the hunt after them never ceased.

Hoping against hope, they had held out as only men of unbounded nerve and sanguine anticipations could have done, until at last they saw staring them in the face nothing but persecution uninvited and pursuit eternal. The sectional spirit was fast wearing out, and those who, immediately after the war, had gladly received and sheltered them, began now to assume the look of waning friendship and granted but a cold and formal welcome. The names of the Jameses were connected with every bold, bad deed, and even those who had trusted them began now to suspect. At home, where they were lovingly greeted, they could not stay; so what was left for them? For them there could be no fixed avocation, for they were liable at any time to arrest, and then would come the trial by the mob.

Some may say "they could have fled to foreign countries." True; but who of us all, having even a lingering spark of manhood, will permit himself to be driven by fraud and injustice from all that he loves and cherishes? It is not in the blood of the Anglo-Norman, the born ruler of the world, to submit to such oppression and become a slave. There was but one thing left for them to do, it was to turn upon that law that hounded them and that society that hunted them, and outrage and defy it. These seem strong words until we apply them to ourselves and reason from our own standpoint, or "coign of vantage."

At this time the Youngers being, if possible, more bitterly hunted and oppressed than the Jameses, had already turned in battle against their enemies. None of their family admit it, and who can blame them! Still, after the robbery at Corydon their friends could not help but see that circumstances like an iron web encircled them and pointed to their participation. Those who pretend to know best, members of the old guerrilla bands, indicate as the parties to this (Corydon) raid Jesse James, Ed. Miller, Clell Miller and two others.

They entered the town whooping and yelling, two staying upon their horses to guard the streets, while three dismounted and entered the bank. That a gentler spirit had charge here than that which commanded at Gallatin, Columbia and Richmond is evinced from the treatment of officers and citizens. There was no unnecessary brutality; no gratuitous murder. There was no reckless firing into streets and houses, and everything was managed in a cool, systematic way. In fact so little had the citizens been terrorized that at last they began to collect, and soon a crowd of them amounting to about two hundred were pressing towards the horses of the bandits still in the streets. Who doubts what would have been the course of the man who killed Martin at Columbia, or the one who murdered Sheets at Gallatin, or of him who led the attack at Richmond? A murderous fire from his deadly revolver, two or more dead citizens, and a fleeing crowd. In this instance the crowd is first warned back, and not heeding this, the leader of the bandits bends low on his horse to avoid all chance of a downward plunging ball killing some distant person. His arm is straightened with a pistol in it, and at the moment it is extended a report is heard, a puff of smoke seen, and the hat of the nearest citizen flies from his head.

"I can do better than that next time, gentlemen!" he said, and the crowd, taking him at his word, began to scatter in flight.

The money (about $40,000[2]) in the bank secured, the other bandits remount their horses and they all go out of town at a swinging gallop. Pursuit is almost immediately organized and the trail is taken, and continues fresh until the pursuers reach Cameron, Mo. Here the trail separates, one part of the bandits turning slightly to the southeast, the other almost south. The pursuers, frightened at their proximity to the dreaded Jameses, and terrified at the tales

[2]Loot amounted to only $6,000 Settle, *loc. cit.*, p. 43.

of their prowess, press on no further in pursuit, but return home.

The wealthy stockholders of the bank put into the field a fine corps of detectives, but nothing ever came of their endeavors. One thing, however, had been gained, the fiercest believers in the James boys had their faith shaken by the circumstantial evidence concerning their participation in this raid.

CHAPTER XV.

BANK ROBBERY AT COLUMBIA, KY.

Situation of Columbia, Ky.—A Sudden Apparition—The Demand on the Bank —A Brave Cashier—His Refusal to Deliver the Keys—His Death—A Combination Lock—The Robbery Does Not Pay—Mr. Garrett Fired On—The Useless Murder—Flight of the Robbers—The Citizens Gather—Their Pursuit—It Ends in the Mountains of Tennessee—Death of One of the Robbers—Who They Were—No Further Results—Not the Work of Missouri Outlaws.

COLUMBIA, Ky., is a pleasant rural village in the county of Adair, which is situated in the central portion of the State. Like most of the small towns of the West it contained one bank, which did quite a fair business, and which was supposed to carry unusually heavy deposits for an institution located in so small a place.

It was on a pleasant day [April 29, 1872] toward the close of the month of transient showers when the staid and peaceful burghers of the village were startled by an apparition whose evil portent was unusual in so quiet and secluded a spot. Two or three gentlemen were in the bank talking with the cashier, Mr. Martin. All at once they were astounded by the appearance in their midst of three men with cocked revolvers.

Seeing that Martin was in charge of the funds, they demanded from him the keys of the safe, but were met with a prompt, determined refusal.

"Open up the safe, then, damn you," shouted one of the robbers, while his companion, to add to the terror of the scene, fired at, but luckily missed, one of the gentlemen in the bank.

"Never," responded the brave cashier, "I'll die first."

"Then die it is, damn you," said the leader, and he placed his revolver close to Martin's head and fired. That brave gentleman sank dead upon the floor without a motion.

What might have happened now, what further unnecessary and brutal murder might have been committed, had not the outside robbers become alarmed, will never be known. They shouted to their companions inside, and, making a last effort to open the safe, they hastily gathered what money they could find, and hurried out. The amount was trifling; the brave cashier had saved his trust at the expense of his life.

Mounting their horses, the five men rode hastily out of town toward the Tennessee line and were never again seen. Who they were will ever remain a mystery, but there are some circumstances that plainly point to whom they were not. One of the parties scouting in pursuit came across a solitary desperado in Tennessee, and, taking it for granted that he was connected with the robbery, fired upon him and mortally wounded him. He was known as "Texas," alias "Sandy," alias "Saunders," but who he was, from whence he came, etc., no one ever knew. He died without revealing the names of his accomplices, if he had any, and if he was engaged in the Columbia robbery, there existed no proof of the fact.

That this was not the work of the Missouri outlaws seems clearly proved by several circumstances, and the first is the utter lack of judgment displayed by these men, indicating a nervousness entirely foreign to the men who had fought under Quantrell.

To the clear, quick mind and intuitive judgment of Jesse or Frank James, or the Youngers, a locked vault and a dead cashier formed an impenetrable combination against sudden robbery. Another thing against the supposition that they were engaged in it is the fact that the murder was not only unnecessary, but foolish, and could not have had any other motive (if there was any!) save revenge, and most certainly none of the Jameses or Youngers had any vengeance to wreak upon Mr. Martin. The work was not at all in the style of the Missouri bandits, and was no doubt the work of native imitators of these desperate outlaws. Probably the deed was done by the followers of Hal or Hub Edmunson, Champ Ferguson or the mountain "boomers" of East Tennessee. Quite a number believe from the course of the pursuit and other indications that it was the bungling work of the "boomers." The best detective talent that could be secured became speedily convinced that this was not the work of Missouri outlaws.

CHAPTER XVI.

STE. GENEVIEVE, MO., BANK ROBBERY

STE. GENEVIEVE is an old French town situated upon one of the gently sloping bluffs of the Mississippi River. Built under the French *regime* it still retains the distinguishing characteristics of that race. Its people and institutions are generally Catholic, and there is a strange rest and dreamy quiet pervading even the atmosphere, and widely at variance with the rush and bustle of the unadulterated American. Quaint, gabled houses, surrounded with spacious gardens, where roses and honey-suckles perfume the mild May air, one can almost fancy one's self in some outlying province of sunny France.

Genial, hospitable people meet with a lingering cordiality, at least of words, unknown to the more dashing American citizen. Neighbor languidly chats with neighbor from adjoining gardens, and chatter in their Creole French as volubly as the saucy sparrows which are adjusting their quarrels and love affairs just without the window, upon its narrow ledge.

On this particular May morning [May 27, 1873], however,

these dreamy people are doomed to be rudely awakened by a terrifying incident, that shall make them move more briskly for the time being, at least, and shall thoroughly awaken them for once in their lives. A band of five well mounted men, each bearing two dragoon revolvers, enters the town at a light trot, and two of them dismount. These two walk briskly past the bank just as its Cashier, O. D. Harris, is entering it to open up for the day's business. Turning, these two enter along with Mr. Harris and a young man, named Rozier. Once inside, the persuasive revolvers of the bandits are presented, and Mr. Harris is requested to "stand and deliver."

"Of course, gentlemen," said he, "of course. You've got the bulge on me and I'll give up."

At this juncture of affairs young Rozier, who had been watching in an agony of terror for a chance to escape, broke through the open door and fled wildly up the street, giving the alarm.

The citizens began to gather, and the robbers having obtained all the money in the bank, about $3,500, took their departure, leading Mr. Harris along with them, presumably as a hostage for the good behavior of the other citizens. Coming up to their comrades, who were holding their horses, they mounted, released Mr. Harris, and after firing a few shots into the crowd of citizens, more for the purpose of alarming than injuring them, they started out of town.

The one who was carrying the booty, either got down to pick up the sack, which he had dropped, or to tighten his saddle, the girth of which had slipped, and in doing so his horse escaped, and started off at a rapid gait. It would not do to leave a comrade in such a strait, so forcing into the service a German who chanced along at that time, one of the robbers accompanied him in chase of the flying horse.

It was overtaken and brought back to where the mounted bandits, gathered around their comrade on foot, were holding the citizens back. Hastily mounting, they were about starting when the German, with a true Teutonic thrift, asked one of the men: "Vat you geef for catching dot horse?"

"Your life, you d—d Dutch s— of a b—?" said the leader as he rode off.

Pursuit was made, but it amounted to nothing. The bandits were heard of here, there, everywhere: like the *ignis fatuus*, they were, if seen at all, always seen at a distance.

It is said that, in leaving the town, the brigands shouted: "Hurrah for Sam Hildebrand!" and upon this slender basis some deduced conclusively the fact that it was the band of this swamp ranger. Others attributed the deed to Cullom Baker, the Arkansas desperado; but there are circumstances that show it, to the careful student, as almost certainly the work of Cole Younger, Bob Younger, Jesse James and Clell Miller. Who the fifth man is admits of a great deal of doubt, but it was either Ed. Miller, Dick Little or Frank James.

The *staying* qualities of the band; their coolness in danger; their perfect nerve in the most trying situation; their rallying around a disabled comrade; a want of unnecessary brutality, and a desire to avoid the taking of human life, show it almost conclusively to be the work of the outlaws above referred to.

CHAPTER XVII.

ROBBERY OF THE HOT SPRINGS STAGE.

A Slight Variation—An Old-Time Conveyance—The Enforced Halt—"Come, Tumble Out Here"—The Line Formed—The Victims—The Amount Obtained—Ex-Governor Burbank of Dacotah a Victim—His Losses—A Chat with the Passengers—Lively Badinage—A New York Man Makes a Modest Request—Sternly Refused—A Horse Trade—One Man's Watch and Money Returned—Release of the Stage—The Bandits Separate—Their Flight—Escape.

A JOLLY lot of passengers were journeying from Malvern, on the Iron Mountain road, in Arkansas, to seek the "respite and nepenthe" of the famous waters of the Hot Springs. It was not a very pleasant morning in January, '74[1], though, of course, the weather was much more pleasant than the visitors had left behind them in more Northern latitudes. By the time the stage had reached the old Gaines' place, in a well sheltered valley, the passengers had fallen into quite a friendly discourse, for there is nothing like an old-fashioned stage coach to break down the barriers of social reserve.

One of the party was dwelling upon the romance of a stage ride here towards the close of the 19th century, and remarked:

"Why, it's like old England in the time of Jonathan Wilde and Claude Duval. I wonder if there are any highwaymen left, as well as stage coaches?"

[1]January 15, 1874. The entire caravan consisted of a stagecoach and two light road wagons. Little Rock (Ark.) *Gazette,* January 18, 1874.

The answer came as if to the "cue," as a theatrical person would put it.

"Pull up, there, damn you! or I'll blow your head off."

The stage was quickly brought to a standstill, its companions a little later submitting to the same treatment.

"Come, now, get out here and form a line," said the leader, pointing a dragoon revolver in at the door.

"Oh, certainly," replied one of the passengers, "can't help ourselves—got to do it."

All alighted, except one paralytic cripple; the line was formed, and a search for money and valuables began, which resulted in netting the bandits, including the money of the express box, about $3,000. From ex-Governor Burbank, of Dacotah, in addition to $800 or $900 in money, they obtained a fine gold watch and a diamond pin.

After having relieved the passengers of their valuables, a sudden thought seemed to seize the leader.

"Are there any Southern soldiers here?" he asked.

"I was one," said George Crump, of Memphis.

Having questioned Mr. Crump as to his regiment, service, etc., the leader gave him back his watch and money, with a few highly complimentary remarks.

CHAPTER XVIII.

FAIR GROUNDS ROBBERY AT KANSAS CITY.

A Gala Scene—Immense Crowds—A Kansas City Carnival—Intense Interest—
Fine Racing—Mysterious Visitors—A Raid—The Cash Box Seized—The
Single Shot—Bandits Retreat—Exciting Pursuit.

KANSAS CITY, in Jackson county, Missouri, is probably the
largest and most flourishing city of its age in the world. Being
the metropolis of a large and wealthy section of country, its merchants are energetic business men, liberal as well as pushing. The
city is the natural market and main shipping point for a magnifi-
cent area of as fine grain-growing country as any in the world.
In addition to its many railroads, it has also the Missouri river as
a line of shipment on to the Mississippi and the Gulf of Mexico.

Many manufactures and other industries have sprung up here
and large capital is invested in them. A spirit of liberality seems
to pervade all classes of citizens, and, as a consequence, in addition to fine stores, residences, etc., they have also one of the
finest fair grounds in the United States. Liberal premiums are
offered in every line, and the display is not only first class, but
the attendance is immense.

The "big day" of the fair is to Kansas City what the carnival
is to Rome. All is jollity, mirth and freedom. The stern severity
of the city ordinances is somewhat relaxed, and mathematical
exactness in the walk of the citizens, or of "the stranger within

the gates," is not demanded. A general good feeling seems to pervade the lively, bustling city.

The "big day" had been a success, the grounds were crowded, and the cash box plethoric with its stores of wealth. The afternoon had worn on and the sun was sinking towards the western hills, but still the people showed no lack of interest. An exhibition, however, was at hand for which they were not at all prepared; something not "in the programme." A cloud of dust is seen up the road, the clatter of hoofs is heard, and a band of seven armed men appear upon the scene. At the gate of the fair grounds three of them dismount, and, approaching the treasurer, ask him to point out the cash box. Showing some little hesitation, he is roughly commanded to give it up. This he reluctantly does and remounting their horses the bandits are off like the wind.[1]

As they rode off they fired, some say, a volley of shots; others say a single shot, as a warning to the crowd that what they had taken with such reckless dash and nerve they were determined to hold to the death. It was not a great while until the pursuer was upon their track, but, like all other pursuits, this was soon abandoned without the slightest results. Some time afterwards it was ascertained that the robbers had ridden only six or seven miles, dismounted, lit a pocket lantern, divided the spoil and separated. Thus all trail or trace of them as a band was lost, and while formidable posses hunted them as an organization, they were each looking out for themselves singly, and thus detection was baffled.

No one knows the amount of money the cash-box contained. It seems that the treasurer made no report until the day's business was closed, so it can only be approximated. It was estimated to be between $8,000 and $10,000.[2]

With regard to this robbery the outlaws themselves are singu-

[1] Triplett's narrative is out of chronological order. The fairgrounds robbery occurred September 26, 1872, before either the Ste. Genevieve or Hot Springs robberies.

[2] For a more factual account of the robbery see Settle, *loc. cit.*, pp. 44-47.

larly reticent, considering the fact that no lives were taken. For this reason it is thought that there must have been collusion with some inside parties, who could, without being suspected, lounge about the fair grounds and observe the manner of taking and disposing of the monies. It is all folly to say that Frank James was in the grounds spying around, for, while brave to desperation, Frank James is the most cautious man alive. If any information was gained by the means suggested, Jesse was more likely to have been the man than Frank.

CHAPTER XIX.

The C., R. I. and P. Train Robbery.

A Train Ditched—The Engineer Killed—The Bandits' Rush—Firing—Still Another Surprise—The Cars Invaded—Expectations Not Realized—The Robbers' Calculations—Western Treasure Looked For—Frightened Passengers—Money and Jewelry Taken—Mounting of the Gang—Their Flight—The Sheriff's Pursuit—Its Results—The Band Reach Missouri—Separate—Disappear.

THE novelty of robbing banks had, by 1873, pretty well worn off. There was but little excitement for the public to take up its morning paper and learn that a bank had been entered in broad day-light, its cashier frightened or killed, its funds packed in a convenient canvas sack, and that the robbers had dashed out of town, rode swiftly until night, separated and disappeared. The papers, unless very scarce of readable items, did not give to such occurrences the flaming headlines that they used to when this mode of robbing was new.

But the time had come when they were to be treated to a really genuine sensation. The knights of the road in "Merrie England" used often to "hold up" the coach bound from London to the provincial towns. This was a gigantic feat for that day, but it was reserved for the Missouri freebooters to originate, develop and put into execution the idea of holding up a railroad train.[1]

[1]Most historians agree that the first post Civil War train robbery was committed by the John Reno gang at Seymour, Indiana, October 6, 1866, on the Ohio and Mississippi railroad.

The time for this novel operation had matured, and about the middle of July, 1873, it was carried out. After canvassing the various localities which were feasible and convenient, they at last selected a place on the Chicago, Rock Island and Pacific road, about a dozen miles out of Council Bluffs, Iowa. Here there was a curve and a cut, and it was thought that the ditching of a train might be accomplished without the loss of human life, for some of the members of this gang were opposed to the useless destruction of human life, not only because it was impolitic, but also that it was not their desire to kill any save a detective or militiaman.

This cut, then, having been selected, the bandits repaired here in ones and twos, reaching the place at night about nine o'clock. Having a late time table of the road, they knew just when the train, for which they were on the look out, would reach the cut, so allowing all the other trains to pass they tore up two of the rails, taking out the spikes, but leaving the rails in position, as they knew that the jar of the train would be sufficient to throw them out of place, and consequently they made no further provision for misplacing them on the approach of the train. Said one of them: "If she goes over safely we'll take it as an omen and let 'em go." "Yes," said another, "but she'll never go over." His prediction was verified. Promptly on time came their train thundering along from the West, like some mighty monster groaning beneath a terrible burden. It strikes the further bend of the curve, and at this point a danger signal that had been placed in the cut by the robbers caught the engineer's eye. As quick as a flash he turned on the air brake, checking the momentum of the train, but not soon enough to avoid the fatal wrecking place. With speed but little abated the locomotive strikes the misplaced rails; a shiver, a slipping of the rails, and staggering wildly she plunges into the cut. A loud, unearthly sigh escapes, as the pent-up steam rushes from the rent boiler, and this noise is rendered more demoniacal by savage yells and the sharp, quick explosions of revolvers.

"What can it be?" ask the passengers; "what on earth can it be?"

Lost in wonder and amazement, they are soon to be relieved of their suspense — that is, if it be a relief to have horrible conjecture turned into actual fright.

At the door of each passenger coach now appears a terrible figure—armed, desperate, determined. A light breaks in upon the minds of the passengers. It is robbery with all of its terrors. It is wreck for this purpose. But to these men what if there may be danger to the passengers—some young and weak, some old and infirm; to the bandits it means the certainty of gain. Gain, it is true, accompanied with dangers to them as well as to the wrecked, but then they are inured to danger. They knew the penalty if caught, but they are willing to risk the catching.

The cars are first thoroughly searched and the passengers despoiled of their money and jewelry, and then the attention of the outlaws is directed to the express and mail cars. Here they are doomed to disappointment. Expecting an immense amount of treasure, they find, instead, but small booty; and so the freebooters, like those who follow more honest, if less lucrative and dangerous avocations, are destined to see their great expectations dwindle away into a rather small certainty.

The engineer of the train lay near his cab dead; the fireman was badly bruised, and also a few passengers. The spoils could not have amounted to over a few thousand dollars.[2]

Mounting their horses, they halted, after a few hours' gallop, divided their spoils and separated into twos to meet again that night. A rapid pursuit was made after them by various officials, but it ended just as such pursuits always had ended.

The bandits fled towards Missouri; the friendly shadows of

[2]This holdup occurred July 21, 1873. It was carried out near the community of Adair on the Rock Island tracks fifty-five miles west of Des Moines, Iowa. A spike was removed from the rail and a "small cord" attached. As the train approached, the brigands pulled the rail out of place, causing the train to derail. The engineer, John Rafferty, was killed when he was pitched from the engine as the train rammed into a wall of the cut. "Six large, athletic men, masked in full Ku Klux style" comprised the force. Frank and Jesse James were the principal suspects. Leavenworth (Kans.) *Times*, July 23, 29, 1873.

the night mantled them; they separated, and singly or in twos rode to their hiding places.

This separation after a robbery was a peculiarity of these outlaws, and it proved their safety in every instance. With all other robbers, fear of the outraged law and the fierce pursuit held them banded together—an object easily trailed and identified. Seven men rob a railway train; seven men, riding jaded but fine horses, are seen, a long distance off, it is true, but still they are an object of suspicion, from the very fact that they are seven, if from no other. Thus, all other bands have sooner or later been captured or destroyed. But now look upon this picture: Seven men rob a train in Iowa to-day, and to-morrow two travelers are seen sixty or eighty miles away, their steeds jaded, but the men jovial and jogging along the road in a quiet, orderly manner—why, Vidocq himself would never connect these two with the other seven. They fully realized the truth of the old adage that "in union there is strength," but they had also learned that in division there was safety.

Who were present at this robbery is so well known that it is useless here to dispute about it, still it is a fact that Frank James and Cole Younger were innocent of it.

CHAPTER XX.

The Train Robbery at Gads' Hill.

Shakespearian Reminiscences—Old Jack Falstaff—A Lengthy Visit—The Entire Population Jailed!—The Generalship Displayed—A Misplaced Switch —A Danger Signal—"Down Brakes"—A Winter Evening—The Train Stops— The First Victim—The Robbers' Tactics—The Express Car—A Broken Safe —Its Contents Sacked—A Search for Pinkerton—The Flight of The Robbers—A Thorough Pursuit—Its Utter Failure—Incidents of The Robbery— Who Were The Robbers?

IN Wayne county, Missouri, on the Saint Louis, Iron Mountain and Southern Railway, in the midst of huge hills and heavy forests, lies a little hamlet, which some lover of the immortal William had christened. Could any presentiment have possibly suggested to his mind that an exploit, by far outrivalling the imaginary ones of the fat, old knight, kindly Jack Falstaff, at the English Gads' Hill, would be here enacted? Not likely, for who, in pondering over the doughty exploits of this slayer of multiplying men in buckram, could ever dream of travellers being waylaid here upon the iron highway in an unfrequented part of the country. Not probable!

But then, again, could the name have, by any possibility, suggested to the outlaws a fit combination of cognomen and place to add still further to the notoriety of a name destined to live for all time, or at least until the English language has gone down into oblivion, and Macaulay's New Zealander has pushed the effete race of the Anglo-Norman from off the face of the earth? Remember that several of these outlaws are men of more than ordinary culture.

But we will leave these reminiscences of the "Swan of Avon;" bury our recollections of *brave* old Jack, and return to our subject.

It was on the 31st day of January, 1874, that Gadshill had a visit. In the history of Gadshill any visit would have proved eventful; but this being no ordinary visit, the interest excited was stupendous. It happened in this wise. About 3 o'clock in the afternoon of the 31st, seven armed men rode into the hamlet, dismounted and tied their horses, leaving one man to guard them. Although no formal invitation had been extended to them, yet they made themselves quite at home, and showed that it was not a mere passing call they intended, but quite a lengthy, if not social visit.

Their first precaution was to scout through the village, not a very onerous task, and secure all of the inhabitants and visitors (amounting to seven or eight). This was a wise precaution on their part, for Piédmont, only seven miles distant, was a telegraph station, and any one who had the slightest idea of the situation could have slipped away to that point, and reached it in time, even if afoot, to warn the down passenger that there was danger ahead.

These prisoners were all put into the station-house and carefully guarded. A signal flag was now set on the track and the lower end of the switch was also opened, so that if, alarmed at any outward indication, the engineer should attempt to run by the station, a ditched train would be the result. But nothing of the kind occurred, and promptly on time the 5.30 passenger from St. Louis appeared, and noticing the signal to stop the engineer whistled "down brakes," and brought the train to a stand-still at the platform.

The conductor, Mr. Alford, stepped off of the cars, was promptly halted, relieved of his valuables and run into the improvised lock-up. While one of the brigands was robbing the conductor, another one had covered the engineer and fireman with a huge revolver, and persuaded them to leave their cab and take a little walk into the woods.

Instantaneously with the work of these two was that of the rest. It consisted in two men placing themselves at the passenger car doors, while another searched the passengers and secured their money, watches, etc.

The safe in the express car next attracted their attention, and a sledge hammer being secured it was broken open and its contents taken. The mail bags were cut open and the valuable letters and packages taken from them.

While searching the passengers each one was asked his name and place of residence. The object of this was made known to one of the passengers, whose curiosity at this strange procedure so far overcame his fright as to cause him to ask an explanation. It seemed that in some way the robbers had got an idea that Allan Pinkerton, the Chicago detective, was on board. It was well for him that he was not, for had he been found it would have required no astrologer to forecast his fate. A bitter hatred existed between this detective and these men, who had so far invariably got the better of the notorious thief-taker.

When the robbers rode out of Gadshill, after releasing all of their prisoners and bidding the engineer and conductor to "pull out," it was black night. No pursuit was attempted from Gadshill, but the train thundered on rapidly to Piedmont, and telegrams were sent in all directions warning every one to be on the lookout for these outlaws. At Piedmont, also, pursuit was organized and the bandits followed to Current river. Even at this distance, only some sixty miles away, two of the outlaws had "vanished into thin air," leaving but five. It is needless to say that the pursuit failed. These were undoubtedly the same men who had robbed the Hot Springs stage shortly before.

CHAPTER XXI.

WHICHER'S DEATH.

The Detective's Doom—His Fatal Error—How He Met His Fate—Cause of
His Employment—Flight from Gadshill Continued—Various Incidents—
Bentonville, Arkansas—The Robbery There—No Efficient Pursuit—The
Trail of the Gadshill Bandits—Their Routes—Allan Pinkerton's Men—
Their Location—Their Inferiority to the Robbers—Death of Captain Lull
—Of Daniels—Wright's Flight—John Younger's Death—Kills His Man
while Falling Dead—Capture of Whicher—His Midnight Ride to Death
—His Body Found.

THE flight of the Gadshill outlaws was continued on through
a sparsely settled country; that of South Missouri, from Current river to the Big Piney in Texas county. They were still five
in number, and seemed to be making for some point in the Indian Nation. Taking Bentonville, Arkansas, in the line of their
retreat, they seemed so little to fear pursuit that here another
outrage was committed. Bentonville lies in the tier of counties
which join Missouri, and is just below the spurs of the Ozark
mountains. It is a small town, prettily situated, and surrounded
by a fairly rich country.

On the afternoon of the 11th day of February the retreating
robbers had reached this place, and riding to the store of Craig
and Son, they dismounted and entered. With drawn revolvers
they enforced quiet on the proprietors and clerks, took all of
the money, about two hundred dollars, and helped themselves
liberally to such goods as they fancied. They next threatened every

one with death if any alarm was made, went out, mounted, and were off. They did not seem to be in any great haste, and when a few pursuers took their trail shortly after, they accomplished nothing.

These three outrages against the majesty of the law and the safety of the people occurring in such rapid succession, and the desperate boldness of their perpetrators, thoroughly aroused the ire of the authorities of Arkansas and Missouri, as well as of the officials of the railway and express companies. Even the United States put its reserve men of the Secret Service at work, determined if possible to repress this rapine and violence.

The States sent posses to the field; the United States its most efficient men of the Secret Service; and the railways and express companies employed the detectives of Chicago and St. Louis. The combination was certainly a most formidable one, and every one now predicted the capture or annihilation of the outlaws.

The trail of the robbers was taken and followed toward the Nation. Here, just at the line, a new idea seemed to have struck them, for they turned towards the north, always by the most secluded routes, on up to and through St. Clair and Jackson counties. Here a division took place, some of the band dropping out here; others continuing on across the river. They had separated and disappeared; it almost seemed as if the earth had opened and swallowed them up.

Pinkerton, incited to furious action by his continual failures, which were greatly injuring his boasted infallibility, determined to secure these men at any cost, so he sent his picked men to Missouri; even sending his brother, William Pinkerton, to Kansas City to establish a headquarters there so that operations might be simplified and results rendered more certain. Captain [Louis J.] Lull, with several assistants, was detached to operate against the Youngers on the south side of the river, while Whicher was to communicate with Jack Ladd,[1] who had been placed at Daniel Askew's, in the immediate Samuels' neighborhood, a year before. This Ladd must have been a man of iron purpose and consummate dissimulation, for he was never for one moment suspected by the Jameses. Working at Askew's as a common hired hand, he was conveniently situated to spy upon the Samuels' household, and could give sure and speedy information of the presence at home of these dreaded outlaws.

When these arrangements were all consummated, Pinkerton is said to have rubbed his hands and said with great glee: "I've got 'em now!" The detective, as the sequel shows, had reckoned without his host. Had the men against whom he plotted been the ordinary thieves of large cities, he would have undoubtedly trapped them; but here he was matched by men of equal or greater skill, more endurance and overpowering bravery. Their unscrupulous readiness to take life was no greater than his, probably not so great, as witness his agents' killing of Little Archie Samuel.

Captain Lull and two others hunting for the Youngers were overtaken by two of their intended victims. Covered with a shot gun, they were ordered to drop their pistols. This they did. One of the Youngers got down to pick up these arms, and John Younger dropped his gun for a moment to quiet his horse. He had made a fatal mistake, for Lull, who was a man of undoubted bravery, hurriedly drew a concealed derringer and fired, striking Younger in the neck, the ball completely severing the jugular vein. It was, of course, a death wound, but so great was the vitality of the man, and so determined his bravery, that in his death agony he drew a pistol and fired, the ball passing through the left arm and into the left side of Lull. Reeling from his saddle he fired twice more, and he and Lull fell at the same instant.

Jim Younger then opened fire on Daniels, who returned it,

[1]There is very little information available on Jack Ladd, if that was his real name. He may or may not have been a Pinkerton operative or a resident of Clay county pressed into service as a spy.

striking Younger and causing a trifling wound. The next shot of Younger struck Daniels in the neck, and he fell dead. The third detective had already fled.[2]

But to return to [John W.] Whicher. After having all the information possible put into his possession, a line of action was determined on, and he departed to Liberty, in Clay county, in order to consult with the officials there.

He called at the bank, stating his object to the president, Mr. [D. J.] Adkins, and was by him advised to consult with Col. [O. P.] Moss, a former sheriff, who could give him full and reliable information. On going to that gentleman and laying his plans before him, Whicher was advised not to undertake the desperate mission.

"You do not know," said this kindly gentleman, "the nature of the risk you undertake; nor can you, who have heretofore dealt only with the ordinary criminal classes, begin to comprehend the cunning and ferocity of these men, who have been educated to combat and strategy as no other men ever have. You need not hope to surprise them; at best you can only hope to elude their suspicion, lucky if you succeed in this. From being continually hunted and trailed by their enemies, it has become almost intuition with them to distinguish an enemy, and, as for daring bravery, they by far surpass any idea you may have formed of them as desperate men."

With such earnest entreaty Col. Moss sought to dissuade Whicher, but in vain.

"I have undertaken this work with my eyes open," said he, "and while I thank you for your evident kindliness, yet I can't help but think you overrate the men and the danger of attempting their arrest."

The Scotch say: "A willful man must have his way"—and so, seeing that Whicher, incited by the hope of earning the large

[2]Lull was using the name W. J. Allen. He was accompanied by a man named John Boyle, who was identified as a private detective. He was using the name James Wright. Their guide was Edwin (or Edward) B. Daniels, a native of St. Clair county. The fight occurred about three miles north of Roscoe, St. Clair county, on the afternoon of March 16, 1874. Kansas City (Mo.), *Times,* March 22, 1874.

rewards offered, would go, the colonel refrained from further entreaty; and Whicher, after changing his clothes, shouldered an old carpet-sack, and taking the afternoon train, soon reached Kearney, a small town within three miles of Dr. Samuel's farm.[3]

Getting off at this place, he enquired for farm work, and then struck out on the road toward Dr. Samuel's. It was growing late in the afternoon, and he found the road a lonely one. He must have been a man of but little nervousness, or the solitary road, winding along the creek and overhung in places with steep bluffs and high, sombre and overreaching woods, must have cast a gloom over his spirits. The allurements of the immense rewards offered, and a cool, undaunted nerve, however, stimulated him, and he walked lightly along, noting every object and every suspicious circumstance, until at last, in passing a dense thicket, a figure confronts him with a drawn revolver.

Ah! Whicher, Fate has overtaken you. Your days on earth are now numbered, but be cool, match the cunning of the guerrilla with the cunning of the detective; the nerve of the outlaw with that of the thief-taker. Do not falter in a single particular— if you do, 'tis death.

Standing grimly in his path, the man with the revolver asks him his business.

"I am seeking work," said Whicher. "I want to get a place on a farm; do you know of any?"

"Yes," said the outlaw. "I know a place for you; a place you will keep all of your life, G— d— you!"

---

[3]Here, again, Triplett has lost the chronological order of his narrative. Whicher arrived in Liberty on March 10. His bullet-riddled body was found the next morning near Independence. It is not known how Whicher came into the hands of his captors after he left for Kearney. He did put in a brief appearance at 3 a.m. the next morning, bound and gagged, and riding a gray horse, closely guarded by three other mounted men. This was at Owen's Ferry across the Missouri river. The party was taken across the river by the ferry keeper who could not, or would not, provide identification of the three guards. Deputy Sheriff John S. Thomason heard the descriptions of the three and decided they were Jesse James, Arthur McCoy, and Jim Anderson, brother of "Bloody Bill." Kansas City *Times*, March 12, 14, 22, 25, 1874; Jefferson City (Mo.), *Peoples Tribune*, March 25, 1874.

"Why, what's the matter with me?" asked Whicher; "what have I done?"

"Enough," said the outlaw, "but come with me," pointing to the woods.

To this command Whicher demurred, saying: "Why should I leave my road at your command? I am a free man and under no obligations to follow you. It is now growing late and I must find some place to rest to-night. If you know of any work I can get, tell me; if not, let me go on my way."

At this point of the dialogue three other armed men appeared on the scene.

"What's the use of bothering the man," said one; "why not kill him here, so we can go on? You know we must be home to-night, and it's a long ways to go."

"No, damn him," said the first bandit, "I've got a few questions to ask him, and he's got to answer them."

Whicher, thinking he might still deceive them, as he had no papers, badge, etc., upon his person, consented to accompany them.

"All right," he said, with a forced smile, "rather than have words about it I'll go with you."

Turning from the road, they all walked back about a quarter of a mile to where a steep bluff overhung a bridle-path in the dark woods.

Here they halted, and the first outlaw, who was no other than Jesse James, began to question the detective.

"Who are you, and what are you doing in this part of the country?" he asked.

"I am a poor man looking for work," responded the detective.

"These are d——d fine hands for a laborer," said Jesse, as he took one of Whicher's hands and examined it.

"I have not always been so poor," said the detective, hoping to excite some sympathy.

"No! nor you ain't so terribly poor now," said Jesse, turning to the other outlaws.

One of these now stepped up to Whicher and searched him, finding, in an inside breast pocket, a heavy Smith and Wesson's revolver. This discovery seemed greatly to enrage the outlaws, and one of them was for killing him immediately.

"No," said Jesse, "I want to ask him some questions; are you from Chicago?" said he to Whicher.

"No, sir!" said the latter.

"Where, then?" asked James.

"From Indiana, sir!" (Whicher's former home.)

"I suppose you'll admit that you are a G—d d—d detective of Pinkerton's," said James.

"No, sir! I am not," said Whicher; "and even if I was, I've never done you any harm."

"No; but you'd like most d—d well to," said Jesse.

"Now, I want to lay down the law to you," he continued, "so that all of your tribe may know how I deal with you fellows who hunt men for money. I know you are all a pack of thieves, from Pinkerton down. I've been in cities, and know that they select all of their detectives from amongst thieves, who are mean enough to turn traitors to their companions. Now, this of itself is enough to condemn you to death, and the fact that you risk your life for money ought to make you willing to submit to it."

Seeing murder in the outlaw's eyes, Whicher poured out a prayer for mercy that was eloquent in its despair. He pleaded not for his life as a coward might, but that he might be spared to his young and loving wife. He painted such a scene of devotion and the suffering his death would entail upon a loving woman, that Jesse lowered his revolver (thinking, no doubt, of one as dear to him as this, and so soon to become the wife of a man whose occupation was as dangerous as that of Whicher), and said: "I can't do it, boys; it's no use talking."

"But I can," said one of the gang, a low, swarthy, ill-favored fellow with a big moustache and high cheek bones, and he drew his revolver.

"Not on my side of the line, Dick!" said Jesse, "not on my side of the line" (river).

"All right, then," said a tall, smoothly shaven man, "we'll take him over the line and do it."

Whicher, seeing that his death had been determined upon, begged Jesse to save him, but the latter, turning away, said: "It isn't for me to say now, ask the rest."

Frank James was not present at this scene at all, although numbers assert that he was an actor in it. When Jesse turned away, the other three tied Whicher's hands securely, placed a gag in his mouth, and taking him a short distance to where their horses were concealed, he was placed on the saddle of one of the horses, his legs tied together under its belly, and the small robber, called Dick, mounted behind him. Regaining the road, they pressed on towards the Missouri river, crossed it, and taking Whicher out into the timber near Blue mills, they there rode under a tree standing near the road. Here the small man produced a piece of rope, tied one end of it around Whicher's neck, and standing up behind him on the horse, secured the other end of it to a limb of the tree. Alighting, he next cut the rope off of the detective's legs and led the horse out from under him, and left him suspended in air. After watching him for some minutes to assure themselves that he was dead, they rode off, firing back at him several times. As they rode off the smallest of the three remarked: "No tender spot in me for a damned detective."[4]

One of the balls fired back at the body must have struck the rope by which it was suspended, for when found, it was lying in the road, a small piece of rope around the neck, another on the limb above it.

As every one knows, the Jameses have everywhere been accused of this murder; but this is not so, for Frank James was not present, and, for the second time in his life (the other will be related in another portion of this book!) Jesse seems to have

[4]Triplett, again, has clothed speculation in the guise of fact. The circumstances under which Whicher was killed are not known. As the Jefferson City *Peoples Tribune*, March 25, 1874, declared: "Whether he was ordered to prepare for his fate, or given some notice of their intentions to kill him, or whether he was shot suddenly while bound helplessly to his horse, is a question that only the three mysterious men know themselves . . ."

given way to the angel whisperings of his better nature, and was willing that his enemy might go in peace.

In speaking of it afterwards, Jesse said:

"If I had killed him before he spoke of his wife, I would never have regretted it, for he was hunting me, and he was a detective taking the chances on his life for the sake of making money, and he had no right to 'squeal' if he got taken in, instead of taking in his man—but," he added, meditatively, "I couldn't do it when he spoke of his wife and how she'd suffer—I couldn't do it!"

Had Whicher known that one of the very men, who accompanied him in his lonely midnight ride to a terrible death, was in Liberty the very day he landed there, he might to-day be alive and happy. But fate willed it otherwise.

At the depot when Whicher's train came in was a plain-looking countryman, who seemed to know no one and who kept his own counsel. Seeing a stranger get off of the train, whose metropolitan air clearly indicated that he was from some city, this plain-looking farmer thought it might be as well to watch his movements. This he did in a slouching, careless manner, not calculated to attract the attention of any one. Seeing the stranger enter the bank, he took a station outside and watched his next move, a hasty glance into the window having showed that the stranger was depositing money.

Leaving the bank, the stranger was next seen in conversation with Col. O. P. Morse [Moss], who was most certainly not a friend of the Jameses. After this conversation was concluded, the stranger disappeared for a short time, and was next seen disguised in a laborer's suit of clothes on his way to the depot, where he took the train to Kearney and to death.

The rest is easily told. The countryman hastened to the Jameses and warned them to be on the lookout, and was even present when Whicher was captured.

Had this detective succeeded in passing unobserved to Askew's, and then joined forces with Jack Ladd, a desperate combat might have been fought between them and the outlaw brothers; but the "sleepless eye" of the detective has never yet proved a match for the wary cunning and watchfulness of these bandits.

John Younger, killed in a gunfight with L. J. Lull on March 17, 1874. Lull later died from wounds inflicted by Younger.

CHAPTER XXII.

JESSE JAMES' MARRIAGE.

Whichers' Pleading—The Outlaw's Bride—A Happy Honeymoon—Courtship Under Difficulties—A True Woman's Love—Devotion to Death—A Woman's Heart—The Marriage Ceremony—Who Was Jesse's Wife—Their Relationship—Mrs. James' Sister—Date of Jesse's Marriage.

IT was but a short time after Whicher's picture of a true wife's distress had granted him a reprieve from death by Jesse James, that the latter married the woman of his choice. And it was a singular union; that of the daring bandit to this gentle woman. It was as if the tender dove should mate with the imperious eagle.

Who shall account for woman's fancies? Who can fathom the depth or reason of her love? Michelet, the tender, old French Philosopher, says of woman: "She reasons not with her head, but with her heart—what with us is judgment, with her is intuition." And he goes on to paint, with gentle touches, her fidelity and devotedness; her sacrifices of self for the object of her love, and the nature at once so passive yet brave in suffering; so active yet yielding in love. He shows that one quarter of her life is a disease, and urges for all of her fancies the tenderest consideration, and for all of her querulousness the profoundest pity. He is right, for woman is as immeasurably superior to man in love, and suffering and devotion, as heaven is to earth. She is the ideal of self-sacrifice, and in endurance a martyr.

Quick to detect the good and slow to believe the evil in a

loved one, the true woman never forsakes him whom once she has loved. To the man this change may come, but no mutation can come to the love of a true woman. Her love is for all time—who knows but for all eternity. The followers of Buddha so firmly believe in the unchangeableness of the love of a true wife that they say "there are no marriages in the life to come—there the woman has become the man's soul."

Miss Zerelda Mimms was a cousin of Jesse James; the daughter of his father's sister, and was named for Jesse's mother, now the wife of Dr. Reuben Samuel. She is a petite lady, slight and graceful, and no man has ever had a truer or more devoted wife than has this outlawed man.

A perfect blonde; of amiable temper, and loving disposition, she was educated at Liberty, Clay Co., Mo. Her mother died when she was quite young, and she was in a great measure thrown upon the care of her sister, who is now married to Mr. Charles McBride, a builder, of Kansas City. Mr. McBride is a man universally esteemed, and his wife, the sister of Mrs. James, is as pleasant a lady as one could meet. Miss Mimms was greatly liked in the large circle of her young friends at Kansas City, and well might she be, for none than she more gentle, kind and good.

There were many suitors for her hand, but the gentle girl had never known but one love, nor could she ever know another. When they were children, she and Jesse had always played together, and the love she cherished for her cousin in her childhood had "grown with her growth and strengthened with her strength."

She had never forgotten his tender care of her, nor his gentle, boyish sympathy with her childish woes and troubles. He had ever been her champion in youth, and in manhood he was her ideal.

Not that she gloried in his evil courses. Far from it, but with the loving charity of a devoted woman she could not believe all of the evil she could not help but hear of her lover cousin.

She had known of the grievous wrongs that had made him a soldier while still almost a child; she had known that he had played the part of a brave and heroic man, while still but a youth;

she had known that he had been hounded from place to place after peace had been declared; she had known him persecuted and maligned, but her trusting heart had never known him evil. To her he had ever been tender as a woman, and how could she believe him cold and cruel?

His wooing was necessarily brief and at long intervals, and in his devotion to his fair cousin he had braved innumerable dangers that a fainter hearted man would have studied long before daring. This he had done, and she felt that it was done *all for her sake!* How could she help but love him, who so devotedly loved her, and who had, in so many ways, proved his love and his devotion?

She had given her consent and at last they determined to marry, and accordingly the nuptial knot was tied and the bridal benediction given on the 24th day of April, 1874, "and the twain became one flesh."

From this time on, "so long as life shall last," her lot is with the outlaw, hunted of men and having no abiding place where he might rest in peace and safety. From this time one she must steel her nerves against the sudden shock of ill report and evil tidings.

From this time she must expect much of grief and of happiness a mere pittance.

From now until her death, or his, she must look forward to many fears alloyed with but little hope; more tears than smiles; more sorrow than gladness.

Has she thought of all this? Aye, but like a true and noble woman she has determined to brave it all for the loved one. Yes, she would brave it all and ten times more; brave agony, shame and death, if it was only to look once into his eyes, his loving arms around her, and hear him call her by that sacred name—that links them together for time and for eternity—WIFE!

Their wedding was of necessity a quiet affair and occurred at the house of a friend near Kearney. The ceremony was performed by the Rev. William James,[1] an uncle of Jesse, who had first fully warned Miss Mimms of the life in store for her. That the warning did not terrify her from her purpose, the marriage shows.

Jesse had prepared a home for his bride, and by pleasant stages they journey thence. Love uplifted them from the sordid cares and bitter grievances of "this work-day world." To Jesse, never given to fear, love had made his courage sublime, for now he had another to care for, and a portion of his bold spirit overflowed into hers and rendered her proof against lowering portents and ill omens.

To each other all in all, and to themselves all sufficient, the very solitude of their new home was an additional charm. What need had they for society; they who had so longed for each other that the presence of another almost seemed a profanation?

Happily the days sped away, and the star light of the balmy nights lent a blessed radiance, as mild yet true as they felt their love to be. The golden days were glorious with promise of a happy future, and no bird of ill omen croaked ghastly forebodings of dire dismay and coming evil.

The sweet fountain of hope, that

"Springs eternal in the human heart,"

warbled only gladsome music, and its gentle rippling answered to the sweet carols of the summer birds.

And yet the time must come, oh happy lovers' when your glorious day shall be changed to darkest night. Many will be the fleeting clouds that shall obscure the radiance of your skies for a brief while, but the "god of day" shall for a time disperse them. Still at last, in an opulent city by the mighty waters of the dark Missouri, the sun of your happiness shall go down in night. Smitten by the traitor hand of a false friend, he that was all to you, oh sad eyed, gentle woman! shall sink from out the ranks of living men.

---

[1]James was a Methodist minister who performed the ceremony at Kearney. Kansas City *Times,* April 4, 1882.

But a loving providence permits no trace of this to shadow your present joy, so love and be loved! Enjoy the sunshine of hope and its golden, glorious summer ere the tide of the years and the frosts of death shall blight and kill. Only the true can truly know that

> "Tis better to have loved and lost
> Than never to have loved at all."

Jesse James in 1875, at age 28, about a year after his marriage to his cousin Zerelda (Zee). *Courtesy St. Joseph (Missouri) Museum.*

CHAPTER XXIII.

SAMUEL'S SIEGE.

Pinkerton's Rage—Defeat on All Sides—His Vindictive Resolution—His Murderous Plot—His Unscrupulous Murder of Little Archie Samuel—The Midnight Assault—Its Horrors—The House Fired in Seven Places—Mrs. Samuel's Right Arm Blown Off—A Night of Terror—Jack Ladd's Assistance —A Revolver Dropped—A Sham Battle—Flight of "Pinkerton's Government Guard"—Death and Anguish in the House—Have the Detectives the Right to Murder?—Their Powers—Jack Ladd Vanishes.

WERE it not for the fact that the incidents related in this chapter are known to thousands, and that they could be proved by many living witnesses that cannot be impeached, the compiler of this work might, with the greatest show of justice, be accused of weaving into the web of a true history some threads of weird and horrid fiction. It can scarcely be credited that such events could possibly occur anywhere in this latter part of the 19th century, except during the barbarous warfare of Cheyennes or Comanches. That it could be the work of men employed by the law to guard the life and property of its citizens almost surpasses belief, yet it is nevertheless absolutely true.

When the news came to Pinkerton that both of his detachments had met with utter defeat, he raged like a caged hyena. His infallibility had become a thing of the past, and the reputation of any mere amateur in detective art seemed likely to rival his. What was to be done? Revenge he must have, even if he had to resort to murder to obtain it. Ah! there was the remedy—he had it at last. He'd smoke the Jameses out like foxes, or kill them in their den.

Calling into requistion the services of the founder and machinist, he planned some infernal machines in the shape of huge hand grenades, and these, with instructions, were promptly shipped to his agents.

Jack Ladd having notified his comrades that he had seen the James boys at home on the 20th and 21st of January, 1875, and that from all indications he supposed they would stay some time, probably a week. At this news there was a gathering of Pinkerton's clans, under the cover of night, by ones, twos and threes. All of this was done with the greatest secrecy, so that no inkling of it might reach the intended victims. Everything was conducted with prudence; no strangers were seen at Liberty or at Kearney; no outsiders were taken into the secret, and only the bitterest of the local enemies of the Jameses had any idea that anything was going on.

It is absolutely certain that the secret had not leaked out, for Jack Ladd had long ago found out who were and who were not the friends of the outlaws. Still, this raid was not a success.

The Jameses were vigilant, shrewd men, and like the wary sailor, may have mistrusted that the deep calm was ominous of a brooding storm. They may have ascertained, too, that dispatches of a peculiar character were passing back and forth; at any rate, when Jack Ladd piloted the detectives and their assistants to the scene, the game had flown.

They were in ample numbers to completely surround the house, and this they did. The time was near midnight when they made their first attempt. In addition to their hand grenades or bombshells, they had seven large balls of cotton "waste," as railway journal packing is called, saturated with turpentine and coal oil. After surrounding the house, they noiselessly approached it, and opening a shutter, they threw in one of their balls of "waste," first having lighted it. The old negro woman aroused the family, and all, including the children, rushed to the scene of the burning. While this ball was furiously blazing, and Mrs. James, Dr. Samuel and the negro woman were trying to put it out, the demons outside —for they can be called by no other name—could plainly see that there were no men present except Dr. Samuel, a kindly old gentleman who was never known to harm a person in his life. *This they could see as plainly as if it was day, as the ball made a very bright light!*

Plainly seeing the women and children in the room, engaged in trying to put out the fire, they set fire to the house in seven places, and threw a huge hand grenade into this room. Their ingenuity was as cunning as it was fiendish, for they had covered the bomb-shell with saturated "waste," so that the family might not suspect what it was, but would cluster round it until it exploded.

Their expectations were fully realized, and at a safe distance outside they had the pleasure of witnessing the consummation of their savage brutality.

Dr. Samuel, in speaking of it, says:

"The bomb-shell was thrown into the room while the fire-ball was still blazing. It was light enough in the room for any person not over thirty yards off to have distinguished our faces. The detectives were not thirty feet distant. Thinking the bomb-shell to be another fire-ball, my wife at first tried to push it up on to the hearth, but finding it to be much heavier than the first one, said: 'Doctor, try and see if you can get it to the hearth.'

"We had used tobacco sticks to get the fire-ball off of the floor and to put out its fire. I still had one in my hand, but found it too light to move the shell. I then got the shovel and began to push it towards the hearth, and just as I had succeeded, the shell exploded. It seemed to me that all at once the room grew black as night; I was blown against the ceiling and heard a tremendous report. Outside I heard several hurrahs, then the groans of my little boy and the agonized cries of my wife, who told me her right arm was blown to pieces. To add to the horror of the scene, the detectives began cross-firing past the house and then left; one man calling out: 'Hurry up, boys, for we'll have to come back again just to keep up appearances.' As soon as they started I went to the door and screamed for help, and at last some neighbors came."

It was a terrible spectacle they found. An aged lady, with her right arm shattered and only saved from death by the thoughtfulness of her old negro servant, without whose aid she must have bled to death before the arrival of the doctor.

Upon the same couch with its wounded mother a poor little child, aged eight years, writhing in mortal agony, his eyes already glazing and the death damp upon his brow. The shell, in exploding, had torn a frightful wound in his left side, and through this ghastly rent was swiftly ebbing the crimson life-tide of this innocent little victim of detective barbarity.

A little negro boy was slightly wounded and two other children badly bruised. Truly this was a night of horror beyond all precedent.[1]

At last the morning came, cold and gray and sad. It found inside the house agony and death, outside, the prints of heavy boots and traces of fiendish preparation. Close to the house, dropped during the horrors of the explosion or the panic of the flight, was found a large revolver branded "P. G. G.," these cabalistic letters being the initials for "Pinkerton's Government Guard." This pistol was taken away by Adjutant-General [George Caleb] Bingham, with the promise that it should be returned, which promise was never kept. Whether he wanted it as a trophy of detective humanity and civilization, or whether he desired to remove an accusing witness, will never be known, for Bingham has long since gone into that other, and we hope better world, "where the wicked cease from troubling and the weary are at rest."

It is a sad commentary upon the then chief magistrate, Gov-

---

[1]The raid on the Samuel farm occurred between midnight and one o'clock on the morning of January 26, 1875. The boy's name was Archie P. Samuel. He is buried beside his mother in Mt. Olive Cemetery in Kearney. Liberty *Tribune*, January 29, 1875.

ernor [Silas] Woodson, that no mighty efforts were made to apprehend the infamous wretches who thus defied all law, both of God and man, and stained the soil of Missouri with a terrible crime, unparalleled for cold-blooded brutality in the annals of the century.

Such crimes as these make us to pause and wonder if the hunted outlaw is not an angel of light compared to this parasite of the law, that under the cover of her mighty shield thus revels in dalliance with attempted arson and base, brutal murder.

The detectives had all fled, and along with the their spy and pilot, Jack Ladd, the hired hand and bosom friend of Daniel Askew. His flight was final, for friend nor foe have ever seen him since.

Mrs. Zerelda Samuel, mother of Frank and Jesse James. *Courtesy St. Joseph Museum.*

CHAPTER XXIV.

Col. Jeff. Jones' Bill.

Proposed Amnesty—The Bill Introduced—The James Brothers Quietly Await
Its Result—Failure to Pass—Provisions of the Bill.

TO say that the news of this outrage, though perpetrated against
the family of the James boys, created astonishment throughout
the State, but feebly expresses the state of the public mind. That
such reprisals might be expected in Zululand, they could dimly
conceive; that they might even be applauded amongst the ferocious
bands of the Apaches and the Utes, they might be made to believe; but that in this, their own State, blessed with education and
refinement, with wealth and Christian civilization, never!

That it could be approved by any, save a few obliquely moral
minds, is impossible of belief, and consequently no one was surprised that a strong under-current of sympathy set in towards
those, whom, as their friends and apologists contended, were

"More sinned against than sinning."

People argued from these revelations that, no matter how
badly the Jameses might have acted, and no matter how slight
their provocation might have been, they could not, by any possibility, be any more radically wrong than these worse than savages
who ruthlessly set about to murder women and children in cold
blood. The very actions of such men as these, operating under

the cover of the law and bearing detectives' commissions, gave color, form and substance to the assertions of the brothers that they could not surrender in safety to the proper authorities to be tried. And it did work a very material change in the sentiments of all law-abiding men, for they argued, and very justly, too, that there was no warrant of the law to put down robbery with arson, and the murder of men by the retaliatory assassination of children and maiming of women.

This opinion was held, not by the vicious classes, who always decry the efforts of justice to suppress crime, no matter how fair her methods, nor how pure her motives, but by all thinking people and fair-minded men of every class and shade of political opinion.

It led also to the introduction in the Missouri Legislature [on March 17, 1875] of an amnesty bill [actually a resolution] by the Hon. Jeff. Jones, of Callaway, who was at that time (1875) a member of the House of Representatives. The United States had already granted a general amnesty to all who had been engaged in rebellion against her authority, and the grounds for the introduction of this special amnesty bill were certainly ample.

A great deal of money had been expended by the State government for their capture, and so far without result:

Judging from experience, the best of guides, there was but little, if any hopes of ever effecting their capture:

It was even doubted if their capture by such methods as that last attempted would not work greater harm to the good name of the State of Missouri than their unrestricted freedom:

Every species of crime attempted and successfully carried out, whether committed by them or not, would be charged to them, and so numerous other criminals would escape:

There was at least some show of justice for their claim that they had been hounded and persecuted by their enemies, and had not been allowed to stay at home in peace and quiet:

By being so hounded and persecuted, they would be deprived of all means of making an honest livelihood, and would thus eventually be forced to become marauders and robbers, even if, as their friends claimed, they were not so now:

Their outlawry was not the result of crimes committed since the war, but dated back to the acts of 1861 to 1865.

Essential portions of the Bill offered by Hon. Jeff. Jones read as follows:

"WHEREAS, By the 4th Section of the 11th Article of the Constitution of the State of Missouri, all persons in the military service of the United States, or who acted under the authority thereof in this State, are relieved from all civil liability and all criminal punishment for all acts done by them since the 1st day of January, A.D. 1861; and

WHEREAS, By the 12th Section of the said 11th Article of said Constitution, provision is made by which, under certain circumstances, may be seized, transported to, indicted, tried and punished in distant counties, any Confederate under ban of despotic displeasure, thereby contravening the Constitution of the United States and every principle of enlightened humanity; and

"WHEREAS, Such discrimination evinces a want of manly generosity and statesmanship on the part of the party imposing, and of courage and manhood on the part of the party submitting tamely thereto; and

"WHEREAS, Believing these men* too brave to be mean, too generous to be revengeful, and too gallant and honorable to betray a friend or break a promise; and believing further that most, if not all the offences, with which they are charged, have been committed by others, and perhaps by those pretending to hunt them or by their confederates; that their names are, and have been, used to direct suspicion from and thereby relieve the actual perpetrators; that the return of these men to their homes and friends would have the effect of greatly lessening crime in our State, by turning public attention to the real criminals, and that common justice, sound policy and true statesmanship alike demand that amnesty

*"Jesse W. James, Frank James, Coleman Younger, Robert Younger and others."

should be extended to all alike of both parties for all acts done or charged to have been done during the war; therefore be it

"*Resolved* by the House of Representatives, the Senate concurring therein:

"That the Governor of this State be and he is hereby requested to issue his proclamation, notifying the said Jesse W. James, Frank James, Coleman Younger, Robert Younger and James Younger and others, that full and complete amnesty and pardon will be granted them for all acts charged to or committed by them during the late civil war, and inviting them peaceably to return to their respective homes in this State and there quietly to remain, submitting themselves to such proceedings as may be instituted against them by the Courts for all offences charged to have been committed since said war; promising and guaranteeing to them and each of them full protection and a fair trial therein; and that full protection shall be given them from the time of their entrance into the State and his notice thereof under said proclamation and invitation."

Colonel Jones, a brave, generous man, one of nature's true noblemen, pressed his bill with energy and with earnest conscientiousness, and his persuasive eloquence secured for it the favorable consideration of the Committee on Criminal Jurisprudence. Colonel Jones was a member of that committee, and his earnest advocacy induced a majority of the committee to report favorably upon the Bill.

Towards the close of the session the Bill came up for its third reading in the House. Of course Colonel Jones gave it his most eloquent and cordial support, and his speech in advocacy of its passage shows the warm, large nature of the man in glowing colors. The opposition came not from the Republican side of the house, and had it depended upon them it is believed that it could have been passed.[1] A Democrat offered, in opposition, the message of Governor Woodson to the preceding Legislature, condemning these

---

[1]Fifty-six Democrats and two Republicans voted for the resolution while twenty Democrats and nineteen Republicans opposed it. Settle, *Jesse James*, p. 83.

very outlaws. Policy prevailed, and this time the door of hope and of reform was forever shut against the outlaws and there was left no possible course for their return to paths of peace and honesty.

Why there should have been any opposition to this Bill, which only exempted them from crimes committed during the war, and still held them liable for any offences they might be guilty of since that time, it is difficult at this late day to imagine.

CHAPTER XXV.

FATE OF DANIEL ASKEW.

Events Following Failure of Amnesty Bill—A Moonlight Night—Part of Daniel Askew in the Samuel's Siege—His Connection with Jack Ladd—Who Led the Detectives—The Fatal Drink—Three Shots—A Dead Man—The Assassins Fly—Henry H. Sears—What He Saw—The Coroner—What He Finds.

THAT the Jameses and Youngers intended to avail themselves of the provisions of this bill, surrender and stand a trial in the courts of law for all crimes charged against them since the close of the war, we have every evidence to believe.

That its failure to pass rendered them more desperate than ever, closing against them, as it did, every opportunity for a fair trial, and every chance to settle down to quiet avocations, no one can for a moment doubt.

Living near the Jameses was a neighbor, named Askew, who had never hesitated to declare his belief in the guilt of the outlaws. This he did in a bold, open way, and the fact that he had never been molested before gives color to their denial of any knowledge of how he was killed, or by whom. True, they now had greater cause to wish him taken off, but then there were others whom his bold, outspoken ways had made his bitter enemies, and amongst these were some of his neighbors, who were concerned in the affair at Dr. Samuel's. These men he blamed for harboring the detectives, and for bringing them to his place, without his knowledge, to rendezvous and organize for that attack. He was a brave man, too, and it is believed by those who knew him best that he would never have countenanced such a proposal as the burning of a neighbor's house and the indiscriminate murder of women and children. *He knew too much,* and fearing he might at the last betray them to the Jameses in order to save himself, the cowards determined on his murder. All of the actions of the assassins go to show that the deed was not perpetrated by the outlaws.

First: the lying in wait at the woodpile, when they could sooner and more easily have dispatched him at the spring, to which they had seen him going.

Second: the hurried volley and the headlong precipitate flight of the assassins, without even waiting to see if they had effected their object.

Third: the call at the house of H. H. Sears, to wake him and tell him they had killed Askew, and the remark, "Say it was the detectives," made purposely to induce the belief that it was the outlaws.

Fourth: the fact that at the time Jesse and Frank James were not in the State.

In speaking of it afterwards, Jesse, as well as Frank, said: "If I had known or very strongly believed that it was he who led the party to my mother's, I would have killed him in a moment; but I never believed he could be such a fool, so I laid all of that work on to Ladd, his hired man."

Askew himself had taken pains to deny all complicity in the raid on Dr. Samuel's, and his word was apt to be taken by those who knew his character as well as did Jesse James. The coroner's inquest developed nothing tending to place the guilt at the door of any certain party, and so found. Who the parties were, who did the killing, will probably remain forever a mystery; but the strongest indications point to the neighbors, who had assisted in the raid, and who, after the terrible termination of that tragic occurrence, had cause to fear, *not only the anger and reprisals of the Jameses, but also the outraged majesty of the law;* hence their desire to remove the only party who knew them, and *this was Daniel H. Askew.*[1]

Some, knowing the absence of the Jameses from the State, have thought the crime committed by some of their old comrades, but this is hardly so, as the work was done in a style entirely different from that of these outlaws.

To the world at large, of course, it was published as another outrage of the James boys, and would have been, even if they had been in Central Africa, instead of a few hundred miles out of the State.

[1]Askew was killed April 12, 1875. Ironically, he had been one of the party of neighbors who came to assist and provide medical treatment for the Samuel family on the night of the raid. Liberty *Tribune,* January 29, 1875.

CHAPTER XXVI.

A Texas Ranche.

Herding Cattle—An Indian Raid—How It Is Done—The Cowboy's Fate—
A Cruel Death—Jesse Strikes The Trail—Overtakes The Indians—A
Running Fight—The Herd Recovered—The Dead Girl—An Attempt at
Revenge—The Return Home—The Burial.

WHEN Jesse and Frank James found that it would be impossible
for them to remain at home in safety, they entered Texas,
and searching for a suitable place for a cattle ranche found one
that could be had on very favorable terms, so they secured it. A
misanthropical Englishman had located in Texas, afar in the western part of it, toward the Rio Grande. "Here," he said, "I will
live a life apart from all I have ever known. If I have any neighbors
at all they will be the noble red men, uncontaminated by the vices
and hypocrisies of the whites. His communings are with nature,
and in him I will find a congenial friend."

He found the Indian most certainly inclined to visiting, if not
very social. The first full moon after locating on his ranche the
Comanches paid him a visit. Not having their visiting cards along,
they left him instead one dead and one badly wounded "cow-boy,"
and carried off a hundred head of his cattle and a few horses.

Shortly after the Kickapoos of Old Mexico, having left their
valley homes on a scouting party, called to interview this genial
old Englishman, and, in addition to raising the greater number
of his remaining cattle, came near lifting his scalp. These amusing

little amenities of Lo made him not only willing, but anxious to
close out his ranche to the first buyer that came along, and he
hailed the advent of Frank James as that of a deliverer. The trade
was effected without much haggling over terms, and the misanthrope
sought the "settlements" with an improved opinion of the civilized
species of the *genus homo*.

The ranche was situated in a lovely valley, the upper portion
of it ending in a short canyon, where from under a steep, overhanging bluff burst forth one of those immense springs, or rather
underground rivers, peculiar to Southern Texas. Thus does the
San Antonio river burst forth a few miles above the lovely little
city of San Antonio, or as the Texan affectionately and lazily calls
it, San Antone. Rising in the park of Mr. Brackenridge, president
of the First National Bank of San Antonio, it meanders gently
through the streets of the city, and adds a piquant beauty to that
quaint, delightful city. Its banks are bordered with Spanish dagger
plants; the long, wide-arching leaves of the banana, and the huge
live oak, with its pendant drapery of Spanish moss hanging like
the gray beard of some picturesque mendicant.

The San Marcos river, the San Pedro, the Cebolo and numerous other of the small rivers burst thus suddenly from beneath
some bluff, or from out some open valley.

It is useless to attempt to describe the beauty of this ranche,
for words fail to put it in its proper colors; suffice it to say that
it was a gem of landscape loveliness.

Here the Jameses found rest, and here they relaxed their vigilance, that, in the more closely populated portions of the country,
truly seemed eternal. Looking only for the monthly raids of the
redskins, they did not fear detection or pursuit from those of their
own race. Knowing that the Indian chooses the season of the full
moon for his forays, and also knowing that during the day he
seeks some obscure covert for rest and sleep, traveling only at
night; the Jameses, fighting fire with fire, adapted their habits to
those of the Comanche. During the day they slept, but when the
nights came and the broad, round moon was in the heavens, flood-
ing the earth with its mellow light, they mounted their horses and

patrolled their ranche. On many of these nights they heard the plaintive howl of the *coyote,* or prairie wolf; or the lonely hooting of the owl. There was a human significance in these mournful calls, that, beginning somewhere near at hand, gradually grew fainter and at last entirely ceasing, were succeeded by the distant sound of hurrying hoofbeats. Then they knew that the red marauder, despairing of success, had fled; and they realized that their vigilance had saved their herd, perhaps their lives. Then they knew that they might relax their guard, and sleep in security.

But even the most wary may be circumvented, and the James brothers proved no exception to the rule. On one occasion there had been the usual savage signals and the usual retreat, and the brothers returned to the ranche to sleep in fancied security. The marauders had practiced a ruse. Their retreat was about eleven o'clock at night, but they returned at two in the morning, and succeeded in driving off every hoof of stock. The herders had released their vigilance when the Jameses had retired, and this was the result.

Rising early the next morning, the herders saw the state of affairs, and promptly reported the loss. These two brothers were not the men to tamely put up with such spoliation, and, arming Juan and Pedro Garcia, all mounted fresh steeds and took the trail left by the flying robbers.

There was no difficulty in following it, and, as the Indians had lost valuable time by having to wait until morning to make their stroke, they were overtaken by their pursuers, who were riding blooded horses, about four o'clock the next afternoon.

About an hour before coming in sight of the rear picket of the Indians, the pursuers saw a ghastly object, that added to their fury. At the side of the trail, near some mesquite bushes, lying upon a worn and dirty blanket, was a sight that might have melted to tears a heart of stone. A female form, that of a girl not over sixteen, lay stark and stiff in death. Her face was regular in feature and in outline; her hair a golden yellow, tinged with a soft red; her eyes blue, and her complexion of the fairest. The right ankle showed a fresh, deep abrasion; and around the left, cutting into the delicate flesh, was a piece of a lariat still attached. There was not a vestige of clothing on her person, nor was any found near her, so it will ever remain a mystery how long this poor girl had been forced to ride in this nude condition. In the left side of the neck was an arrow; just beneath the heart, and in several other parts of the body, were sticking others. It was easy for any one, familiar with the traits of the pet of the Indian bureau, to conjecture what had been the fate of this poor girl before death came to her relief.

Truly "it was a sight to stir a fever in the blood of age," and it fired these daring men to frenzy.

"By G—!" said Frank, "I'd hunt 'em now, if the trail led on and into hell!"

"Yes," said Jesse, "and when we find 'em, we'll remember this," pointing to the dead body.

Removing the arrows as gently as possible from the wounds, they took off two of the blankets strapped behind their saddles, and placing the body upon one, reverently covered it with the other. Cutting a few boughs from the chapparal, they then strewed them over the blankets, and said as they left: "If we live to come back, we'll bury you."

Mounting their horses, they were soon again in chase. At last, rising a gentle slope of the prairie, they saw, not more than a mile away, the band of savages furiously driving the cattle. When they saw that they were pursued, the Indians, eight in number, immediately made preparations for fight.

Three of them continued to urge on the cattle, while five of them dismounted and got their rifles ready for action. The Jameses did likewise. At the first fire the Mexican herders shot wildly, missing of course. Jesse, who had aimed at a very large Indian, had the satisfaction of seeing him fall. Frank's fire brought down one of the Indian horses. The next fire produced no noticeable results, but one of the herders, the youngest and the bravest, Pedro, with the face of a girl, but the brave heart and true soul of a noble man, fell, mortally wounded. Crossing himself like a true Catholic, as he was, he had only time to gasp: "Mi madre! — adios!" and his soul had sped to its final account.

Infuriated at this, the brothers made a dash on their horses, to get in their "revolver work." How this might have terminated none may ever know, for, when within two hundred yards of the enemy, Jesse's horse received a slight, but painful wound, and stumbling, the girth of his saddle broke, and he fell to the ground. The Indians were rapidly firing, and fearing that Jesse was wounded, Frank rushed to his aid.

The Indians who had been driving the cattle, seeing how matters stood, determined to take a hand in the fight, and matters looked decidedly badly for the two brothers, for Juan, after the death of Pedro, had fled.

A brief consultation of the Indians as the two parties met, and they were preparing for a rush that must have ended in the death of the brothers, but just then a loud shout is heard, and coming up at a swinging gallop a band of the old Baylor rangers, under Captain Hays, is seen. By this time Jesse's saddle girth is repaired, and he and Frank join in a pursuit that resulted in the death of every Indian.

Returning with the rangers, who were ten in number, the various incidents of the happy meeting were explained. Journeying back by the same trail over which they had pursued the enemy, the body of the unknown girl was buried upon the lonely prairie where she died.

Nothing marks her last, lone resting place, save a pile of stones, heaped upon the shallow grave to preserve it from the desecration of that plain's hyena, the *coyote*. No carved epitaph to tell the story of her name and life, no monumental urn to hold the mouldering dust; but the All-seeing Eye of the "Ancient of Days" beholds her, and her troubled spirit rests within the bosom of "the lowly Nazarene."[1]

[1]Stories of the James brothers in Mexico and at the rest ranch have been handed down from biographer to biographer without any support in fact.

CHAPTER XXVII.

Stage Robbery Near San Antonio.

Holding Up A Stage-Coach—How It Was Done—The Passengers—Who They Were—How Treated—Jim Reed Shot—His Alleged Confession—"Give A Dog A Bad Name," etc.—Who The Robbers Were—Various Incidents.

WE had at first determined to make no mention of this outrage, thinking that at this date no one could believe that the Jameses and Youngers, (who at the time were promptly accused of it!) were present at this robbery. Still we do find some who insist that they were the leaders in the affair, so we here enter for them the plea of "not guilty."

It was on the 7th day of April, 1874, that the stage between Austin and San Antonio was robbed. Five masked bandits advanced up the road, and meeting the stage presented their pistols and ordered a halt.

"What do you want?" asked the driver. "What do you mean by stopping this coach?"

"We mean to hold you up, G— d— you! so keep your mouth shut, or we'll make you!"

He was then ordered down and made to open the stage door. Two of the bandits were now on one side of the coach; two on the other, and the fifth one was at the horses' heads. The passengers were now ordered out and formed into line, and when satisfied that all were in line the two bandits on the opposite side rode around, alighted and began to search the passengers for money and jewelry. The ladies in the party were treated with great respect, but were forced to give up their valuables with as little ceremony as their male companions.

With some of the latter quite amusing dialogues were held. Amongst them was one between a robber and Bishop Gregg of the Episcopal Church. When told by the robber that he must give up his watch and money, he asked the leader:

"Do you mean to rob us?"

"We intend to relieve you of your surplus funds and your useless jewelry," responded that individual. "You can call it robbery if it suits you."

Here the Bishop stated to the robber his calling, a minister of the Gospel, and begged to be allowed to retain his watch, a valuable present from some friend.

"*You* don't need a watch," said the bandit; "Christ didn't have one! Your money, too, we'll take, for you are commanded when you travel to take no purse or scrip. If you live by the Book you must abide by it!"

Mr. Brackenridge, president of the First National Bank of San Antonio, was relieved of his wallet, containing about $1,000.

There were eleven passengers in all, and none of them escaped search and spoliation. The mail bags were cut open, and all valuable letters and packages appropriated. Even the trunks of the passengers were taken from the boot and rifled.

Having secured all of the valuables in the party, the outlaws now cut out the two lead horses from the stage team, and left them to drag the heavy four-horse coach with two horses.

The time the robbers held the coach could not have been less than two hours, but the road was a lonely one, and no travelers chanced along to see the bandits or their prey.

The delay occasioned by the team of two horses having to drag in a load for four, gave the robbers a start of a day and a half. Pursuit was attempted, but it can't be conclusively said that they were at any time on the trail.

A desperado named Reed was suspected of complicity in the outrage, and was mortally wounded in an attempt to arrest him. It is doubtful if he was engaged in the affair, and a confession pretended to have been drawn from him prior to his death and implicating the Jameses and Youngers was all "bosh." Even if such confession was ever made, and this is greatly to be doubted, it was false in every particular.

The robbery bears no evidence of the handiwork of the Jameses, except the coolness of the perpetrators, and this alone is not sufficient grounds for the belief. It is now certainly ascertained to be the work of Burton, *alias* White, and a band of amateurs organized by him. Jesse James was in Missouri at the time, and *the very day the robbery occurred was in Kansas City.*

CHAPTER XXVIII.

THE MUNCIE, KANSAS, TRAIN ROBBERY.

Planning the Attack—Selecting the Ground—The Approaching Train—The Precautions Taken—The Train Stops—Boarded by Bandits—The Express Car Detached—Sacking the Safe—Conflicting Accounts—The Amount Realized—A Woman in the Case—An Enraged Lover—A Reckless Ride—It Ends in Arrest—Search at the Station—Its Results—Gold and Jewelry—McDaniels Taken to Kansas—The Lawrence Jail—Escape from the Guard—A Week's Respite—Resists Arrest—Death—Who Planned the Raid—Who Carried it Out.

IN a small house in Kansas City a few desperate and daring men sat planning an attack on a railway train. The chances of reward and the dangers incident to the attempt were fully canvassed. Several plans were suggested as the proper point for the attempt and several avenues of escape considered. But one mode of attack was spoken of, the old one long since familiar to every one. After debating the merits of various f' ces as the proper point to hold up the train, all finally agreed on Muncie.

Muncie is a small station in Wyandotte county, Kansas, containing a water-tank and a few houses, and lying in a dense growth of timber and thick brush. This was a good place to secrete their horses, and it was this consideration that led them to finally fix upon this as the scene of operations. Arriving at this point shortly before the train bound East was due, they hitched their horses, and for fear that the train might not stop for water, though this was almost invariably the custom, they placed an obstruction upon the track and took the further precaution of flagging it.

Promptly on time it appeared, approaching rapidly from the West. It was the 18th day of December, 1874[1], and in some mysterious way the bandits had received an intimation that a large treasure safe would leave Denver on the 12th *via* the Kansas Pacific Railway, and consequently they knew that it was due at this point (Muncie) on the afternoon of the 13th.

That they did have an intimation that this treasure would be forwarded from Denver their action plainly shows. When the train came thundering along it seems that their precautions to stop it were not taken in vain, for there being an abundance of water in the tank of the locomotive, the conductor had determined to run through to Kansas City, only five to six miles distant. No sooner had the train stopped, however, than one of the bandits leaped up on the engineer's cab, another cut the express car loose from the train, and the engineer was forced to haul it away from the other cars. It was now entered by the robbers and the messenger made to open his safe. The information of the bandits at the time of the C., R. I. and P. R. R. robbery was defective; here it realized their most sanguine expectations. There was $30,000 in gold dust and over $25,000 in gold coin and currency. Some of the passengers were robbed of their money, but were allowed to retain their watches. In the express car was considerable jewelry, and this was taken.

Having completed the robbery, the bandits hastened to their horses, and mounting, fled towards the Kansas river bridge, crossing into Missouri. During their retreat they overtook a farmer named Steele, and exchanged one of their jaded horses for his fresh one. The train made rapid time to Kansas City, and the alarm was widely spread. A posse of twenty or twenty-five men started out in pursuit. The trail was easily found, and it led towards and through Westport, and then in a southeasterly direction. "Making for the Blue" was the inward exclamation of the members

---

[1]The robbery occurred on December 8. Leavenworth *Daily Times*, December 11, 1874; reward notice in "Governors Correspondence, Thomas A. Osborn," archives department, Kansas State Historical Society.

of the posse. The day succeeding the robbery two of the gang were in Kansas City; one of them lying quietly at his home, the other in his usual haunts, the city slums.

Some French philosopher says that whenever there is any trouble it is always safe to ask: "What was the name of the woman?" Without accepting or denying the truth of this allegation, one of the brigands would, no doubt, most willingly have endorsed it, when he was arrested "on a big drunk" and taken to the police station. "D—n all women!" exclaimed Bud McDaniel most heartily on this occasion.

"Who was Bud McDaniel, and what did he and his woman have to do with the subject in hand?" Patience, gentle reader! Bud McDaniel was one of that class who, "like the lilies of the valley, toil not, neither do they spin," yet in some way manage to exist. He was a believer in that scriptural injunction: "take no thought for the morrow;" though it is extremely doubtful if he knew that the Scriptures contained such a passage. He was part loafer, part gambler, part pimp and part thief. Like all of his class, he had a girl, and like all of her class, her habits were not the most domestic; so Mr. Bud McDaniel should neither have been surprised nor angry, when, calling on her on the 15th day of December, 1874, he was informed that she was "not at home." At this his feelings were outraged; here he had brought down a buggy to take his girl out for a ride, and only to find out that he had had his trouble for nothing. To a gentleman of the McDaniel class there is but one resort in these desperate emergencies. He felt that he must "whoop it up with the boys;" must "fill his keg" — in plain English, must get drunk. This he proceeded to do. Driving recklessly up and down the streets, taking in all the "dives" and saloons, he is soon in good case to have a charge of "drunk and disorderly" and "reckless driving" preferred against him. Accordingly he is arrested, taken to the station, and then searched preliminary to being locked up.[2] In the first pocket they investigated

[2]William "Bud" McDaniels was arrested in Kansas City on December 10. Wyandotte *Herald,* December 17, 1874.

they found money, in the second, money; in the third, money; in all money! Mistaking him for an ordinary "prospect," he "panned out" a perfect "bonanza." They had supposed they would find on his person some ten or fifteen dollars, but there was over one thousand. In addition there was some jewelry. On being questioned as to how he got it, he said he bought it for his girl, to make her a present. Being questioned as to where he bought it, he could give no satisfactory answer, and eventually it was recognized as some of the spoil of the train robbery. A part of the money found on his person was gold coin, and no one doubted but that Mr. McDaniel had been an assistant in "holding up" a railway train, rather a bold feat for one of his caliber.

He was taken to Lawrence, confined in the jail there, and indicted by the grand jury. Like Mark Tapley, he came out strong in adversity. No threats nor inducements could make him betray his confederates, and his stern and stubborn refusals under any and all circumstances "to give away his pals," as he expressed it, cause admiration for his courage and fidelity, even though displayed in a bad cause.

When the time for his trial came on, one of the sheriff's deputies started with him from the jail to the court-house. Going peaceably along a few yards, McDaniels made a desperate break for liberty, and succeeded in escaping. Had he possessed the cool judgment of the Jameses he need not have been captured a week later. We say captured, but it was only his dead body that was captured, he being mortally wounded in the attempt, and had that supreme felicity of the Western desperado — the pleasure of "dying with his boots on."[3]

[3]McDaniels made his escape from the Lawrence, Kansas jail on June 27, 1875, after he and other prisoners subdued a guard. The next day he was wounded by a German farmer west of Lawrence and lived until the next evening.

Some writers also credit the James gang with the robbery of a bank in Corinth, Miss., the day before the Muncie holdup. For an analysis of the two robberies, see Jeffrey Burton, "Attributed to the James Gang," *The English Westerners' Brand Book*, v. 6, no. 4 (April, 1964), pp. 1-11.

CHAPTER XXIX.

HUNTINGTON, WEST VIRGINIA, BANK ROBBERY.

The Ohio River—Chesapeake & Ohio Railway—Location of Huntington—Its Inhabitants—Its Bank—The Robbery—The Flight—Pursuit—"Yankee" Bligh, the Louisville Detective—In the Mountains—Death of Thomp. McDaniel—Game to the Last—Capture of Jack Keen—His Statements—Newspaper Accounts—Escape of Two of the Gang into Missouri.

"THE beautiful river," as the first French explorers of the then wilderness lying along its shores called it, certainly merits this complimentary title. Clear as a crystal, the smoothly flowing waters of the Ohio sparkle brightly in the sun, or ripple under the gentle influences of peaceful zephyrs into thousands of lines of light and shade, and dancing on beneath the silvery moonbeams, its flowing is as limpid as the radiant waters, that cheered and refreshed our first parents in the garden of Eden.

Lying upon one of the banks of this lovely stream, in Cabell county, West Virginia, is the charming little town of Huntington. It is also reached by the Cheasapeake & Ohio railway. The town has a beautiful location, being seated in the midst of overhanging trees, and its yards and gardens are filled with fragrant shrubs and lovely flowers. Its business was very good indeed for a town of its size, containing, as it did in 1876, about three thousand inhabitants.

A bank with a moderate capital enabled its business men and the surrounding farmers to transact their financial affairs with the outside world. The cashier of this bank was Mr. R. T. Oney.

Amongst the denizens of Huntington was one Jack Keen, a citizen of the Bud McDaniel type in every thing, but nerve. Mr. Keen, like all men of his occupation, was rather peripatetic in his habits, and was often missing from his home. These absences, however, produced no alarm in the minds of his fellow-citizens, who doubtless thought of him, as has been said of some enforced absentees from home, that he had "left his country for his country's good." One of his absences, however, was productive of unusual results, for, during its continuance, he recruited a band of kindred spirits to the number of four, including himself. These men arrived together in Huntington, and one fine morning made a descent on the bank of which Mr. Oney was cashier.

They came into the town quietly, but all mounted. There was no sudden entrance with whoop and yell and the firing of pistols, but they discreetly rode up to the bank, and two dismounted, leaving the other two to hold the horses. These two remained on horseback. The dismounted robbers, once in the door, drew their revolvers and covered Mr. Oney and a friend of his who happened to be in the bank at the time. The contents of the safe were rapidly transferred to a sack, and they hastily joined their companions, who had begun to fire on the gathering citizens. Mounting their horses, the four men galloped out of town, firing a few shots as they went to intimidate the people.[1]

In this instance a most vigorous pursuit was begun, and kept up with energy, courage and perseverance, resulting in partial success. [D.G.] "Yankee" Bligh, the great Louisville detective, was engaged in the pursuit, and the whole country was aroused. Telegrams were sent in every direction, and a systematic hunt was organized, that produced good results.

The outlaws were sighted often, but whenever pressed closely would make a stand. They early had to abandon their horses,

---

[1]The Huntington robbery occurred on either September 5 or 6, 1875.— Settle, *Jesse James*, p. 87; George Selden Wallace, *Cabell County Annals and Families* (Richmond W. Va., Garrett & Massie, 1935), p. 180.

as well as their contemplated line of retreat, and take to the mountains of East Tennessee and those of Kentucky. Ten days had now elapsed, and still the wood-craft and cunning of the robbers eluded the vigilance of the hundreds of their pursuers. It seemed a mystery that they had not been captured long before. This tenth day, however, was destined to prove eventful. For Thomp. McDaniel, one of the flying robbers, the "Ides of March had come."

The trail of the robbers was never allowed to become cold, and daily reports of their whereabouts and the direction taken by them were made to "Yankee" Bligh, and thus it was easy to form some idea as to what points they would pass. The last report had stated them to be heading toward Pine Hill, Ky. The people in that vicinity were on the look out; amongst the rest J. W. Dillon and his brother.

They had stationed themselves in a dense thicket, at the intersection of two woods roads. Lying behind a large log, noiselessly watching the roads, they saw, by the pale moonlight, four men advancing towards them. At the intersection of the roads these did what prudence should long ago have suggested, that is they separated; two of them taking the road angling off from the brothers; the other two coming directly toward them. They had held a short consultation at the forks of the road. What was it? Were they appointing a rendezvous, or were they for the first time deciding to separate and thus try and baffle pursuit? It matters not; to one of them its results were destined to be fatal.

When the brothers Dillon saw two of the bandits coming towards them they took aim and fired. What was their surprise to see the two men, they expected to fall, turn from the road, and rush in the direction pursued by the other robbers. One of them, however, ran as if injured, and after waiting a short time they returned home. The next morning they were up and out early to see if their firing had been entirely in vain. No! Upon the twigs and leaves a plain trail of blood is visible, leading into a cornfield. Following this up they came to one of the bandits terribly wounded.

To their credit be it said, they did not abuse the dying man, but gave him every attention, and procured for him the services of a surgeon. It is said that in the delirium precedent to his death the outlaw made frantic inquiries for "Bud." Thinking that, as death was so rapidly approaching, he might want to make a confession, they asked him: "Who is Bud?" To this he gave no reply. Being further questioned concerning his confederates, he looked firmly at the questioner and replied: "I'll never do my partners dirt. I'm dying. I know it. But I'll never squeal!" (The slang word for confessing.) At this there was a rattling in his throat; a long, deeply drawn moan, half sob, half sigh; a straightening of the limbs, and the bandit knew more of the infinite mysteries of the beyond than does the most learned doctor, or the most erudite theologian—he was dead! As he had lived, so had he died; revengeful to his foes; with lax ideas as to the rights of person and property; faithful to his confederates; and game to the last.

If the newspaper reports are to be credited, a singularly dramatic incident occurred on the day succeeding the outlaw's death. The solitary bandit had in some way found his companions, and the three made their appearance at Mr. Dillon's house for the purpose of obtaining a last look at their dead comrade. When they called, no one was present except a few ladies. As can well be realized, their sudden appearance frightened and surprised Mrs. Dillon greatly. In a gentle, respectful manner they asked the privilege of seeing the dead bandit. This Mrs. Dillon refused, explaining that there were no men at home, and that the coffin lid had been closed, and the remains were ready for burial.

"Excuse me, madam," said the leader, "but it is absolutely necessary that we should see him. We are sorry to disoblige you, but really we cannot take a refusal."

Being badly frightened, she consented, and taking the three into another room, she procured a screw-driver, with which they opened the lid of the coffin. On seeing him, the leader seemed in great grief, and said: "He does not look like he did before. Poor fellow, he must have suffered terribly."

At this the leader, a large, tall man, shed tears, stood awhile in the greatest sorrow, and thanking Mrs. Dillon, walked away gently, bidding her good-bye. They entered the corn-field and disappeared. During the day a dispatch was sent, asking for succor, in anticipation of an attack. None was made.

After wandering about for the next day, they must have found it necessary to separate and each one shift for himself. This was most likely done, for one of them, Jack Keen, was caught in Tennessee, and the other two escaped. Jack Keen had, when captured, $4,000 on his person.

The two who escaped were, without doubt, the same two who assisted in the Gadshill affair; the same who had already disappeared at Current river when pursued in conjunction with the other five. Their names none of the other bandits have ever told, and it may never be known who they were and where they went.

Jack Keen was taken back, tried, and sent to the penitentiary for twelve years.[2]

Of course the first cry was: "the Jameses and Youngers again." They were not concerned in this robbery. In the first place Frank and Jesse James were at that time living in Tennessee, near Nashville, and Jesse, under the name of J. D. Howard, was engaged in a flour speculation, shipping to Savannah, Georgia. In the second place the description does not suit them. In the third place they were riding inferior horses, a thing the Jameses never did when on a raid. In the fourth place their marksmanship with revolvers was too poor.

There were some points of resemblance, very stong in fact, between this work and that of the Jameses; for instance: their coolness under fire; their physical endurance; their devotion to their comrade, who was a Missourian, as were most likely all but Jack Keen.

One point of their work was unlike that of the Jameses, they

---

[2]Jack Keen, or Thomas J. Webb, stood trial at Huntington and on December 4, 1875, was convicted and sentenced to fourteen years in the state penitentiary. *Ibid.*

did not scatter soon enough and thus place in the way of pursuit the most formidable barrier.

It has been pretended that Jack Keen said that Frank James and Cole Younger were there, but this is extremely doubtful; and even if it were so, it would be no evidence, as it might be merely to make himself appear as the comrade of such notorious men, or it might have been done to shield his comrades, who were actually engaged in it.

CHAPTER XXX.

OTTERVILLE TRAIN ROBBERY.

Otter Creek—The Bridge—Heavy Woods—Watchman Arrested—The Danger Signal—The Train Halts—The Express Car Robbed—Passengers Spared—The Telegraph at Work—Indiscretion of Hobbs Kerry—Arrest at Granby—His Confession—Heavy Rewards—Detectives in the Field—The Pursuit—Usual Results—Discontinued.

IT had now been quite a while since a train robbery had occurred, and the banks were so well and strongly guarded that it it seemed as if this method of raising money by the bandits must be abandoned. The last attempt, though not perpetrated by the Jameses, had proved so disastrous as to deter even these bold men from lightly entering into another operation when the risk was so decidedly against them. Their policy in robbing a bank was at its heighth, but the ability to resist and pursue was becoming stronger every day. Their method of attack had sprung forth fully matured at its very inception, as Minerva from the brain of "cloud-compelling Jove;" but while their science could not advance in the slightest, that of their enemies was becoming better developed constantly. The telegraph could be brought into effective service; the country could be easily and widely alarmed; special trains could be sent to cut them off; fords and ferries could be guarded, and in a thousand other ways they could be balked, surrounded and killed, or captured.

The scheme was an alluring one, but in it lurked greater and

greater dangers. Men were no longer smitten with sudden surprise at the sound of horrid oaths and yells in the quiet streets;
they could no longer be terrorized by a reckless, random firing
of dragoon revolvers. The novelty of the thing had worn off, and
people began to prepare for it. They cleaned up old and rusty
rifles; they freshly loaded long disused revolvers; and the wary
bandit could easily see from the handwriting on the wall that this
industry was rapidly nearing its end. If done at all, they would
have to seek distant States, where no attack was anticipated, and
in consequence no defense would be prepared.

They thought the matter over, reckoned up the arguments for
and against the various modes of "making a raise," and finally
settled on another train robbery.

The mode decided, the next thing was to select the proper
place for a bold and paying stroke of business. Where should it
be? In some manner—no one knows how, and the bandits have
never told their most intimate friends—they ascertained that a
large amount of treasure would pass over the Missouri Pacific
railway on a certain day in July, 1876

Learning this, they promptly acted upon their information, and
riding in ones and twos, they reached their rendezvous on the
7th day of July, just at nightfall. Their meeting place was near
Otterville, in Pettis county.[1] Here they went into the heavy timber, and having arranged the details of the attack and the subsequent flight, they secreted their horses, and threw themselves
upon the ground, some of them securing a sleep that would
certainly be needed. It is useless to say that Hobbs Kerry, a new
man, and the only one, by the way, who was captured, did but
little sleeping on this eventful occasion.

Something more than a mile east of Otterville is Otter creek,
which is spanned by a railroad bridge. Before striking this bridge,
the Western train, bound for St. Louis, must pass through a deep,
rock cut. Below this cut, to the South, the robbers hitched their
horses, and lay concealed until the proper time. Great caution was

[1]Otterville is now in Cooper county, Missouri.

always used by the engineers in approaching this place, and the slightest signal would be sufficient to stop the train here. At the bridge is stationed a watchman, whose duty it is to cross and examine the bridge just before and after the passage of each and every train.

According to the newspaper reports and the tale of Hobbs Kerry,[2] which is partially substantiated by the statement of the watchman; Charlie Pitts and Bob Younger arrested this watchman, and after taking his lantern forced him, under threats of death, to tell them his mode of signals. They then securely tied him, but offered no other violence.

By this time the party gathered at the cut, with the exception of Hobbs Kerry and Bill Chadwell, who were left to guard the horses and to keep them in readiness. Having looked well to their arms, etc., the bandits now anxiously awaited the coming of the train, which was due between 11 and 12 o'clock.

At last they hear the low rumble of the train, which gradually increases, until, coming nearer and nearer, its roar is like that of the gathering storm. Charlie Pitts is now sent forward with lantern, and the approaching train stops just at the mouth of the rocky cut, and is instantly boarded by the robbers. The coach doors are guarded, an occasional shot is fired, and the maneuvers of the train robbers generally carried out.

The passengers were not harmed in the slightest, nor even robbed, as the bandits seemed to fear they would lose too much time, so a break was made for the express-car, which they knew to be rich in spoils. The messenger was compelled to open his safe, and even after it was emptied of every thing of value, there was an additional search to see if the messenger had not hidden away some portion of his trust. Nothing further being found, the booty was placed in the ever-present sack and the outlaws disappeared from this car.

A loud whistle called in the others from their posts on the

[2]Kerry's confession may be found in the Kansas City *Times*, August 15, 1876.

platform of the coaches, and all faded away into the silent shadows of the night. A death-like stillness pervades the scene, until
the engineer and fireman having released the watchman, and the
three having removed the obstructions from the track, the train
sped onward once more.

As soon as a station was reached, the news of this daring
outrage was telegraphed to St. Louis, Kansas City and over the
country generally.

The whole time of the robbery was only about one hour, so
that it must have been at least one o'clock A.M. before they had
started in their flight from this scene of pillage. The amount realized had been about $15,000. Had the passengers been searched,
the amount would have been largely increased, as a New York
sporting man had in his possession over $10,000 in cash, besides
quite a number of goverment bonds; several others were flush of
money, but luckily they escaped.

The express companies offered heavy rewards; the railways
joined with them, and the state, too, added to these offers. The
best detective talent of Chicago and St. Louis turned out in force
to hunt for the outlaws. The citizens, the sheriffs and their posses,
even the notorious Bacon Montgomery, with a squad of twenty
or thirty men, turned out to engage in the hunt, which proved
about as effectual as the ridiculous "pistol play" of the train boy.

By daylight the next morning, according to Hobbs Kerry's
statement, they were all twenty miles away. Here they rode into
a deep wood and the spoil was divided; Frank and Jesse James,
Cole and Bob Younger and Pitts taking the lion's share. During
the whole ride Kerry, Chadwell and Miller had no opportunity
of carrying the sack. The division was made by Frank James
The jewelry captured was divided between Frank and Jesse James,
Cole Younger and Charlie Pitts.

The division over, the bandits separated; Kerry, Chadwell and
Pitts striking towards the south-west. Cole Younger and Frank
and Jesse James rode off together in one direction and Bob Younger
and Clell Miller in another.

Kerry and his two companions proceeded in the direction they had selected without molestation. Reaching Grand river, it was forded, and on the other side of it the bandits sought shelter, and lying down upon the ground they obtained a sound sleep. The next morning it was seen that Kerry's horse was used up and could go no farther. Several plans were suggested by his comrades, who did not want to leave him alone, but Hobbs decided to hide his saddle and bridle in the brush, turn his horse loose, and strike the railroad. This he did at Montrose, on the Missouri Kansas and Texas Railway. From Montrose he went to Fort Scott, Kansas, and saw no more of his comrades, whom he left in the Grand river bottoms. At Fort Scott Kerry bought a good suit of clothes, throwing away his old ones. From this point he went by train to Parsons and stayed there that night. From Parsons he went to Vinita, on the St. Louis and San Francisco and the M., K. and T. roads. From here he proceeded to Granby. This point he made headquarters, and branched out in various directions; his principal pursuits seeming to be drinking and gambling and boasting. In his drunken moments he talked often and boastingly of his "nerve," where he'd been, and who was with him, etc. At first, thinking such talk the mere drunken vagaries of a foolish man, no attention was paid to it; but his flushness of money at last caused him to be suspected. He was arrested, tried, and got four years in prison:[3] He "squealed" on his companions, and the events which transpired at Northfield, and the parties engaged, confirm his statements.

The parties engaged in the Otterville robbery were Jesse and Frank James, Cole and Bob Younger, Clell Miller, Charley Pitts (or W ls), Bill Chadwell and Hobbs Kerry.[4]

Charlie Pitts and Bill Chadwell, after separating from Hobbs Kerry, had made their way to Cherokee, Kansas. From here they

[3]Kerry was arrested at Joplin, Mo. Kansas City *Daily Journal,* October 18, 1879.

[4]Clell Miller was really McClellan Miller, Charley Pitts' real name was Samuel Wells, and Bill Chadwell was actually William Stiles. Settle, *Jesse James,* p. 215n22.

went to Coalfield. Owing to the treachery of Lillie Beamer, a widow whom Pitts had deceived, he was captured on Spring river. He had eighteen hundred dollars on his person when "run in," and whether this had anything to do with his escape soon after will now never be known. Chadwell was pursued closely, but having taken Mr. Weller's advice to "beware of the widers," he made his escape.

The other bandits dispersed quietly to their usual hiding-places and were safe.

CHAPTER XXXI.

THE NORTHFIELD BANK ROBBERY.

It is singular with what persistance the bandits denied their presence at some robberies, at which there was neither bloodshed
nor brutality, and yet tacitly admitted theid participation in others
equally as bad or worse. Even to their most intimate friends and
nearest relatives the Jameses and Youngers strenuously denied all
participation whatever in the Hot Springs stage robbery, and also
in the Otterville expedition. Why this is, no one can tell, unless it
is that, having extended a general denial at the time, they have, in
order to be consistent, continued to disclaim them ever since.

Even without the revelations of Hobbs Kerry, there were other
circumstances that pointed to them conclusively as the daring opera-

tors who risked their lives and liberty for the sake of gain. It is true that, being obliged to keep ever out a line of paid pickets and places of rendezvous, the costliness of these adjuncts to safety was enormous, and it is believed by those who best know them, that it was only when money was at the last ebb with them that they threw themselves into the saddle to execute some boldly planned stroke.

The mere sake of gain seemed not to form the temptation, as many suppose; it was a living that was the inducement. Cut off, especially of late years, by their actions from all honest modes of gaining a livelihood, it was in the struggle for bare existence that they perilled everything. Had only a greed of money possessed them, it would have been an easy matter for them to have robbed the passengers at Muncie, Otterville and other places where they spared them; and, too, they could with perfect safety have preyed upon solitary travelers, without the risk to themselves of pursuit by the hired mercenaries of the express companies. Their plan in robbing seems to have been as little as possible to injure the individual, and to strike only wealthy corporations, that themselves had the taint of monopoly or oppression, hanging about them.

That this cannot in the slightest degree be justified, of course all honest men must admit, still they may have hugged the delusion to their souls that it was more honorable to spoil a bank or express company, than to rob a solitary passenger on the highway. The greater ease with which the one increases its money may have caused some special pleading.

It may be said that they showed a brutal and reckless disregard in the taking of human life. Not all of them. Jesse James was not by nature cruel, and has been known to spare his deadliest enemies; while Frank, as is well known, never uses force save to repel force. If the truth could be ascertained, it is extremely doubtful if the crime of deliberate murder could be fixed upon either of these men.

But to return to our subject—the scene of the next expedition of these freebooters. Hobbs Kerry, in his statement, has named the two Jameses, the three Youngers, Clell Miller, Bill Chadwell, Charlie Pitts and himself as the operators in the robbery in the rocky cut near Otterville. Some doubts having been expressed as to the accuracy of his disclosures, he remarked: "Well, you'll find out soon if I am telling the truth." On being pressed further, he pretended that he had nothing more to tell. It may have been that he had no intimation of the raid into Minnesota, for he was hardly the man such prudent operators as the Jameses and Youngers would take into their confidence; still he might have gained some inkling of it, and if so, "his prophetic and oracular soul" did most truly shadow forth results. After Northfield there were but few doubts.

To many it was a mystery why Jesse should have called to his aid so weak a person as Kerry, and it is difficult to determine. The number was certainly sufficiently large without him, and it caused a loss of money to the others in the division. Some say that Chadwell and Pitts refused to go unless Kerry was given a show, but no one knows. It may have been the "beginning of the end;" the weakening of judgment and division of councils, that marked the waning power of the bandits. Be this as it may, he did not, owing to circumstances over which he had no control, accompany his comrades in their next ride, but secure within the walls of the penitentiary, he had cause for congratulating himself on his enforced absence from a ride that, if it had not brought him death, would at least have given him a life-time in the Minnesota penitentiary.

When another raid was contemplated, a council was held and various points were suggested as proper for the attempt. Chadwell, who had graduated as a desperado from rough and tumble combats and horse stealing forays in his native state, Minnesota, was for giving that section a "shaking up." He argued that his thorough knowledge of the country, and friends conveniently located in out-of-the-way places, would ensure a safe retreat, and he knew, he said, that after the wheat harvest was marketed, the banks would be bursting with money. He made a speciality of arguing his intimate knowledge of every secluded road and by-path into and out of the state; if they would just gather the spoil, he would bring them out safe enough. He forgot to tell (and they seemed to have overlooked it) who would bring them out safely in case by any possibility *he* should happen to be killed.

Cole Younger was for a bolder move. Tired of this continual riding and raiding, he had made up his mind to make one more grand stroke, secure a big booty, and retire to some foreign country, since he could have no peace in this. With this aim in view it is perfectly natural that he should desire to make this next stroke not only a successful one, but not a gathering of trivial spoil. It is said that he urged some rich town in Canada. In support of his proposition, and against that of Chadwell, he insisted on the fact that the Canadians were a people less inured to fire arms than any of the Americans, certainly less so than the hardy borderers of Minnesota, and that, in consequence, a rush such as they contemplated would utterly terrorize them and place them completely at the bandits' mercy. They are, said he, a quiet, orderly people, not used to the pistol and knife combats of the Americans; they are men who settle a difficulty with their fists, or in their courts, and half a dozen desperate and well-armed men could ride through the biggest city in Canada and come out alive. You will find on the other hand, that the people of Minnesota, like all borderers, are inured to sudden broils, and that the explosion of pistols in their streets will not terrify them; and besides, he added, by selecting Minnesota we place an immense number of railroads and telegraphs between us and retreat.

The discussion was long and ardent, but at last it was settled that the section proposed by Chadwell should be the next scene of action. They thought that being so remote from the various fields where they had displayed their successful daring, they could take the people completely by surprise, and that before they could recover from their amazement and organize an effective pursuit, they would have struck a safe line of retreat under the guidance of Chadwell.

An order to march was given soon after this decision was arrived at, and an advanced guard, supposed to have been Bill Chadwell and Cole Younger, took the lead, followed a day or two later by the other bandits in couples. These did not go to the same roads, but took as many various paths as possible. A long ride was before them, so the utmost care was taken of their stock; no unnecessary haste being displayed to reach Mankato, the appointed rendezvous.

Proceeding leisurely along, their route marked by no urgency of haste, and their conduct of the most orderly nature, these men might well have been taken for land buyers, well-to-do farmers, or small country merchants. No brawling, drunkenness, or disorder marked their course. Going quietly along, offending no one by act or word, they stopped at quiet inns and farm houses, shunning the larger cities that lay in their course. Some might have wondered at their strange pertinacity in caring for their own steeds; they might also think it a little strange that these horses that never seemed to go out of a plodding walk were groomed as the jockey grooms the racer, and fed as that pet of the turf is fed. Outside of this there was nothing unusual in their manner, though occasionally a connoisseur in horse-flesh might view with delighted eyes the long barrel, thin limbs and velvet coats of these horses; some of which were fit to make a race almost for the price of a king's ransom.

But had these been the merest hacks that ever dragged a cart, their gaits could not have been more sedate on that long walk, or jogging trot to Mankato. The men, too, while riding like centaurs, yet took every care of themselves, and early hours, abstemiousness and temperance had left their bodies in splendid condition. To two of them the country through which they had passed seemed to present an object of absorbing interest. From the top of every hill they mapped upon their minds its salient features; the water courses, the belts of timber, the swamps; nothing escaped their eagle eyes. Could it be that some gloomy presentiment had shown to them that there would be dire necessity for all of this knowledge? No! for it is doubtful if, in the open air, these men of iron nerve ever know gloomy forebodings any more than they experience physical fear.

On they journeyed, each day bringing them nearer to the place of meeting; every hour the hand of Fate drawing nearer and nearer to the ominous moment of defeat and flight. At last they reached Mankato. Near here resided one of Bill Chadwell's friends, and at his house they could gather secretly and freely discuss their further plans. On arriving they found that their *avant couriers* had in view three places: Mankato, St. Peter and Northfield, and it was to discuss the selection of one of the three that this council was held.

Again there was division in the ranks of the robbers, for each place had its attractions. Some favored St. Peter for one thing; some Mankato, for another, and finally all settled down upon Northfield as *the* point. Clearly the hand of Fate was in the thing, for, although Mankato was a larger town, yet it is extremely doubtful if either here or at St. Peter they would have encountered such prompt and sudden resistance and pursuit. Had there been no such man at Northfield as Dr. [Henry] Wheeler to organize resistance, by showing that a bank-robber was only mortal and could be killed as well as another man, it is almost certain that the bandits would have scored another escape.

In fact, the duration of their flight in their wounded condition, and handicapped by a terribly injured and supposed to be dying comrade, shows what might have been effected by them if sound and well. More nerve than they had is impossible to mere human beings, but had they had less, and had made immediate flight after finding an impenetrable safe and while their band was still intact, their chances for escape would have been infinitely greater than after waiting as they did. But those outside would not fly from their comrades in the bank, and those inside were so infuriated at the cashier's obstinacy that they never seemed to fancy that the citizens had risen until, rushing to the door, they saw their dead and wounded comrades.

Just before leaving Missouri on this raid a letter appeared in the *Kansas City Times*,[1] denouncing Hobbs Kerry's revelations as "all lies." What the object of this could have been, supposing the communication to have been genuine, is left to conjecture. No great urgency of denial of the Kerry statement was demanded, for any other train robbery was as bad as this one, and some worse, and certainly no sane man would think that a man of the native sense

---

[1]Two letters from James denouncing Hobbs Kerry's confession appeared in the *Times*. The first, dated August 14 at Oak Grove, Kansas (Mo.?), was published August 18. The second, dated August 18 at "Safe Retreat," was published August 23, 1876. Kerry's confession appeared in the *Times* of August 15, 1876.

and judgment of Jesse James could hope to establish a September *alibi* by a letter dated the 18th of August. The conjectures by some in regard to the actions of these bandits have been so ridiculous that it is wonderful that some of them had not said that it was called out by the fact that he could foretell that while all of the other parties named by Kerry would be killed or captured at Northfield, he and Frank would escape.

Having selected Northfield for their attempt, they divided into two parties, in order to approach the town without exciting suspicion. Some say they divided into three parties. Northfield is a town of some 2,000 to 2,500 inhabitants. It is situated in Rice county, on the line of the Milwaukee and St. Paul Railway. Cannon River is a beautiful little rivulet, which runs through the town. It is spanned by a fine iron bridge, and is the thoroughfare for crossing teams, footmen, etc. It contains, in addition to stores, schools and mills, a flourishing bank, the First National of Northfield.

Three of the bandits, who had taken dinner in the town, rode liesurely up to this bank and hitched their horses. Here they talked quietly for some time, looking occasionally up and down the streets. A shrewd observer might have noted some anxiety in the eyes of these pretended cattle buyers, who seemed to be awaiting the coming of some one.

Their waiting was not doomed to be of long duration, for all at once a rumbling noise is heard, growing louder and louder until three men are seen rushing, like the on-coming storm, across the bridge and towards the bank. As soon as they cross the bridge they begin firing their pistols, and their savage yells ring out on the air. With their coming the three men talking quietly at the bank rushed into that institution, and with drawn revolvers demanded its monies. Met with a square refusal, they endeavor to intimidate the cashier by drawing a knife across his throat, slightly wounding him. Still refusing, they turn their attention to one of the other parties in the bank, a Mr. [A. E.] Bunker, and as he flies they fire, wounding him in the shoulder. No attention seems to have been paid to Frank Wilcox, a companion clerk of Bunker.

After the cashier's refusal to open the safe they seemed to have desisted from molesting him, and one of the bandits seeing the outer vault door open, went in to try the inner. While doing this [Joseph L.] Haywood, the cashier, is said to have sprung to the door and attempted to close it on the robber, but was prevented by Charlie Pitts. It is now said that they heard cries from their comrades outside, and seizing every dollar in sight they hastened to the door. Some say that no signal at all was given, but that they found it useless to stay, since they could neither open the safe themselves, nor force the cashier to do so. Most accounts seem to agree that the bravery or foolhardiness of the cashier caused his death. Brave to rashness, he neglected the old Grecian proverb, "to build a golden bridge for a flying enemy," and as the last robber was just about reaching the door he sprang to a drawer where he kept his revolver, but before securing it the rear robber turned, and divining his purpose, fired and killed him. No matter by what name his act may be called, J. L. Haywood died like a true, brave man; his courage dauntless and his trust intact.

On the outside, at the beginning of the dash, three men had ridden across the bridge and into the public square, to guard the approaches of the bank, and keep the streets clear of citizens. Almost at the same time they were joined by two others, who had swept down a different street, and the five deployed in the square, firing, whooping and yelling.

For a moment, and it was a moment only, the citizens seemed paralyzed by fear, and then there was a hasty search for long discarded arms and ammunition. Amongst those who succeeded in securing them were Dr. Wheeler and Messrs. Stacey, [A. B.] Manning, Bates and Hyde. Dr. Wheeler had selected for his stand a room in the hotel (the Damphier House), and throwing up a window began firing with a breech-loading rifle. His first victim was Bill Chadwell, the guide of the expedition. An evil omen! a heavy ball pierced his breast and he fell from the horse he was mounting without even a groan.

Mr. Bates was in the second story of Hanauer's clothing store and Manning kept his position in a door-way on the side-walk.

He it is who fired the shot which killed Clell Miller. At the time Miller was riding rapidly across Division street, and at the fire he clenched the bridle reins, checking his horse and half turned in his saddle, feeling for a pistol, and then reeled and pitched out of his saddle to the ground. Seeing him fall Cole Younger rode up to his body, and dismounting saw it was all over with him. He then unbuckled Miller's revolvers, took them himself and rode back to the others.

Bob Younger was dismounted, and standing behind his horse firing. His horse was killed by Manning, and Bob retreated to the shelter of some boxes under an iron stairway, and from here opened an ineffectual fire upon Manning. Seeing the danger of the latter, Dr. Wheeler fired on Younger from his window and broke his right arm. With the cool nerve and steady bravery characteristic of the man, he charged his pistol and began firing with his left hand. Bates was standing inside of his store with his gun raised, ready to fire, when Younger's bullet grazed his cheek.

Seeing that they could not stand the rapidly increasing fire of the citizens, the bandits turned in flight.

Here the horse of Jim Younger jerked loose from him, and escaped, but was not noticed by the others (he being in the rear), until they heard him call:

"Help me, boys! don't leave me here shot."

Cole Younger did not hesitate a moment, but dashing back to him, helped him on to the horse he was riding, and again turned in flight.

While this was going on, a Norwegian named [Nicholas] Gustavson was mortally wounded. Ordered indoors, he either did not understand the command, or did not care to obey it, and was shot by one of the robbers.[2]

In their flight from Northfield, the bandits took a westwardly course, and went along at a full gallop for about two miles. Here they made a slight halt to examine their wounds. These were many and various; from the bird shot of Stacey's double-barrel gun to

[2]The Northfield raid occurred September 7, 1876.

McClellan (Clell) Miller, a member of the James-Younger gang, was killed at the Northfield, Minnesota bank robbery on September 7, 1876.

the balls of Wheeler's breech-loading rifle. Remounting, they galloped on to a little place called Dundas, and again halted here, as some of their wounds were bleeding terribly. Their only surgery was cold water and tight bandages. At this point Jim Younger had grown so weak from loss of blood that he had to be placed on a horse before one of the others, and his horse led.

Going on this way, they met a farmer hauling hoop-poles. Without consulting him as to the desirability of the proceeding, they took one of his horses, and proceeded on their way.

Again they halted to dress their wounds, and it is astonishing how rapidly they were going, considering these halts and the condition of the men. A farmer who met them said that one was holding one arm in his other hand, and the blood was streaming over his horse and down into the road. A comrade was leading his horse. Another bandit, supposed to be Frank James, had a compress around his leg, and all appeared to be stiff and sore. They reached Shieldsville that night before dark, having made over twenty-five miles. They went on boldly through this town.

To stimulate pursuit, rewards were offered by the State, the Northfield bank, and at least one railroad, the Winona & St. Paul.

At, or rather beyond, Shieldsville, the bandits had a brush with a party of citizens, twelve in number, but the latter speedily retreated. In this skirmish one of the robbers' horses was killed, but there was no thought of deserting him, or their badly wounded comrades. Riding up to the dismounted man, another bandit takes him behind him, and their flight is continued.

From Shieldsville the route lay through La Seur county. By this time there were fully 500 men between them and the line of their retreat. A posse, guarding a ford on French Creek, fled on their approach, and they crossed without molestation. Here they took a night's rest. The next day they had struck a heavy belt of timber, but had to abandon it. Had they been able to keep to a southwestwardly course they had some chance of escape, but confused by the heavy shadows of the dense timber and the cloudy weather, they seem to have lost their course and they were all surrounded in the timber on Blue Earth river, six days after they began their flight. From this point on, the accounts vary; none of them being accurate, so far as the James boys are concerned.

When surrounded in the woods on Blue Earth river, a council was held, and it was decided that if they all continued together, they could not hope to escape, and in consequence, separation was the only remedy if any expected to get away in safety. This, however, was not deemed the proper place for this separation, so the six bandits continued on together.

A few miles northeast of Mankato, they came upon a man named Dunning, who was most likely scouting for them. They covered him with their revolvers, and forced him to keep quiet. A consultation as to his fate was held, and the unanimous verdict was death.

Dunnning, however, who had nothing of the Roman about him, begged long and earnestly for his life. His voice was broken with sobs, and the tears streamed from his eyes. Being moved by his fright and his prayers, the bandits consented to let him go, on condition that he was not to mention where they were, nor even the fact that he had seen them. This he gladly consented to do, and swore by all that men hold dear and sacred that he would keep his promises. As soon as released, he hurried to his companions, and informed them of the whereabouts of the robbers, also giving a complete picture of their crippled condition.

This stimulated the pursuit, and parties were pushed in every direction through the timber. After a slight rest, they marched painfully on, and on the night of the 13th of September they passed through Mankato. Here they took to the back streets and reached the bridge at the further end of the town.

They anticipated trouble here, as they supposed the bridge would be guarded, but passed over securely. It is likely that on their approach the guard had fled, for entering a melon-patch, they secured some melons, and at a house secured one chicken, and were looking for others, when they saw a crowd of men on their trail, most likely led by the bridge guards, who had seen them cross, but feared to stop them.

Rapidly pushing on, they eluded pursuit, and the next day entered the timber on the Blue Earth river. They crossed that stream and continued their flight. Here in this timber it was concluded to separate, as matters could not be more desperate, so it was agreed that the two Jameses should go due South, the Youngers and Charlie Pitts West. In this was they hoped to so divide up the forces of their enemies, and confuse pursuit, as to insure the safety of one, if not both parties.

From this point we shall first follow out the fortunes, or rather the misfortunes, of Pitts and the Youngers, and then return to the Jameses.

The circumstances attending the flight of the latter seemed for a time to draw away the entire pursuit, as the people appeared to think the whole band had gone, or would go due southward; hence for a short time the Younger party seemed to have a certainty of escape. This might have been, had they been in any physical condition to make speed a possibility. Footsore; without sleep or food, save such articles as they could secure raw, and not even a sufficiency of that; desperately wounded and without surgical aid, they were in a horrible condition. Even strong, hearty men, with full supplies of edibles, might well have despaired, if cooped up in swamps and forests and hunted by hundreds of pursuers. It was enough to cause the heart of the boldest to sink, but famished and worn; without food or sleep, the indomitable courage of these men asserted itself. They would never surrender till the last; while they could drag one foot after another, no matter how great the pain, they would stagger on.

The *ultima thule* of their retreat was destined to come at last. When the Jameses burst through the line of the hunters and drew their fire and pursuit, the Youngers and Charley Pitts kept on through the forest to the West. Passing on through Blue Earth county, they entered Watonwan county. They had chosen woods, swamps and thickets for their paths, and had struck the low swamps of the Watonwan river.

On the afternoon of the 21st, just fourteen days after the Northfield raid, their trail was struck by a scouting party under Sheriff McDonald, who was coming from the southward. Following fast and hard upon them, he surrounded them in a swamp, where they had determined to try and secure some rest. This swamp was but a few miles from Madelia. There was a large force with McDonald, nearly two hundred, and having put a cordon of pickets completely around the swamp in which the bandits lay concealed, he gave the order to close in upon them on all sides. At last they had narrowed the circle so as to include only a small thicket, and into this they poured volley after volley. It seemed as if nothing mortal could live under this terrific fire, but the answering shots showed that some, at least, of the men were yet alive, and that the mere force of superior numbers did not daunt their boldness.

During this firing, one of the posse was seriously and one slightly wounded. Charley Pitts, struck by a heavy ball, fell to rise no more. A low moan, a slight shiver, and all was over with him. The next bandit wounded was Jim Younger. A ball of large calibre from a heavy breech-loading rifle shattered his lower jaw-bone, inflicting a frightful wound. Bob was shot through the arm, and Cole received seven wounds.

It was a desperate, determined battle, made by men as desperate and determined as earth ever saw, but the old luck that had attended them had fled forever. Resistance was useless, and Cole Younger, having emptied his revolvers, threw up his hands.[3] He is said to have told some one that with these revolvers he had never before missed a man inside of one hundred yards, and yet that he emptied them into that body of men at less than half that distance, and never killed a man. "I knew then that it was fate, and so I surrendered."

The sight that greeted the eyes of the captors was a terrible one. Charley Pitts lay dead; Cole Younger, the only one of the brothers able to stand, was bleeding from seven wounds, which he

[3]It was Bob Younger, not Cole, who stood up and surrendered the wounded bandits.

bore with the stoical courage of a Western Indian. Bob and Jim lay upon the twigs and leaves, moaning in what almost seemed the throes of death. Everyone said of Jim, "He can't possibly live." They didn't know the nerve and vitality of these brothers.

The men were mere shadows—they had not had a meal in weeks; they had not had a night's sleep in the same length of time; their shoes were worn from their feet; their clothing torn to tatters—they needed food, rest, the aid of the surgeon, the care of the nurse; they needed everything.

Their eyes were blood-shot from want of sleep, and inflamed with the fever of their wounds; their clothing was stiff and glued to their persons with their blood. They had no lint for dressing, no linen for bandages. They had long ago torn up their handkerchiefs and shirts, and were now bandaged with coarse strips of linen dusters. One would have said, men cannot stand this and live; the picture is too horrible! But then these men did stand this and live, and under it all plodded wearily on, day by day, and night after night, stopping ever and anon to make a stand against their flushed and eager pursuers.

It is a wonderful chapter of human endurance, this retreat of these bandits from Northfield. It is almost past belief, and mayhap in less than half a hundred years it may be scouted at by the sybaritic American of that better day, and yet it is not in the slightest degree exaggerated. This chapter furnishes, too, besides its picture of wonderful daring and endurance, an example that in a different way might well be copied by better men. Had they sought safety in selfish flight, leaving their wounded to their fate, these men might easily have saved themselves, but this was not written in their bandit creed.

To "spoil the enemy, but stick to the friend," they made the groundwork of their faith, and acted conscientiously up to it. The annals of heroism furnish no grander example of unselfish devotion to their chosen friends, and we must allow that that heart is not altogether bad in which can harbor such noble virtues as undaunted courage and undying fidelity.

Their lives, or portions of them, were doubtless wild, but who shall judge them so harshly as to say that the "little leaven" of these divine qualities, courage and true faith, might not, under varying circumstances and more propitious fates, have so leavened the whole man that he would have been an honor to his country and an ornament to society? Who knows, or who shall judge?

Posse members who captured the Younger brothers at Madelia, Minnesota on September 21, 1876. L to R, Sheriff James Glispin, Captain W. W. Murphy, G. A. Bradford, Ben M. Rice, Colonel T. L. Vought, C. A. Pomeroy, and S. J. Severson. *Courtesy State Historical Society of Minnesota.*

Cole Younger, while serving time in the Stillwater Penitentiary.

Robert Younger, while serving time in the Stillwater Penitentiary; 1890.

James Younger, while serving time in the Stillwater Penitentiary; 1889.

CHAPTER XXXII.

The Flight From Northfield: Continued.

The Jameses break through the Line—Fired On—Wounded—Their Course—
Difficulties—Strike the Wilderness—A New Idea—A Change of Route—A
Sudden Possession—The Posse Satisfied—A Night's Rest—A Square Meal
—The Deserted House—Costly Clothes—Lord Byron's Poems—A Blessed
Bible—The Pursuers Pass—A Friend in Need—Primitive Surgery—Ride to
H——.—Board The Cars—Fort Dodge, Iowa—Change Cars—Illinois Central
Railroad—Chicago to Cairo—The Ohio Steamer—Louisville—A Good Rest
Baltimore—Well Once More—Return Home— Conflicting Accounts.

WHEN the Jameses took leave of the Youngers, their old comrades upon the field of battle and companions in many an
expedition, they gazed long and earnestly at each other. All felt
that this parting might be their last on earth, and the deepest emotion pervaded the heart of each. For the moment wounds, famine
and fatigue are forgotten; even the tireless ardor of the pursuit
fades from their minds, as scenes and incidents of other days take
its place. But this is no time for long partings. In action men ever
of the briefest speech, even the little they now have to say seems
to choke them with emotion. Pressing their hands in a warm clasp,
each hurries away with the simple words: "Good bye, boys; God
bless you!" When the parties were about to lose sight of each
other they turned, waved their hands, and the next moment they
were shut from view by intervening timber and tangled thickets.
Turning due south the Jameses plunged deeper and deeper into
the woods, but at last they see men stooping down as if searching

for them. Summoning all of their strength and energy they rush towards them; the posse fires a hurried volley, one ball striking Jesse James in the side and Frank in the thigh. After firing they turned in flight, running in a northeasterly direction and calling to others. Hurrying on the two brothers strike a small watercourse, and wade down it for about a mile. Coming out they step on to the root of a tree, thence on to a fallen log, and hurry on still to the south.

That night they had some rest and a chance to dress their wounds. They then hastened on, and about two o'clock in the morning, having covered their trail as well as they could, they entered a thicket. They lay here until about seven, getting another much needed rest and a refreshing sleep. At seven o'clock they were just about to start out, Frank very stiff and sore, when they heard voices towards the east. Peering cautiously through the bushes, with their revolvers ready, they saw four men coming towards them, minutely searching the ground for "signs." Passing close by the thicket and seeing no tracks, they stopped for a moment and then moved on. Their halt was a supreme moment in their lives, for had they entered, it is doubtful if any of them had lived to tell the tale. After they had passed some half hour Jesse and Frank, hearing no further pursuers, started on after them until they reached a small but deep stream (probably one of the branches of the Blue Earth river). Here the pursuers, or rather now the followed, who had been going west, turned due south. Halting but a moment, the Jameses followed after them until nearly nightfall, when fearing that the posse might return, the brothers penetrated deeper into the wood and secreted themselves. This precaution was taken none too soon, for they had scarcely got under cover when the very four they had been following were seen returning. As they passed back they were heard to say: "It's impossible; they can't escape. They are sending out men everywhere to the west and south."

Here they passed out of hearing, but what they had said was enough to suggest to the fertile mind of Jesse an expedient that had at least a showing of success. He proceeded to counsel with Frank in regard to it. "You have heard," he said, "what these parties say—now what do you think of us starting due east from here, walk steadily all night and lay up. We will go down towards the south for a few miles, then strike out a little north of east if any thing, lay up to-morrow and get a good rest and something to eat, if possible, and then we can determine what we will do." Frank agreed to this plan, for the reason, as he said, that one course was as bad as another. They immediately proceeded to put this scheme into execution.

They were now on the north side of a strong stream of water, probably Elm river, and they struck due south until they reached its banks. Here they stumbled on a camp of their hunters, and hurrying on they had barely reached the bank of the stream, when looking back, they saw their pursuers charging in on them. There was no thicket in which to hide, so into the stream they went, wading along its north bank until they found a place they could dare to cross. They managed to get over without swimming. Where they crossed was about midway between Horicon and Westford, but nearer to Horicon. One of these towns is on the south and one on the north side of this stream. Coming up the opposite bank they were seen and fired at.

In order to baffle pursuit they started west towards Horicon, but after going a short distance they lay down upon the river bank for a short rest. They now determined to re-cross the stream, and under cover of the steep bank to wade down past the camp of the enemy. This they succeeded in doing, and after wading for a mile or more they crossed over to the south side, taking great precautions to leave as little trail as possible.

They now struck due east, and walked as rapidly as their sore condition would admit, and having secured a couple of chickens at a lonely house along the road, they continued on until morning, drying their clothes and cooking their chickens at a fire that some one had built. This food greatly benefitted them, and going deep into a belt of timber they had a long sleep. Awaking about twelve o'clock they trudged on, still keeping to the east. On this trip, so far, they had met but two persons. One of them, a Norwegian, paid no attention; the next, an American, eyed them suspiciously and spoke to them, but Frank answering him in German he must have been satisfied, as he passed on muttering:" a d—d Dutchman!"

They made good time that day, and got a loaf of bread and some milk from a poor looking house by the road, Frank bargaining penuriously for them in broken English. They were in a tight place, and they knew appearances must be kept up, as they could not afford to throw away a single point. Plodding along this road, they had towards evening entered a gate leading to a house some hundred yards off of the road. Their intention was to get supper, but they found no one at home. While sitting down on the doorstep resting, Frank caught sight of a band of five men riding up the road. He knew that they could not yet have seen him, so stooping he ran around the house, and seizing the first implement he could find, which by the way was a rake, he began tugging away at some dead flowers with might and main.

"Hello!" shouted the leader of the band as they rode up, "do you live here?"

"Oh, yaw!" said Frank, straightening up, "I leefs here."

When saying this, Frank knew his risk, for the leader might live in the immediate vicinity; still it was but a chance, and he was willing to chance it

"Can we get some supper to-night?" asked the leader.

"Nein," said Frank, "der olt vomans don'd vos at home."

The band passed on, and the brothers proceeded to investigate the contents of the kitchen safe standing on the porch. They proved ample for a fair meal, and they tied up enough to last them for another, and leaving a sufficiency of change on the plate to largely pay for what they had taken, they went back to the road, walked on, and at about two o'clock in the morning entered some woods, and slept until eight. They now arose, ate what food they had with them, and again taking the road pressed on. Frank had cut a cane, and limped very perceptibly.

They met several people this day, one of them a woman in a sort of a dog-cart. Still retaining his German accent, Frank asked her the name of the next town, and its distance, and was told that it was Blue Earth City, and was distant some five or six miles.

Fearing from its name that it was a large town, they waited until the woman was out of sight, and then turned out of the road, bearing to the left between that town and Walnut Lake. Finding a detached farm house, they got some provisions, and asked for work. If these people had ever heard of the Northfield bank robbers, they certainly did not suspect them to be this honest Dutchman and his shabby-looking partner. Here Frank, after much bargaining, succeeded in getting a pair of overalls and a canvas jumper, or jacket. These he rolled into a bundle and carried along.

At the first opportunity these were donned by Jesse, and going through the same programme at the next house, Frank secured some of these articles for himself, and also a calico shirt for each. They now felt so well rigged out that they entered a little store at Clayton, and bought a coarse hat and a pair of shoes each.

They now had the appearance of the yeomanry of the country, and meeting a man who had a team of fair-looking horses, they bargained for them and bought them very reasonably. They knew from the farmer's moderate price for his team that he suspected nothing. Accompanying him home, so that he need not leave his wagon in the road, they got a fair meal from him, and buying two old saddles he had, they again took the road.

Comfortably, or at least not suspiciously dressed, not suffering for food or sleep, their spirits began to rise to the usual level; still they neglected no precaution. They now stopped always at farm houses, and never rode after night. When they entered a room to sleep, their first move was to rumple the bed-clothes, turn them partly down, and lie down upon them dressed, for fear their wounds, which still bled a little, might betray them.

For the first two days after procuring their horses, they met numbers of men in small squads, returning, as they supposed, from the hunt after the bandits. None of them seemed to suspect, even in the slightest, the honest Dutchman and his companion jogging soberly along. We say none. The second party they met, consisting of eight men, riding four abreast, did stop them to ask them if they had seen any men on foot.

"Oh, yaw," said Frank volubly, "shust lots of dem."

"Which way were they going?" again asks the leader.

"Vell," said Frank, shrugging his shoulders, "some von vay, some de odder—shust efery vay."

Not gaining the desired information, they rode on, but Frank, looking to each side of the road with his eyes cast as far to the rear as possible, saw them halt, the leader put his hand on the cantrell of his saddle, and turn to look at them again. Settling back into the saddle, he said something to the others, half turned his horse, then turning on his way, they rode off.

When he noticed the movements of the party, Frank did not turn in his saddle, nor move a hand, but a cold glitter began to steal into his eyes, and he said: "If we can't run, Jess, we can fight!" and on they jogged. The leader of the posse will probably never know how near he was to death that day.

They had now passed on through Winnebago county, Iowa, and into Kossuth county, following one of the branches of the Des Moines river. They were not molested at all now, for the pursuit was, as they could ascertain daily, far to the West and Southwest. They had entirely baffled the hunter, and were now almost in safety. Every day would come tidings that they were seen; one report would make them going in the direction of Sioux City; another towards Council Bluffs; but none represented them as going East. Their boldness, as much as their cunning and cautiousness, was fast carrying them out of their difficulties.

The day after passing into Kossuth county, they stopped at a neat, little roadside cottage for supper and a night's lodging. There was an air of refinement about the place not ordinarily met with in so wild a country. The pictures hanging on the walls; the books scattered on the tables; the exquisite air of neatness, all spoke of people who had moved in the higher walks of society. Taking up one of the books from the center table, a volume of Lord Byron's Poems, Frank turned to the fly leaf. The name and former residence recorded there struck him at once:

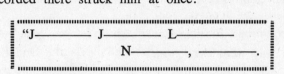

"J———— J———— L————
N————, ————.

Could it be possible, he asked Jesse, that any of the L————s, of N————, lived here? He would look further. The old family Bible, blessed book! was lying there, and he rapidly turned to the family records. "Why, it's a brother of the very man I know," he said. His mind was made up as to what his course of action would be. When the gentleman of the house came in he dropped his German brogue and asked:

"Is not this Mr. L————, of N————?"

"That is my name, sir!" said Mr. L————, "and N———— was formerly my residence. I left there, however, some years since, and so have not kept up my recollections of the people, and I must say you have the advantage of me."

"My name is Hall," said Frank, "my companion is Mr. Howard. We are travelling to look at lands for the purpose of buying."

"I rather thought you were Germans," said Mr. L————, a little suspiciously.

"Oh, yes," said Frank, laughing heartily, "that is a little ruse of mine. We find the country people so excited over some horse thieves and robbers that it was difficult to get entertainment, so we affected the honest German dialect to avoid suspicion."

This explanation, together with Frank's hearty enjoyment of his little joke, soon dispelled any suspicions Mr. L———— might have had, and before bed time Frank and Jesse, who both knew all of Mr. L————'s connections and relatives near N————, had fully convinced him that the Halls, Howards and L————s were of blood kin.

The next day Mr. L———— was anxious to have them remain some time; make him quite a visit, in fact, and see if they could not find some land in his vicinity that would suit them.

Telling him that they had already bought some wild land in Winnebago county, and that they had even now been longer from home than they anticipated when they set out, they proposed leaving. Ascertaining that Fort Dodge was the nearest large town, and that their host had business to transact there, they decided to wait until the next day before setting out. When morning came they insisted on Mr. L———'s hitching *their* team to his wagon, as they would go from Fort Dodge East by rail, and if he would not take care of their horses they would have to leave them in a livery stable. They would like to leave them with Mr. L———, they said, until they returned, which would be after closing up their affairs East; they would give Mr. L——— the use of the team for its board. This arrangement being made, they jolted into Fort Dodge in a lumber wagon, and from there, after thoroughly refitting themselves with clothes, under garments, etc., they took the Illinois Central Railroad for Chicago.

Neatly shaved and dressed in a becoming manner, these men would have been taken anywhere for well-to-do farmers, looking after a cattle shipment, or country merchants going to some big city to buy goods. After getting on the train, Jesse remembered that in the fob pocket of the overalls he had discarded at the clothing store, were two twenty-dollar gold pieces. This, in addition to the price paid for his present suit, made it a rather costly one, but considering the $40 "a sop to Cerbeus," his regrets were but few.

In Chicago their first care was to seek a surgeon. This they did, not as you, gentle reader, might have done, in the highest ranks of the profession. No! they looked for one of those, whose practice in the slums has taught him to keep a quiet mouth, if he would wish future fees. They secured a man that just suited. It took much whisky to put his nerves in trim, but once the shaking hand steadied, and the torpid brain aroused with fresh venom of the serpent which had numbed it, he was a master of his art. He was no soft-spoken Esculapius, fit for ministrations at the dainty couches of sybaritic invalids, but he was one of those minds that clearly and accurately grasped a situation, but whose terrible love for drink had brought him down from a good practice to his present level. His rude, abrupt manner he had absorbed from his later patients, but he knew his science thoroughly, and under his treatment Frank and Jesse felt as though they were being ministered to by an angel.

In a few days they had become so nearly well that they determined to leave Chicago. Paying their doctor liberally, they went down to Cairo, and from there took passage on an Ohio river steamer for Louisville. On the way up some sharpers "picked up" the brothers for a game of poker, but before reaching Louisville, the gamblers had lost over a thousand dollars to them.

At Louisville they stopped some days, and then they separated; Frank going to Baltimore, and Jesse to Nashville.

Thus ended the Northfield raid and retreat. Of the eight who had entered the town well armed, splendidly mounted, and full of health, strength and vigor, two had fallen dead in its streets torn through with rifle balls. The six who had, though desperately wounded, been able to ride out of the town, had suffered untold agonies, and had endured fatigues that seem impossible. Of these six one more was killed outright, and all received additional wounds. Three of them were captured, with revolvers empty, and unable to drag themselves farther. Only two escaped, and that but by a boldness no others would have dreamed of. Had they not baffled pursuit with their superior wood-craft and infinite cunning, they too would to-day be languishing in the cells of the penitentiary at Stillwater. Had they continued their flight to the south, or west, their escape could only have been effected by a miracle, as there were fully fifteen hundred determined men between them and safety. It was only by baffling their hunters at Horicon, and putting them on a false trail, that they succeeded; and their skill and patience in working back through the cordon still advancing was most marvelous. The men camped at the creek, where they crossed, were confident they could capture them. At early daylight they divided; one squad taking the north side; the other, the south side of the creek. At Horicon those on the south received tidings of gladness. An old lady was certain they went through; she had heard the guns fired, and about an hour or so after, there was a terrible fluttering amongst her hens, and then she heard all of the dogs barking. Some friendly owl, no doubt, had created a diversion in their favor. The next morning they did eat chicken, but it was not this old lady's.

Their promptness in acting on their sudden resolve to strike eastward, alone prevented their being captured the very next day, for they would, in either going south, or west, have come to open country that afternoon, and here they would have been surrounded, and captured or killed. They were heard of everywhere towards the west, south and south-west, *but not a soul had ever seen them from the time they burst through the cordon of the pursuers and sought the covert beyond them.* After this, with the exception of the night they crossed the river and were fired on, they were never seen, and then were but dimly seen as flitting shadows. It was an escape without parallel in all the history of flight and pursuit of which the records anywhere make mention.

CHAPTER XXXIII.

UNION PACIFIC TRAIN ROBBERY.

The Great American Desert—School Days—Ogalalla—The Sioux Hunting Grounds—The Camp—Texas Cattle—The Cow-Boy—His Character—Jim Berry—What He Bought at Ogalalla—Big Springs Station—The Ambush There—The Through Train—The Attack—Wells, Fargo & Co.'s Express—The Robbery—The Inevitable Sack—Train Released—Flight Over The Plains—Berry's Proposal—The Clue—Buffalo Station—The Guard of Soldiers—Berry Visits Missouri—Gold for Greenbacks—A Tale of The Black Hills—The Suit of Clothes—The Order—His Friend Seized—Sheriff Glasscock's Posse—What They Did—Berry Trapped—His Wound—His Wife—The Spoil—Berry Dies—Sam Bass—Billy Hefferidge—Jim Collins—Jack Davis—The Unknown—Who Was He?

IN the school geographies of our childhood's days, with what lingering interest did we use to gaze on that mysterious stretch of land in all the maps of the West, big enough for an empire, colored a suggestive yellow and branded the "Great American Desert." In underlined strips, running, at intervals, transversely across it, were the cabalistic words: SIOUX, CHEYENNE, BLACK FEET, etc., etc. When our lesson came to this section we invariably knew it well, and our teacher must certainly have wondered at our numerous questions and our suddenly awakened interest in this rather dry study. For days after passing over this "Great American Desert" — on paper — many were our meditations concerning this land of mysteries, and we made vague plans to explore it, "when we were men." Alas! when we were men that vision, like many another of childhood's trusting fancies, had fled forever. The

"Great American Desert" had become a respectable combination of States and Territories, innocent of simoons and oases, of date-palms and Bedouin Arabs. The gazelle had given place to its near relative, the antelope, and the date-palm had been misplaced by the less romantic and picturesque sage-brush.

Of all our childish illusions in regard to this "desert," but one remained, and that the most visionary and least substantial of all. The "Great American Desert" did and does present an occasional mirage, as wonderful as any thing that far-famed Sahara can do in that line. But the substantials have departed forever.

It was in the golden days of "the mild September," 1877, so say the newspapers (for we do not pretend that we have, in regard to this robbery, any private information, or in fact any save that furnished by the papers of that date!), that a jovial party of "Cow-boys," or "Stockmen," as they are called, camped near Ogalalla, Nebraska. The party consisted of seven, and they desired to take a good rest, so they said, before starting back across the trail to Texas. They had made their sales; the prices were satisfactory and they were returning satisfied. The trail over which they would return had been the former hunting ground of the Ogalalla, Minniconjou, Brule and other bands of the Sioux and their allies and neighbors, the Cheyennes. With the exception of a few small bands of renegades these Indians were now quiet on their reservations; still the "Cow-boys" must sleep lightly on their long ride, if all would get through safely, hence their halt for recuperation. These men from long association seem to absorb part of the character of the animals they herd: they become quick, lithe and agile; they lose all sense of fear; they become inured to hardships and delight in broils and dangers.

Abilene first, then Ellsworth, Great Bend, Dodge, etc., knew him, and found him what might be classed, "a hard citizen." He is nervy: Wild Bill, midway in his career of blood and murder, found that out at Ellsworth, when cool Bill Thompson made him "take water."[1]

Tom Carson,[2] the Kansas bully, found one too many of him, when he "jumped" a quiet stranger in a small saloon, only to fall back dying from a quick revolver shot. He might drink; he might gamble; he might fracture individually and collectively all the commandments of the decalogue, but he *would* fight. It was his one redeeming trait; his solitary virtue, "midst a thousand crimes."

Amongst the Cow-boys who had camped at Ogalalla was one Jim [James P.] Berry, a native of Callaway county, Missouri, and who had, it is said, been one of the rough-riding, hard-fighting guerrillas of Bill Anderson; Jack Davis, of or near Fort Smith, Arkansas, a man of not over good reputation, was another; Billy Hefferidge, "a hard citizen" from Pennsylvania,[3] Jim [Joel] Collins, a brother of Brad Collins, and Sam Bass. There were two others, but they were unknown.[4] One of these two is supposed to have been afterwards killed, but his partner was never known. Some have tried to identify him and Jesse James as the same, but at that time Jesse was at Nashville, Tenn., as can be easily proved.

Jim Berry was well known along the line of this division of the U. P. road, and had been in business at Plattsmouth, Neb. It was a purchase of his at the store of Mr. M. F. Leech, at Ogalalla, who knew him well, that first turned attention to this party of

[1]There is no evidence that Billy Thompson, brother of Ben, ever faced up to James Butler "Wild Bill" Hickok. For a reliable study of Hickok see Joseph G. Rosa, *They Called Him Wild Bill* (Norman, University of Oklahoma Press, 1964).

[2]Tom Carson had been one of City Marshal Hickok's deputies in Abilene, Kansas during 1871. He was arrested in 1872 for shooting with intent to kill, but escaped jail and fled town. Nyle H. Miller and Joseph W. Snell, *Great Gunfighters of the Kansas Cowtowns, 1867-1886* (Lincoln, University of Nebraska Press, 1967), pp. 64-74.

[3]Hefferidge was at first identified in local papers as William Cotts or Potts of Pottsville, Pa.

[4]There were only six members of the gang, not seven as Triplett states. Besides those mentioned here the robbers included Tom Nixon. Charles L. Martin, *A Sketch of Sam Bass, the Bandit* (Norman, University of Oklahoma Press, 1956), pp. 15, 16.

campers as the robbers.

Stepping into Leech's store shortly before the train was stopped, Berry and his companions bought some large, red cotton handkerchiefs. Not a very weighty purchase, you will say; that of half a dozen cotton handkerchiefs—not particularly—and yet it caused the death of at least five men. The tale will be told further on.

West of Ogalalla, about twenty-five miles, is situated the station of Big Springs, Nebraska. It is about like all other of these small stations along this route, in the barren districts, possessing, as its name implies, a liberal supply of water. On this account it is a place at which all trains, both East and West, stop, in order to procure supplies of water from its never-failing tank. The Pacific express, on its way East, just at nightfall on the 17th [18th] day of September, 1877, proved no exception to this rule. Coming to a full stop on this eventful evening, she was taken possession of by seven armed men, *all masked with red cotton handkerchiefs!*

Their tactics differed somewhat from those of their brethren in "the States." Four of them guarded the engineer and fireman; one guarded the conductor and rest of the crew, and two men searched through the cars, robbing the passengers. As one of them collected the spoils, he handed them to his companion, who put them into the inevitable sack. Before they got through, it resembled the bag of the prestidigitateur, as it held a little of everything, some of the frightened passengers contributing keys, letters, etc., etc.

While this was going on, the four who had the engineer in charge entered the Wells, Fargo & Co. express car, and rifled its safe. Having secured all of the valuables on the train, the robbers rode out into the shadows of the night, and the train was allowed to proceed on its way, which it promptly did.

At Ogalalla and at Brule the news was spread that night, but, of course, no pursuit could be made until morning. The cow-boys were found to be in their camp the next morning, and there was nothing unusual to be seen there.

Mr. Leech, of Ogalalla, had had some experience with border bandits, and he was secured to hunt up the robbers. This he proceeded to do, and set about securing a number of good men to accompany him. Amongst others, he saw Jim Berry hanging about amongst the crowd, which had collected when they heard what was going forward. Jim Berry, being an old acquaintance, spoke to Leech about it, and asked him if it was true that he intended to organize a party, and go out in pursuit of the train robbers.

"That's what I am," said Leech, after the emphatic manner of the plainsman.

"You don't think you'll catch 'em, do you?" asked Berry incredulously.

"If I don't, I'll try mighty hard," said Leech.

"I wonder if they wouldn't give me a show to go along, too?" said Berry; "what do you think?"

"I don't doubt it," said Leech, "and pay you well for your time and trouble."

"Well," said Berry, turning off, "I'll see."

He couldn't have seen it in a very good light, for he did not go; and when Leech and his party started for Ogalalla to strike the trail of the bandits, Jim Berry and his party stayed two days longer, then broke up camp and disappeared.

Leech had a special train furnished him to go to Sidney, from which point he supposed the robbers had operated. On the way, he stopped at Big Springs, to look carefully over the ground. Here was no sign, but while searching around the track a piece of red rag was detached from a tie by his foot; it fluttered in the wind, blew away from him, then an eddy of the air brought it back, and after hovering in the air for a moment, it fell at his feet. Idly stooping, he takes it up—a thought strikes him—for Leech was a born detective; not one of the kind who discover a robbery by having planned it beforehand themselves.

He looks at this rag carefully; he has seen it before—yes! it is a piece of one of the handkerchiefs he sold to Berry and his party!

He puts it in his pocket, says nothing, and goes on to Sidney, where a careful search reveals not the slightest trace. He next steams back to Ogalalla. Here he visits the cow-boys' camp, and finds amongst the debris of the camp what he never even hoped to find, a handkerchief! Do not smile, my friends! a handkerchief, as those familiar with the fate of Shakspeare's gentle Desdemona know, is no trivial affair. A handkerchief is at once the most alluring and yet the most fatal web that ever came from the loom. In beauty's hand it leads us on to love and folly; in that of the captain of the file its fall means death by the swiftly flying bullet; in that of the headsman its wave means blood and saw-dust; a covered basket and a headless corse.

But to return to this hankerchief: it is torn, therefore it is worthless; it is worthless, therefore it is thrown away. Fool! that handkerchief to thee is priceless, for it will cost thee thy life!

Leech finds that the fragment of Big Springs accurately fits the torn handkerchief of the camp. The clue is had; the pursuit follows. The whole thing is as dramatic as a tale of Emile Garboriau!

Leech next hunts for the trail of the cow-boys, and at last finds it. With the tenacity of the blood-hound this born detective follows the scent. If they keep their present course they will pass through Gove county, in the state of Kansas, striking the Kansas Pacific road somewhere near Buffalo station. He telegraphs his surmises, and follows ever on. Several times he is near to his prey, and he saw them when they divided up the spoils.

His escapes from being caught watching them were numerous. This would have meant a sudden death, but he never faltered. At last the band divided, Hefferidge and Collins going through Buffalo station, where they were followed by the patrolling soldiers on the look-out, and killed*[5] Bass, Davis, and the other two escaped into Texas. Berry made for Missouri.

It was supposed that he would go to his home in Callaway

---

*It has since been strongly asserted that the two men killed here were innocent men, who made a fight to save themselves, as they supposed, from robbers. [Triplett note]

[5]Collins and his partner were killed while resisting arrest by a posse under Sheriff George W. Bardsley, of Ellis county, Kans., and a group of soldiers from Fort Hays commanded by Lt. Leven C. Allen, 16th infantry. Hays City (Kans.) *Sentinel*, September 28, October 12, 1877.

county, so telegrams were sent on ahead, warning the authorities. Being seen at Mexico, in Audrain, the adjoining county to Callaway, a watch was kept upon him. He was known to have been in the Black Hills, so when he appeared at the bank with gold to exchange for greenbacks the suspicions of Mr. Robt. Arnold, the cashier, were not aroused. Berry had told to some friends that he had made a "strike" in the hills. He celebrated his big luck in a big drunk, and wound up with leaving his measure with a tailor for a suit of clothes, and then he went to his home in Callaway.

The sheriff, Mr. Glasscock, knew of Berry's whereabouts, and had been advised of the robbery and his complicity in it, and he only waited for an auspicious time to attempt the arrest of his man. He had ascertained that Berry had ordered a suit of clothes made, and he told the tailor to notify him whenever they were called for.

After going home and sleeping off his drunk, Berry seems to have become quite cautious. He did not call for the clothes himself, but after waiting some time he sent an order for them by a friend of his named Casey, or Kazey [R. T. Kasey]. When the order was presented, the sheriff was promptly notified. The sheriff and a Mr. Carter went over to the tailor's shop and arrested Kazey. He then summoned three other men, named respectively Coons, Steele and Moore. Kazey was now compelled to act as guide, and the party set out, on the night of October 14, '77, the sheriff riding by and keeping a close watch upon his guide to see that he played no trick.

The ride was long and tedious, and it was not until daylight the next morning that they came in sight of Kazey's house, where Berry was stopping. Here they halted, took Kazey into the woods and tied him to a tree, Steele being left to guard him; the others were stationed at different points where it was thought they might be useful. To each one the sheriff spoke, cautioning them if they saw Berry to first halt him, and if he made a fight to try and kill him: if he ran, on being halted, they were to shoot him in the legs. Berry was known to be a dangerous man, and these precautions were not amiss, for Berry had often boasted that he was the best man in Callaway, and that was a county prolific of fighting men.

They now kept quiet for a considerable time, watching the house for developments. While doing so, they heard the neigh of a horse some distance off in the woods. Thinking that there were enough to watch the house, the sheriff took Moore with him and started in the direction of the sound they had heard. They crept on for about two or three hundred yards, and on crossing a fence they came on to fresh horse tracks. Following these a short distance they heard the snort of a horse, as if some one were approaching it. The sheriff crawled through the bushes on his hands and knees for thirty or forty yards, and then rose up and looked toward the sound. He could see a portion of the side of the horse. Throwing off his hat, Glasscock cautiously crept some thirty yards nearer, and again rising he saw Berry untying the horse.

Having loosened the animal, Berry started to lead it towards Glasscock, but the latter, fearing he might become suspicious and mount and escape, ran rapidly toward Berry with both barrels of his gun cocked. Berry did not notice him until they were within twenty feet of each other. Here the sheriff called a halt, and Berry dropped the horse's halter and started to run. In his excitement Glasscock fired wild, the charge passing over Berry's head, but the next load struck him in the left leg below the knee, seven buckshot taking effect. Berry fell writhing to the ground, and attempted to draw his pistol as the sheriff came up, but was unable to do so. Moore rushed up just about as the sheriff was disarming his prisoner. Berry, whether from humiliation at being taken alive, he having often boasted that he could not be, or from the agony he suffered from his wounds, begged Glasscock to dispatch him.

It was but a short time until the other members of the sheriff's posse had arrived on the scene, and a thorough search of Berry's person was made. Belted around him, under his clothing, they found five packages of $500 each, and in his pocket book $300; making the entire amount $2,800. They also got a fine gold watch and chain.

Berry was now removed to Kazey's house, and a messenger was dispatched in haste to Williamsburg, the nearest town, for a surgeon to attend to his wounds, which caused him excruciating agony.

After breakfast Glasscock and Moore proceeded to Berry's house, in order to thoroughly search for the remainder of the money, as it was supposed that the share of Berry would amount to nearly, if not quite $10,000.

While searching the house and its surroundings Mr. Glasscock incidentally asked after Mr. Berry, but was told by his wife that she did not know where he was, but thought, as she had not heard from him for a number of days, that he must have left the country.

Mr. Glasscock then produced the watch taken off of Berry and showed it to his wife. She turned deathly pale, and a little child standing near recognized it immediately as her papa's.

Seeing the evident distress of Mrs. Berry, the sheriff kept her no longer in suspense, but gave her full details of the occurrences of the morning. Her sobs and tears, and the weeping of the five little children were enough to move a heart of stone, and giving her what little comfort he could, the sheriff and Mr. Moore, after searching everywhere and finding nothing, quietly returned to Kazey's.

What had become of the money Jim Berry had secured at such a terrible expense? Was it secreted, and its whereabouts known to his family? Or had it been squandered in bacchanalian orgies, and bouts at the faro table? No matter what way it had gone, Jim Berry kept a still tongue to the last, and died with the secret in his breast.

When Glasscock and Moore returned to Kazey's, it was determined to procure a conveyance and take the wounded man to Mexico, and accordingly this was done. He was kept, under guard, in a room of the Ringo House, and had medical attention, but he continued to sink. It may have been that his wound was necessarily mortal; or his late debauch may have left his system in no condition to recuperate: be that as it may, on the 16th day of

October, 1877, Jim Berry—"Bad man" Jim, as his associates on the plains called him, passed

> "Beyond the frost-chain and the fever,
> Beyond the ever and the never."

He had enjoyed his ill-gotten gains just one month, lacking one day. Striving at the last moment to make a "pistol play," he had gone under with his boots on, and his days of train robbing were over.[6]

Sam Bass is supposed to have passed in West of Buffalo Station, and after innumerable dangers, and terrible fatigue and suffering, at last reached his headquarters in Northwestern Texas. His escape was but for a short time. Being hunted by the Texas rangers for crimes committed in that State, he was killed in the early part of 1879.[7]

Jack Davis, becoming disgusted with the cowardice of Sam Bass in the latter part of 1878, left him, and disappeared. Since that time no trace of him has ever been found. His reason for leaving Bass was that the latter would not stand with him to fight a sheriff's posse near Weatherford, Texas.

The man designated "the Unknown" has been the subject of a great deal of discussion in detective and other circles. Was it Jesse James? It was not—that is all that this sketch pretends to tell. As we said at the beginning of this chapter, we have no *inside* information as to who were, nor all of those who were not, present. We are only able to mention with certainty some who were not, and amongst them Jesse and Frank James, who were both in or near Nashville, Tenn., on the 17th day of September, 1877.

We could hazard a rather close guess, we fancy, as to who the unknown man was, and don't think we would be far away in saying that it was a man that Jesse James has been accused of having killed, but whom we know to be alive and well to-day.

[6]Berry's capture, as described by the Mexico (Mo.) *Intelligence*, October 14, 1877, appeared with other items about his death, in the Hays City *Sentinel*, October 19, 1877.

[7]Sam Bass was killed July 10, 1878.

As stated in a foot note, there is very grave cause for doubt as to young Collins and his partner having had any hand in this robbery. Many suppose that, being on the way home with a large amount of money, and seeing strange men bearing down upon them, they made up their minds that they were robbers, and so made fight, and were killed.

This statement, also, is given for what it is worth, as it is only a gleaning from a newspaper, and we have no private or reliable information on the subject.

The organizer of the movement, the great Unknown, we believe to be alive to-day, but not living in either Missouri or Texas.[8]

[8]Undoubtedly Triplett used this entire chapter for filling, since it has no relationship to the story of Jesse James.

CHAPTER XXXIV.

The Glendale Train Robbery.

About The Minnesota Raid—New Men Needed—The Recruits—The Dead—
Character of Pitts—Chadwell—Miller—Kerry—The Ford Family—The
Older Members—Charlie—"Cap"—Bob—Mrs. Boulton—Her Character—
Not Like Caesar's Wife—Her Lovers—Dick Little—Woot Hite—A Dandy
Bandit—Rivalry—Murder—The Robbers' Ranche—The Good Book—Glen-
dale—Surprise—The Red Light—The Down Train—The Halt—A Smashed
Door—Ford's Brutality—Flight of Bandits.

THE disastrous consequences attending the fatal expedition into
Minnesota, which had ended by the almost total annihilation
of the band, made it necessary to recruit additional members, if
any bold strokes were to be attempted in the future. Knowing
that the railroad companies would eventually be obliged to carry
armed squads for the defense of their safes and passengers, and
feeling the inability of five men to both beat back the attack of
this squad, and at the same time secure the booty, the Jameses
and the Youngers began at Muncie, and at Otterville to gather
recruits, who would have sufficient nerve and boldness to "stick,"
and whose fidelity could be depended on, if they should happen
to be captured.

In this way Chadwell, Pitts and Hobbs Kerry and later, the
Fords, were taken into the band, and put upon their trial. Dick Little or Liddil and Jim Cummings, as well as Ed. Miller, had been already tested, though in no very important matter. In Pitts and Chadwell they felt that they had secured valuable aids; the one was hot

blooded, sarcastic and cruel; the other cool, easy tempered and laughing, but both were men of great determination and undoubted courage.

True they could neither ride like the Jameses and Youngers; nor, like them, was their aim with the revolver rapid and unerring, still they were men without fear and whom nothing could induce to betray a comrade.

Had the Northfield raid been a success, the old mystical number of five, or seven, would have afterwards been changed to eight, and no doubt many and desperate would have been their raids. Luckily for the railroads and banks this combination was destined to be broken on its second trial far to the north, in Minnesota. It is a mystery how Hobbs Kerry happened to get into so formidable a band, for all seem to have known that he was but a weak disciple. True he was game enough for the broil, for, like Chadwell and Pitts, he had been thoroughly tried in the mining camps of Granby, Joplin and Carbondale, but he was not made of the stuff that could endure fatigues and hardships, and his soul was not filled with that "thieves' honor," that will suffer death before it yields to betrayal.

Now these fiercely tried comrades were all gone: the Youngers, with whom they had ridden side by side in honorable battle, as well as in many a nocturnal foray, "to reap where they had not sowed," and in other ways to despoil individuals as well as corporations, were now resting quietly, if not calmly, behind the bars of the Stillwater Penitentiary. Clell Miller, their childhood's playmate; brave, generous and true, even if misguided, was mouldering into dust.

Charlie Pitts and Bill Chadwell had carried their shares of good and ill, their virtues and their crimes, into the misty shadows of the outer world.

Who should be the next to undergo the dread novitiate and graduate as full fledged bandits. Ed. Miller had already served with them, and so had Dick Little, but this latter they doubted. They found in him a vanity inordinate, and an overpowering self-esteem. Fancying himself a Don Juan or an Adonis, no considerations of decency or propriety would cause him to let slip an opportunity to attempt to fascinate the opposite sex. Small, swarthy and forbidding of aspect, he had the high cheek-bones and small, restless eyes of a Malay pirate, yet no power on earth could convince him that he was not absolutely irresistible.

Jim Cummings, while brave as a lion, and as true as steel, was as surly and sulky as the typical "bear with a sore head," and while he could be depended upon, yet he was entirely too full of whims requiring humoring and absurd projects demanding curbing. Out of conceit with the world, Jim was in love with himself, and if he was not petted and humored like a girl, he "sulked in his tent" like the mighty Achilles before the walls of Troy.

These three discordant elements must be pacified, however (if only long enough for a single stroke), and others added to them. But where to find the others? The McDaniels were dead; Shepherd and other guerrillas of old days had been approached, but some were conscientiously honest men, and the others could not see a sufficient percentage of profit to justify the risk of death or perpetual imprisonment. If a new gang was gathered around this small, remaining nucleus, its members must come from amongst untried, raw recruits, and not from the old veterans the leader would have preferred.

There was a family living at Richmond, Ray county, Missouri, whose names were Ford. If domestic warfare was the proper school of bold and daring men, here was a chance to obtain them. The elder members of the family were eternally engaged in domestic bickerings; burdening the courts with their unsavory law-suits. One member of the family, the widow Boulton, or Moulton,[1] was a buxom, healthy-looking woman of about 25 or 26 years of age. Coquettish in manner, but countryfied in appearance, her husband had either levanted in order to escape the miseries of marital life; or else a kind Providence had most mercifully removed him from a land of widows and trouble to one where "there is neither marrying nor giving in marriage."

This widow had three brothers, called "Cap," Charley and "Bob," and a delectable set they were. The widow herself was a rather well-

[1]Martha Bolton, widowed sister of the Ford brothers.

formed woman, of passable face, and her reputation, to say the least of it, was not exactly that which Caesar demanded in a wife; for it could not, by any stretch of the imagination, be said to be "above suspicion." This widow kept, in conjunction with two of her brothers, Charley and Bob, a ranche, or rendezvous, where the bandits were entertained at any and all times. The latch string was always on the outside, the robbers had the run of the house, made themselves quite at home, in fact, and many a time when the detectives and sheriff's posses sought them far to the southward, in Texas, or the Indian Territory, they were here safely ensconced at the gentle widow's, drinking in the sweet music of her dulcet tones and other things fully as liquid, and rather more intoxicating.

This entertainment was ostensibly free, but the munificent gifts of the grateful outlaws made bandit tavern keeping a lucrative business for this amiable trio. It was more than hinted that the widow was liberal of her favors to these dashing free booters, and in consequence mortal rivalries soon arose. Some of them paid high for kisses and caresses, however, and in one instance, if not more, they cost a human life. Woot Hite had dared to rival the dandy highwayman, that Adonis of bandits, Dick Little.[2] Creeping one night lightly to his room, Dick and Bob Ford put a pistol to his head, and he was soon weltering in his gore.[3] That house, since the occupancy of the Fords, had been the scene of divided plunder, drunkenness and lascivious debauch, in which the syren, Boulton, was the central figure; now it had witnessed the basest treachery and cold-blooded murder. Scout the Bible as we may, it teaches, best of books: "the feet of the strange woman take hold on hell."

One, *if not three,* of the Ford boys accompanied the bandits on their next expedition. All agree that Charley was there, and sought, by his uncalled for brutality towards the express messenger, to prove himself "one of the boys." Some of the unguarded expressions of

[2]Triplett uses Little and Liddil interchangeably.

[3]Robert Woodson "Wood" Hite, a cousin of the Jameses, was killed in a gunfight with Bob Ford and Dick Liddil in Martha Bolton's kitchen, December 4, 1881. St. Joseph *Weekly Gazette,* April 13, 1882; Kansas City *Times,* April 4, 1882.

Jesse seem to point to the fact that Bob and Cap also were present. Two brothers from Kentucky, Clarence and Woot Hite, were also present. Little had drummed up some recruits, who were along, and there were quite a number, some seven or eight men, to be tried and then sifted down, by discarding the weak-kneed and untrustworthy, until the maximum of their number was nine.[4] It would be an easy matter, after they had passed through the ordeal of holding up a railroad train, to determine who possesed a sufficiency of cool determination and daring valor to make a first-class highwayman.

Jim Cummings's nerve was known to be good, and Dick Little, who had ridden with the Jameses before, had performed the lackey offices entrusted to him in a commendable manner. Barring an uncontrollable desire to make love, in and out of season, Dick Little had been a serviceable man to the Jameses and Youngers. They had found him a hired hand at Bob Hudspeth's, in Jackson county, and a few dollars, judiciously presented to him at various times, had bound him to their interest, and he made for them a valuable spy and messenger. Had the bandit leader pandered more to this fellow's self-love and vanity, and less often wounded his *amour propre,* he might have been alive to-day—but of this anon!

It is extremely doubtful if Jesse James himself knew all of those who were present at the Glendale robbery, they had been so hurriedly and widely gathered. Even if he had known them, it is certain that, although in the bosom of his own family, he would never have called the name of a single one of those, who, having taken one chance in a venture of this kind, concluded to retire from so perilous a trade.

This was an invariable custom of the Youngers and Jameses, so that no obstacle might be thrown in the way of the neophite bandit's return to the paths of honesty. If he stuck, well and good; if not, why, let him go in peace.

---

[4]Neither of the Ford brothers was present at the Glendale train robbery. The band consisted of Jesse James, William Ryan, Dick Liddil, Wood Hite, Ed Miller, and Tucker Bassham. George Miller, Jr., *Trial of Frank James for Murder* (E. W. Stephens Publ. Co., 1898), pp. 283-305.

In the Western portion of Layfayette county, Missouri, lies a
small village called Glendale. It is situated upon the Chicago &
Alton railway, and is some twenty miles from Kansas City. The
situation of the town is as romantic as its name, and it is shadowed
by high hills covered with dense forests, and broken by ravines and
abrubt bluffs. It would be difficult, even in the wild, mountain re-
gions of Southwestern Missouri, to find wilder or more rugged
scenery. The very place, you will say, for some terrible deed of blood.
Yes! or for holding up a railway train.

No better spot for the latter purpose could possibly be selected,
for it offered every advantage for the approach, the attack, and the
retreat; three very important factors in the element of success, and
always looked for by the cautious general, who leads his forces on
to expected victory. If the general who planned this *coup* had made
one fatal selection, he at least did not intend, in this instance, to ex-
pose his troops to unnecessary dangers. The men he led at Northfield were hardy veterans; those he had marshalled to this attack
were but unseasoned recruits.

The place, as we have said, was well chosen. It was in a deep
cleft through the hills, whose heavily timbered sides afforded ample
cover for both men and steeds; there were only a very few persons
in the hamlet, it being merely a flag station, and so the interference
of armed bodies of citizens was not to be dreaded.

The method of the robbery is variously told, but the essential
details of each story are admitted by the actors to be substantially
about as follows:

Riding to within a short distance of the village, the horses were
securely fastened, and a guard left with them, and the rest of the
party make their way into the town. Here they divide—part going
to the store, and securing all of the inhabitants, who were there
congregated. These are now marched to the station, which the rest
of the party have already reached. These latter have arrested the
operator and station agent and a minor official of the road, and
have cut the telegraph wires. The prisoners are then locked up in
the freight room, and a guard left to watch them.

All is now in readiness for the train; the agent having been compelled to arrange his danger signals, so as to halt it, and as a further precaution, a few ties, rails, etc., are used to obstruct the track.

The bandits have not long to wait. Soon, in the distance, is seen the single, glowing eye of the iron Cyclops. A low, humming noise, as of a gathering storm, strikes on the ear, a continuous running sound is heard leaping along the rail, and louder and louder grows the rumbling; brighter and brighter glows the fiery eye, until, at last, a mighty shriek is heard, and a few seconds after the train stops at the station.

As the conductor leaps on to the platform to ascertain the cause of the unusual stoppage, the bandits rush out from their concealment in the depot's shadows, and one of them salutes him by clapping a pistol to his head, at the same time giving his lantern a kick that shivered its globe to pieces, putting out the lamp. Simultaneously the engineer's cab was taken possession of, a heavy firing being kept up to intimidate passengers and train men.

The engineer, under threats of instant death, is ordered to bring the coal hammer from the tender and burst in the door of the express car, which the robbers find securely locked. Securing the heavy sledge used to break the large lumps of coal, the engineer is brought to the platform and made to break in the door. Resisting bravely at first, the sturdy ash at last begins to yield to the heavy, rapid strokes of the sledge.

When the splintered pieces of the door begin to fly into the car, the messenger, hastily unlocking his safe, takes from it all of the money, stuffs it into a canvas sack, and re-locking the safe, springs to the other door of the car to try and escape. Too late! Charlie Ford and two other robbers spring into the car, and seize the flying messenger.

"Give up the keys of your safe, you ———!" said one.

"What do you want with my keys?" said the messenger.

"None of your d—d business, you son of a b—!" said Charlie Ford, striking him over the head with a heavy revolver.

Reeling from this cruel and unnecessary violence, Grimes delivered up his keys, the blood all the while streaming from his face. A thorough search resulted in the securing of $30,000.

"Is that all?" asked Ford, who seemed determined to distinguish himself by his brutality. "I've a d—d notion to shoot you!" and it is said that had he not been prevented, he would have done so.

The terrified passengers had waited in an agony of suspense, expecting every moment to be made the subjects of spoliation; but the booty secured in the express car, it appears, satisfied the greed of the bandits, and no search of the passengers was made.

The train was now released, the guards called in, and taking to their horses, the bandits vanished away in the darkness of the night, while the train thundered on to the next station to spread abroad the news of still another train robbery.[5] "These train robbers die hard," was the muttered ejaculation of many, as they read their morning paper at the breakfast table the next day.

The $40,000 offered caused great activity amongst the detective forces; but everybody being on the lookout for the Jameses alone, the Fords, Littles, Cummings, and the rest of the smaller game, went safely and quietly back to their homes, and no doubt joined most heartily in the bitter condemnation of those terrible outlaws, the James brothers.

Truly Colonel Jones' Amnesty Bill most fairly presented the matter, when it declared that attention was drawn from all other malefactors by the cry of the James and Youngers.

[5]The Glendale robbery occurred October 8, 1879.

CHAPTER XXXV.

GEORGE SHEPHERD'S FEAT OF ARMS.

Marshal Liggett—His Determination—Arrangements—The Printed Slip—A
Meeting—Rogues' Island—Short Creek—The Bank There—Camp of the
Bandits—A Dramatic Scene—The Chase After Shepherd—The Wound—
How Jesse James Was (not) Killed—Jim Cummings in Chase—Shepherd's
Flight—Was it All a Scheme?—The Two Accounts—Who Believed Shep-
herd—How He Acted—Mrs. Samuel's Visit to Kansas City—Meets Liggett
and Shepherd—A Prior Meeting.

MARSHALL James Liggett, of Kansas City, a bold, energetic
man, had made repeated efforts to get upon the trail of the
bandits, and had spent time and money in the endeavor to over-
take and bring to justice these desperate brigands. To calm determination, Liggett united an eager impetuosity, and the outlaws had
no more determined foe in all the land than he, not even Pinkerton, the Chicago detective. His warfare against them, though, would
never countenance such illegal and barbarous methods as were used
on the night of the 25th of January, 1875. His warfare was that
of man against man, and with the courage and energy of a man
would he pursue it.

Thinking that one, who had ridden with the Jameses in their
old guerrilla days, might possess as much of woodcraft and of
cunning as they, and that no doubt he would be as well posted
as they in the forests and fastnesses to which they invariably retreated after their raids, he looked around for such a one.

In Jackson, or any of the Western counties of Missouri, it was not difficult to find these men, for almost every town contained one or more of those who, under Quantrell, had ridden to the fiercest battling ever known to man. In every hamlet were quiet, peaceful men, following the various avocations of life, who had performed deeds of valor that, at the time, had electrified a continent. The war over, these men had been enabled to come quietly to their homes, and there permitted peaceably to remain, consequently they had made the best of citizens. Had such a course of life been permitted to the Jameses and Youngers, what an amount in treasure and good name it would have saved to the State of Missouri.

Liggett had not far to look, for right under his hand was George Shepherd, quietly living in Kansas City. This man was brave as a lion. In war he had been a hero; now none than he more quiet. Bold as any of the desperate band that followed the ebbing and flowing fortunes of the daring Quantrell, he could handle a horse or a revolver with any bandit of them all; and as for fear of any living man, he did not know what fear was. His exploits during the civil war would fill volumes, and Cole Younger said of him that he was the coolest, bravest and most adventurous man that ever followed Quantrell. Such praise, coming from the lips of such a man, most certainly set the seal of confirmation, if any was needed, upon the desperate bravery of this man.

The question in Liggett's mind was: would he undertake this enterprise? Would he forget the old-time ties that had bound them together as closely as brothers in that daring band? It was a hard question to determine. If Shepherd would earnestly and honestly undertake the mission, he might accomplish something—but would he?

When it was announced that Liggett had secured the services of George Shepherd, many said: "Now you will hear of some re-results; now they have got a man on the trail that knows every thicket and forest, every lane and by-path in Missouri." They argued that it would be an easy matter for George Shepherd to enter their camps and ferret out their plans, find out their hiding-places, betray their friends, and so completely out-general them that they could easily be exterminated or captured. George Shepherd was to be the ferret that was to drive them from their coverts and their hiding-places, so that the terriers of the law, placed in readiness, might pounce upon and destroy them. A very neat programme, indeed; a very comfortable arrangement!

On the other hand there were men who shook their heads when it was told that George Shepherd had turned hunter, and intended first to worm himself into the confidence of the bandits and then betray them. These others said: "It is not in the man. Even if he undertakes this thing in good faith, there isn't in the composition of George Shepherd enough of the stuff that enters into the make-up of the detective to enable him to carry it out. He may go into it in good faith with Marshall Liggett, but when he meets the bandits, shakes their hands and breaks bread with them, that very moment Liggett loses his detective, and you'll see it."

These believed that there still lingered in George Shepherd that peculiar sentiment of honor which, though possessed by all honest men, is called "thieves' honor," probably because it is the very last to abandon a man, and is consequently retained in some measure by all save the utterly lost. Believing this, they knew that, once in the presence of the men he had set out to hunt, there would flash on his mind in a moment the nature of the task he had undertaken. It is only the city detective, most often himself a renegade thief, who can enter with zest into the excitement of thief-taking. It is only he who can glory in treachery, even towards the criminal and abandoned. To all, save minds of his kind, there is something so repulsive in fireside treachery that most men would rather endure the prevailing evils of dishonesty than to undertake, of themselves, the peculiar detective methods of its suppression. So they reasoned of George Shepherd, that his was not the soul for this sort of business; and so believing, they did not hesitate to declare that his employment would prove a failure. Those oblique minds, which could see nothing dishonorable in the basest treachery, if only it was practiced against a criminal, hooted at the idea of such finely drawn points of honor, and knew it would be a success.

There is no doubt a class of people whose moral faculties are so obtuse that they are unable to judge of the honor or honesty of any thing, and allow the law to be the sole arbiter of their consciences. These men will lie, if it suits their purpose, because, luckily for them, there is no law against lying; but these men will not swear to a lie, for fear they might be made to legally suffer for perjury. These men, too cowardly themselves to take human life, will employ and countenance the assassin, under the mistaken idea that the law gives to power the authority to commit assassination, in order to avenge murder.

Some of these peculiarly constituted moral monstrosities have attained to dangerous eminence and power; others are only the admirers and apologists of those above them. It is, however, a terrible commentary upon the boasted enlightenment of our people and the widely vaunted superiority of our methods of government, that men of this class can ever attain to social or political prominence and distinction.

In detailing the mythical adventures of legendary heroes, their historians have held themselves bound to no very strict limits of probability, and in recounting the alleged deeds and adventures of George Shepherd we do not feel that we should be held to the strictest chronologic accuracy; in fact we think we should be permitted to roam at will amongst the fancy painted scenes presented in the narrative of the undoubtedly brave, but also undoubtedly imaginative Mr. Shepherd. In the words, not aesthetic, but rigorously descriptive of the Western man: "George Shepherd had bit off more than he could *chaw*." He had, in undertaking to betray his former comrades, attempted a feat at which "his gorge did rise," and which he found at the very outset so distasteful that he determined to shirk it. The reader should not suffer himself to be misled in this matter; it was not fear of the Jameses, or of any one else, that made the job distasteful. Had it only not been his former friends he was sent out to hunt, he would have entered into it body, mind and soul, and it would have been strange if early and good results had not been obtained.

Feeling that he could not carry this thing through, Shepherd had too much of a false pride to permit him to go boldly to Liggett and tell him that the job was one not suited to his tastes; he even feared that his hesitation might be attributed to cowardice, so he went forward in it, trusting to luck to let him out of his dilemma in an honorable, or rather a creditable manner. With this reliance upon chance, he continued upon his career in search of the train-robbing, bank-raiding bandits of Missouri.

From the very beginning his narrative assumes the romantic, if not the marvelous, and shows a robust fancifulness and fertility of invention, that might, with proper training, have placed Mr. Shepherd in the front rank of American novelists. Provided with a supposed newspaper cutting, very cleverly prepared under the direction of Mr. Liggett, which stated the fact that suspicion pointed strongly to George Shepherd as one of the Glendale train robbers, and that this, taken in conjunction with the known sympathies of the man, and the little service he had done the state of Kentucky in her penitentiary, had induced the authorities to arrest and hold him for trial, etc., etc., etc. The trap was skilfully baited, and the game took the hook, like eager trout. Making his way to Mrs. Samuel's, in Clay county, he displayed the newspaper clipping, told of its injustice, and poured forth a voluble lament over the immensity of his own wrongs and those of the other former guerrillas, and wound up with the request to be permitted to see Jesse, as he intended to enter his gang and avenge upon society its cruel injustice to himself and friends.

His ruse succeeded, and he was blindfolded (we are now giving his own account of the matter!), led to a great distance, halted, and the bandage removed from his eyes, and he found himself in the presence of the dread outlaw! Could this account be more "stagey," even if told by some melodramatic detective behind the footlights? Why it is the regulation way of entering the robbers' den in all the blood and thunder tales of Beadle and of Buel. But to continue: his reception was not at all pleasant. Jesse did not rush forward, throw himself on Shepherd's breast, and call him his long lost brother. Instead, he looked coldly upon Mr. Liggett's detective; and the gang began to debate as to whether it were best to "blow him at the moon" with their revolvers; whittle him into mince-meat with their bowie knives; or only tamely to hang him, as is the mode in more law-abiding communities. At last, however, by a liberal display of his newspaper clipping, which proved a veritable "open sesame" to the bandits' hearts and confidences, as well as to those of "their sisters, their cousins and their aunts," he was received into full fellowship, was invited to take off his overcoat, and if he could find a convenient "knot on a log," to hang up his hat and make himself at home.

This he did, and the first act of the drama ends as it should, the curtain going down on a peaceful scene of jollity and content, the detective happily ensconced in the den of the robbers he has selected as his victims. *En passant,* we think it would have been safe to bet that had a band of Pinkerton's or McDonough's detectives run in on this sociable tea-party, George Shepherd would have fought as desperately against them as any James, Cummings, or Ford in the gang. Any such stimulus or excitement as a sudden attack then would have proved irresistible to Shepherd, to whom a state of combat is a normal condition, and whose nerves of steel only relax in the absence of danger; and it is safe to say that he could no more have resisted the temptation of taking a hand, had any chance have so precipitated such a conflict, than the hungry eagle can resist the opportunity of pouncing upon his quarry. Fate, however, kindly withheld this entanglement, and George is to day an inhabitant of cities—honest, brave and true, instead of a reckless highwayman.

Having obtained from the bandits a knowledge of their future plans, he secured permission from them to go to Kansas City; telling them that his object was to get an outfit, but really to reveal to Marshall Liggett what he had discovered. Now this of itself ought to have been enough to convince any sane man either that Shepherd had not seen James; or if he had, that James fully understood him, and was giving him this liberty for purposes of his own; or else that he and Shepherd had a full understanding. We cannot easily believe that Jesse James had grave suspicions of Shepherd, which a trivial clipping from a paper quieted so easily that he would let him go without protest from his camp *right to the place from which he pretended to have been hunted,* and yet had no further suspicions aroused. It is imbecility to suppose this of the shrewdest and most suspicious man, that ever led a band of outlaws, as Jesse James undoubtedly was. The most reasonable supposition is that George went to where he knew he could get a clue to Jesse's whereabouts; that he entered camp, as an old time comrade, still one who preferred to lead an honest life; that instead of a bandage over his eyes, he went in boldly, with his eyes open; sat down without fear, and had a long talk with "the boys;" that he spent the night with them, and talked over the many scenes of battle and ambush and marching they had together been engaged in, and that finally pulling out the newspaper clipping, instead of saying: "Boys! I've fled to you to seek safety; count me in as one of the gang," he merely said to them: "Cute trick, ain't it?" and explained the whole dodge.

How easy then to say to the bandits, after the joke had been thoroughly enjoyed: "Now, boys, you know me, and you know that the war hasn't left me with any money—you know that I have a living to make, and can't be choice about the employment I accept, and so I've taken this place of detective under Liggett, and I intend to hunt you, but not by coming into your camp, and eating and sleeping with you, and then betraying you: that I can't do, but if I can catch you squarely, I'll make the hunt, and the best man wins." It might even be agreed between them that in order to start fair they should all repair to their old coverts at the same time, and there separate; they to save themselves, if they could; he to run them to cover, if possible.

Shepherd went into Kansas City, had a long conference with Liggett, and left to join the bandits, mounted on a good horse and wearing two heavy revolvers.

It is said that he mentioned to Liggett several points on their Southward trail at which they could be seen, but this every sensible man must feel inclined to doubt, although Mr. Liggett himself is said to have authorized this statement. If he had notified Liggett of these points, at which secreted parties might see them pass does any one suppose that Ligget would not have had his men concealed there and taken in the entire party? Liggett had been wild to capture these men; not so much on account of the rewards, though that was a great inducement, as of the honor and renown it would confer upon him. Burning with the desire to so distinguish himself, is it likely that he would have let the gang slip through his fingers? Not at all: the first point indicated would have found Liggett and his posse lying in wait, and their sudden attack, combined with the surprise of Shepherd turning traitor, would have produced wonderful results.

All this though did not happen, and one account speaking of it says: "Marshal Liggett, acting upon this information, proceeded to the point designated, and at the hour named he had the *satisfaction* of seeing a party of armed men cross at the previously announced place, and among them recognized his chosen detective, Shepherd." Easily satisfied, Marshall Liggett! no doubt he was delighted when they had got out of sight, and absolutely enraptured when they had been gone for twenty-four hours. If this account does you justice, Marshal Liggett! it is no wonder *you* never captured the Jameses. But we believe this whole tale to have been bosh.

To follow the romance of Mr. Shepherd:

On to the South speed the bandits. Unable, however, to pass so delectable a spot as Rogues' Island, which, we are informed, is situated in the Marais des Cygnes river, somewhere near Fort Scott, Kansas, they camp there one night on their way to Short Creek, Kansas, a lead-mining town, in the same belt with Granby and Joplin, Missouri. They had matured a plan to rob the banking house of Street & McArthur, and intended to put it into effect Sunday evening, November 2d, at 3 o'clock p.m.

The party, according to his statement, consisted of Jesse James, Jim Cummings, Ed. Miller and Sam Kaufman. Frank James was not with the party, he having taken no hand in the Glendale business. It is supposed that the person he took to be Sam Kaufman was in reality Billy Blackmore.

The plan to rob the bank was known to the authorities, but they frustrated the plot for the capture of the outlaws by putting the selected posse on guard early in the morning, instead of waiting until near the time indicated—3 o'clock p.m.—to place their men in ambush.

Is it Virgil or Horace speaks of the "golden mean?" Here we find the Short Creekers as much too anxious, as Marshal Liggett was too dilatory, in taking these bandits in. Jesse James, like a prudent general, went into Short Creek that morning to take a last look over the ground preparatory to his attack, and while there, saw the placing of the guard and other preparations for a warm reception. Being of a modest, retiring disposition, he did not care to have any great noise made over his visit, so he concluded to defer it for the present, at least.

This disarranged completely the plans of Shepherd, for Jesse James, on his return to camp, moved to another location, some miles away, fearing treachery. Had this not been done, Shepherd had arranged for the annihilation of the entire band, and in this wise:

He had placed his two aids, Mike and Tom Cleary, in ambush, and his intent was to proceed to the camp, pick a quarrel with Jesse on some pretext or another, shoot him, and fly. Of course the "avengers of blood" would be hot upon his trail, and he intended to fly so that they would fall into the ambush already prepared, when they would all become victims to his skill and strategy.

How well it looks on paper! But, the camp being so suddenly moved, all of his plans were frustrated, and a new campaign was necessitated. He was equal to the occasion. He sought the new camp of the bandits, and found them on the move. They were riding in open order through the timber, the parties being placed, respectively, as follows: Ed. Miller on the right, James and Shepherd in the centre, and Jim Cummings and the unknown rode to the left, the intervals between the three parties being about one hundred yards, but all were in plain sight.

They had reached a point some twelve miles South of Galena, still riding in the same order, when Shepherd pulled up his horse, allowing Jesse to get a few paces in advance, then pulled his pistol, and shot him in the back of his head, the ball taking effect one inch behind the left ear. Jesse plunged headlong from his saddle, and lay motionless on the ground. Shepherd sat looking at the body for nearly a minute before he moved, or either of the outlaws made any attack.

Then Ed. Miller started towards him in a walk, and shortly afterwards Jim Cummings and the unknown were after him in full chase. His horse was better than that of the unknown, but not so fast as Cummings', and while he distanced the first easily, the last gained rapidly on him. As the pursuit was narrowed down to one man, Shepherd wheeled, and prepared to fight, but received a ball through his leg in so doing. The next instant he fired, striking Cummings in the side, who then reeled in his saddle, turned his horse and fled. Shepherd rode into Galena, put himself under the care of a surgeon, remained two weeks, and returned to Kansas City.

About the only variations of this account are those which change Mike Cleary's name to Ed.; make Marshal Liggett to send three men to get the satisfying sight of the passing robbers, while he has Shepherd locked up in jail in Independence; vary the name of the town from Short Creek to Empire City, and make Shepherd to have given vent to the following rather florid piece of decla- mation: "Damn you, Jesse James! thirteen years ago you killed my cousin, Frank Shepherd," before doing his pistol act.

The whole thing is bosh from beginning to end; and if there is a grain of truth is the entire fabrication, it is astonishing what an immense superstructure of fiction this atom of actual foundation has been made to support. The whole tale is a transparent romance that ought not to gull a ten-year-old child; but there are some grown men, especially a writer pretending to have private and reliable information in regard to the lives of these very men not obtainable by others, who has pinned his faith to this report, and on the strength of it has everywhere proclaimed, as if absolutely indisputable, the fact, first, that Jesse James was dead, and after- ward that he was a paralytic inbecile from the effects of Shepherd's shot. To those parties who came in daily contact with Jesse James, and whom Jesse often asked to see if he really had been wounded, as he himself had never found it out, this wound, or even the slightest scar of it, was always invisible.

The wound on Shepherd's leg was made, how? No one knows. Whether, in order to strengthen the tale he intended to tell Liggett and publish to the world, he shot himself, or whether he held out his leg and let Jesse James shoot him; or whether he shot himself accidentally; or whether he was shot accidentally or purposely in some brawl, it is hard to determine. He succeeded in convincing Liggett of the truth of his tale, and several alleged colonels swore by it for a year or two, but in the light of recent events have been compelled to relinquish their belief.

When Mrs. Samuel, Jesse's mother, visited Kansas City to see Liggett after the reported shooting, she first saw Shepherd, and he knew by her looks when she met him that she had seen or heard from Jesse since the reported killing. Matters looked badly for Shepherd, and he appealed directly to Mrs. Samuel to save him from his awkward dilemma. It suited her purpose to do so, and, too, she pitied the evident distress of a brave man in difficulties; so when she saw Liggett, and he asked her what she thought of Jesse's death now, she *believed* it, and Shepherd was saved from disgrace. It ended as all farces ought to, and the curtain went down on every body smiling and happy.

CHAPTER XXXVI.

WINSTON, MO. TRAIN ROBBERY.

Location of Winston—Features of the Country—How the Robbery Was Planned—The Waiting Horses—The Dead Conductor—Accidental (?) Killing of McCulloch—Messenger Murray—Ford Again to the Front—Safe Rifled—Amount of Money Secured—Wild Surmises—Abused Stories—Who Killed Westfall—Was It For Revenge?—Dividing the Plunder—Escape of the Outlaws—The Usual Talk of the Indian Territory—Where the Thieves Did Harbor—Who They Were.

THE next train robbery was destined to occur at Winston, in Daviess county, Missouri. This village is situated well for the operations of the bandit, being convenient to the heavy timber and dense undergrowth of the Grand river and its tributaries. This would furnish most excellent hiding places for any stock the robbers might need in their foray, and besides, if an accident should happen to overturn their plans, it would afford an excellent opportunity for their escape. Their horses would need cover to hide them from the inquisitive eyes of the villagers, and then, too, it might become necessary for a hurried flight, such as the Jameses and Youngers made from Northfield, and as no place promised greater facilities for both, Winston was selected.

A new gang was here to try its hand at the fascinating pursuit, which had so long been held as a monopoly by a few experienced operators. The pupils intended to eliminate themselves from the control of these "older, if not better soldiers," and set up in business for themselves, and Winston was the place selected for the opening

PROCLAMATION
$5,000⁰⁰

REWARD

FOR EACH of SEVEN ROBBERS of THE TRAIN at WINSTON, MO., JULY 15, 1881, and THE MURDER of CONDUCTER WESTFALL

$ 5,000.00

ADDITIONAL for ARREST or CAPTURE

DEAD OR ALIVE
OF JESSE OR FRANK JAMES

THIS NOTICE TAKES the PLACE of ALL PREVIOUS REWARD NOTICES.

CONTACT SHERIFF, DAVIESS COUNTY, MISSOURI IMMEDIATELY

T. T. CRITTENDEN, GOVERNOR
STATE OF MISSOURI
JULY 26, 1881

of the campaign. No matter what may be said to the contrary, neither Jesse nor Frank James was present at Winston; it was a venture of Dick Little, the Fords and Jim Cummings; and this insubordination of his troops led to the deadly enmity between Jesse James and the rest of the outlaws. They never, with the probable exception of Charlie Ford, paid to him as leader one cent of the tribute levied on the express company at Winston. He was not even notified of the planning of the affair, nor was the time of its intended completion ever intrusted to him.

He was purposely ignored in the entire arrangement, which was the concoction of the combined intellects of Jim Cummings and Dick Little, who were, as they said, tired of playing second fiddle to a man, who was no better schemer nor fighter than they were. Of this fact they intended to convince him, and not only him, but some of his admirers. Dick's vanity had been too often hurt by Jesse, and his jealousy too often aroused, not to make him a secret but bitter enemy of his leader, and he found Jim Cummings with a grievance easily worked up into positive hatred. Thus matters stood when the new firm opened business as train robbers, under the style and name of Little, Cummings & Co. There was one thing, however, that they did not care to assume, and that was the responsibility for any stroke of business they might do; so they considerately allowed that to fall, as of yore, upon the old firm of the James brothers.

Every thing had been put into perfect order for this first piece of business, which they determined should be a grand success. Their horses had been brought up and secreted in the heavy timber, and a sufficient guard left with them to keep them in perfect readiness for any emergency. The camp having been established, the men scattered to take the train at different points, for they had determined to inaugurate a new method of carrying on the business, as they fancied it would not only be more expeditious and safer, but it had about it the charm of novelty.

A part of the crowd got on as far up as Cameron and part at Winston, two of the latter taking their station on the front platform of the baggage car, where they could easily climb on to the tender, if need be, and thence into the engine. It might not be necessary to do this, however, as from the advantage of their position they could compel the engineer to do as they wished, and if the engineer and fireman in a moment of desperation should jump from their cab, the robbers could cut the baggage car loose from the run-away locomotive and thus eventually stop the train.

The rest of the robbers were arranged as follows: Three of them were seated in the smoking car and two stood on the rear platform of the baggage car. Their idea was to so quickly rob the express car, that they could be ready to jump off at the bridge with their booty as the train slacked up there, hence the disposition of the men as stated. This was an improvement on the James and Younger method, as will be plainly seen, since it would enable the bandits to rob the train without stopping it, thereby rendering the discharge of fire-arms unnecessary, when it was likely to attract a crowd and hasten pursuit. Another thing: by this plan they would leave the train at the bridge, take to their horses, and be off with a good start before any alarm could gather a crowd and put pursuers on the track. It was a progressive idea; it rendered train-robbing safer and entailed less expenditure of muscle and ammunition.

Its brutality was destined to increase along with its accession of ease and safety at an equal pace. As the conductor entered the car in which the three ruffians sat he called out "tickets," and proceeded to take up the fares of the passengers. He had already passed half way or more down the length of the car, when the largest of the robbers, a big burly fellow, rose in his seat, and turning around drew his revolver. Calling to [William] Westfall, the conductor, he said: "Here, G—d d—n you! you are the man I want," and fired at him, the ball taking effect in his shoulder. Seeing that he was to be murdered, Westfall made for the rear door of the coach he was then in, and had just reached the door when one of the thieves, a small man, fired at him. He stumbled through the now opened door, and fell first to the platform and thence to the ground.

Next there was a rush into the baggage car, and in the firing that took place a stone-mason named [John] McCulloch was killed.

It has been the general belief that his death was the result of an accident, but those who are more intimately acquainted with the fiendish cruelty and bravado of Dick Little and the Fords can easily believe that it was intentional, being done not even to terrorize, but for the mere love of killing. Another thing, too, they intended at all costs to others to make this robbery a success. They intended to show Jesse James that there were others besides himself who could plan and carry out a train robbery.

When they entered the express car the messenger, [Charles] Murray, was first struck over the head with a heavy revolver and then asked to give up his keys. This of course he did, and the safe was speedily rifled of its contents. The amount obtained is variously estimated at from $8,000 to $15,000. It was placed in a sack, and the train, which had stopped a short distance from the town, was again set in motion, until it reached the woods in which the robbers' horses were concealed. Here they forced the engineer to stop, and leaving the scene of their rapine and violence, they ran to their horses. The state of their trepidation is proved by their cutting their bridle reins, instead of taking time to untie them, in order the sooner to make their escape.[1]

Their course, as well as can be ascertained, was around Cameron, and then almost due South to the Missouri river, where they disappeared. The hunt again was made for the Jameses in Clay and Jackson counties, in the Indian Nation, and in Texas. No one visited the ranch of Mrs. Boulton, or searched the house of Mattie Collins Little at Buckner. The crossing of the Missouri river by the entire gang is all nonsense; it was never done. Dick Little and one, maybe two others, did cross it; the rest stayed on the North side, and joined in the cry of "the Jameses."

In the brush where the horses were tied, the following letter is said to have been found:

Kansas City, July 12.

"CHARLIE:

"I got your letter to-day, and was glad to hear that you had

[1] The Winston robbery occurred July 15, 1881.

got everything ready in time for the 15th. We will be on hand at that time. Bill will be with us. We will be on the train; don't fear. We will be in the smoker at Winston. Have the horses and boys in good fix for fast work. We will make this point again on the night of the 16th. All is right here. Frank will meet us at Cameron. Look sharp and be well fixed. Have the horses well gaunted, for we may have some running to do. Don't get excited, but keep cool till right time. Wilcox or Wolcott will be on the engine. I think best to send this to Kidder.

"Yours till and through death,

"SLICK."

This letter was written in order that it might make this business seem a stroke of Jesse James, and it was purposely dropped. None of then ever kept a letter any longer than time enough to read it and become familiar with its contents, but this letter was, when found, four days old.

It is not at all in the style of Jesse James, who would have said all that is in it in half the number of words. Its phraseology is not like his. The allusion to Frank is done to further the plan of throwing this job on to the Jameses. Part of it is ridiculously silly, for instance, where it says: "We will make this point again on the 16th." This was done in the hopes that pursuit would be held back for at least one day, by which time, or long before it, they would be safely at their homes, chuckling at the pursuit of the omni-present Jameses.

Of course there are numbers who will believe nothing else but that the Jameses were the originators of this outrage, and that they were present to carry it out. If nothing else should cause a doubt of their presence, the fact of the want of coolness on the retreat should do so. When had the Jameses ever shown so great a dread and so feverish a haste? Men, who had ridden through showers of bullets, and who, under fire from a regiment, have been known to get down and aid a fellow-comrade, or (a point of honor with the guerrillas!) secure the revolvers of a fallen friend, are not apt to take so panic a fright as that which possessed these men, who for the first time depended on their own nerve and judgment in their onset and retreat.

The nonsense of Westfall's death being a sacrifice to the vengeance of the Jameses is too silly for belief. They well knew who it was that piloted the detectives to their mother's home, and were not idiotic enough to blame Westfall for what he never did. They were too well posted for that, for they knew beyond the possibility of a doubt that Jack Ladd was the pilot on that occasion. Had he been on the train, and either of the Jameses present, he would have died as sure as fate, but neither had any cause of quarrel with Westfall.

The Jameses had never been unnecessarily cruel or brutal, and had they been present at Winston, there would have been no murder committed there. The very descriptions of the ruffians, who did the killing, exonerates Frank and Jesse James; neither of whom could be called a big, burly man, nor a small man, both being men of a size classed as medium. Jim Cummings, Charley Ford and Dick Little were the master spirits of this expedition, and on their skirts rests the blood of Westfall and of McCulloch. Interested parties will strenuously deny this assertion, but a cool and candid consideration will convince any one that it was not the work of the Jameses.

To some, of course, the fact that a train is robbed is at once conclusive proof of the presence of the Jameses, and they will go to work to deduce, or if necessary to manufacture evidence tending to show that they must of necessity have been present. Of this class are the men who could, at a moment's notice, give you any number of very cogent reasons why George Shepherd's tale was bound to be true in every particular.

The record of the Jameses, since they were forced into outlawry, has certainly been sufficiently burdened with crime, without making them to bear the sins and outrages of every bad man whose viciousness led him to the commission of pillage and of blood-shed.

Study the Winston outrage over closely, and it presents no mark of the handiwork of the James brothers. The unnecessary brutality and murder; the precipitate haste; the mode of operating, and the evident trepidation and panic hurry of the flight, do not characterize any of their outrages.

CHAPTER XXXVII.

BLUE CUT, MO., ROBBERY.

The New Leaders—Their Enmity Against the Jameses—Charlie Ford—Dick Little (or Liddil)—Jim Cummings—The Conference—Revolt—A Bungling Job—Blue Cut—Location—Number of the Bandits—17th September, 1881 —"Danger Ahead"—The Conductors' Warning—Its Good Results—Freight

Train Flagged—Barton's Peril—The Bandits' Speech—Bold Threats— Brutality—Attempted Murder—Small Booty—Pursuit—Why It Failed— Who Did the Deed—Absence of the Jameses—This Fact Proved—Course of the Robbers.

THE new hands had had a taste of the sweets of independence and of money easily though guiltily acquired. Unlike those of whom this thing had ceased to be a novelty, these novices longed to again try the uncertain fortunes of the road.

Jesse James had sworn vengeance against Jim Cummings, Dick Little and all of the bandits, in fact, who had added to his evil reputation another stigma, and had caused him additional danger by the outrage at Winston. Of the spoil none of them, with the possible exception of Charlie Ford, had ever tendered to him the smallest fraction, although they all traded for safety on his name. To Dick Little and Jim Cummings, at a stormy meeting between the three, he plainly laid down his ultimatum, that another outbreak of the kind, and the first time he met them somebody would die. So the meeting ended, no promises having been asked or volunteered.

To any one familiar with the characters of Dick Little and

Jim Cummings, it would have been an easy task to read in their faces that they did not intend to submit to this dictation. They knew that they would have to look out carefully for themselves, but they expected to be able to do this, as they could, at any time danger became imminent, deliver Jesse up to the law, and so save themselves. Trading on this idea, they determined, in opposition to, and most likely in consequence of his command, to show to the world another bold stroke of genius, though in this instance, as at Winston, they were willing that to the world in general, and the detectives in particular, it should appear as the work of Jesse James. The job, however, was so bungling a piece of work, that it did not delude even the merest novice in detective science into the belief that the Jameses were present.

Blue Cut is about two miles West of Glendale Station, the scene of a former robbery on the Chicago & Alton railway. It is a cut in a hillside; on the South the wall of the cut rises to the height of twenty-five or thirty feet, while on the north side, owing to the steep slope of the hill, it is barely eight or ten. From Independence, in Jackson county, the cut is distant some six or eight miles.

This was the place selected by this newly-organized band for the second in a series of robberies they had planned and contemplated carrying out. From the very inception to the completion of the job, there was shown an utter want of judgment, and even common sense. A great number of men and boys had been drummed up by Little, Cummings and Ford, the idea being held out to all that Jesse James was to be the leader in the enterprise. This was not only talked to all whom they approached, but it was boldly and openly announced before even the consent of the party approached was obtained. The idea evidently was to have it thoroughly impressed upon the minds of every one that it was the work of Jesse James.

It was on the night of the 17th [7th] of September, 1881, that the robbery occurred. It was only about two miles below this point, and two years before this date, that the Glendale train robbery had happened, which was still fresh in the minds of every one.

The bandits had possessed themselves of a red lantern, the universally accepted signal, amongst railroad men, of "danger ahead." One man was stationed on the track at the cut with this signal lamp. The track was also obstructed with ties and other debris, so that even had the danger signal not been heeded, the train must have come to a standstill or have been wrecked. When the train began to slow up the conductor went forward, saw the obstructions on the track, the red light, and the armed men swarming around.

Hastily making his way back through the cars, he warned every body as he went that the train was in possession of the robbers, and advised them to hide what they could. This thoughtfulness on his part saved a good deal to the passengers under his care. He had made his way through the train to the Pullman sleeper, when he was halted by a ruffian with two revolvers, who ordered him to throw up his hands and get into line with the engineer and mail agent, whom they had already secured.

Mr. [Joel M.] Hazlebaker signified his willingness to do so, but asked permission to first go back with a lantern and signal the freight, which was following them, and would run into them if not warned of the stoppage. This the robber agreed to, as it endangered himself and comrades as much as it did the train men and passengers; so getting one of his brakesmen, a young fellow named [Frank Burton] Barton, he started back around the curve to stop the train, which was rapidly bearing down upon them.

The bandits lining the south hill side did not understand this move, and opened a rapid fire from shot-guns and revolvers upon the brakesman and conductor. Scared nearly to death, Barton leaped into the engine cab in an agony of terror. The engineer shouted to them not to shoot the boy, that he was only going back to signal the freight and save the lives of the passengers.

At this explanation one of the robbers on a car platform called to those on the hill to cease firing, and in a moment all was quiet again. This enabled the freight train to be stopped, and none too soon to prevent a terrible catastrophe. The utmost exertions of the engineer and brakesmen stopped the train within a car length of the Pullman coach.

When the robbers got to the express car they found Henry Fox, messenger in charge. In addition to his own safe he had charge of another, but it was luckily so covered with boxes, chicken-coops, bundles, etc., that it was never discovered. The doors of the car were securely fastened, but this was no protection; for a coal-pick was handed to the engineer of the train, and he was ordered to force it in. The baggage man knew that the door could not long withstand the attack, so he opened it, and he, the engineer, mail agent and express messenger, were covered with the bandits' revolvers.

Right here a proceeding took place which would never have occurred had either of the Jameses been along with the gang.[1] One of them, a tall man, and evidently the leader, began in a very dramatic strain to orate before the parties under guard. He told them that he was the man that had killed Westfall at Winston, and claimed that Westfall brought on his own death by trying to draw a revolver on him. He said: "But you fellows have acted decent, by G—d; and if you don't go to making G—d d—d fools of yourselves you won't get hurt." Continuing his rhodomontade, he said that he didn't want to hurt any of the railroad boys, but that he was going to make it hot for the d—d Chicago & Alton railroad, because it had dared to offer rewards for him and his men. They intended to burn every freight train on that road, he said, if they had to ditch them first and burn them afterwards.

Here he was interrupted by Dick Little asking where the express messenger was.

Fox, who had sense enough to see that his silence would only infuriate the ruffians, and could at best but delay the rifling of his safe, stepped forward and told them that he was the messenger.

"Get into your part of the car, then, and open your safe," said the tall man.

[1] Conductor Hazlebacker, in an interview with a reporter, stated he did not think the leader of the gang was Jesse James though the robber kept declaring he was. Kansas City *Times*, September 8, 1881.

"Yes! and you'd better be d—d quick about it, too," said Little, "we've got enough of this foolishness;" and in order to hurry him up Little began beating him over the head with his revolver, talking very loudly and swearing all the time. Making what haste he could, Fox opened the safe, and taking out the packages handed them over to the ruffian.

"Is this all you have?" he asked, and seemed to be furious with rage at the small amount they had secured.

"It is everything there is," said Fox.

The naturally brutal nature of the ruffian seemed enraged beyond measure at the trivial haul they had made, and he began to give vent to his fiendish displeasure by beating Fox over the head again with a heavy revolver, and at last wound up by firing a shot at him, which just grazed his ear, as he lay prostrate upon the floor where a blow from the pistol of the robber had stretched him.

While this was going on at the express and baggage car, the passengers were being jerked about, hauled rudely out of their seats, and stripped of their valuables. Thanks to the timely warning of the conductor, the passengers had had time to secrete the greater part of their money and jewelry before the search began, so this robbery was destined to be a disappointment all round.

Not satisfied with one thorough search of the sleeping-coach, they made another, tearing the bunks and bedding apart and searching everywhere for spoil. They seemed to think that somewhere, if they could only stumble upon it, fortune lay hid, waiting for them. The sleeper was about the worst disarranged coach that ever bore the name of Pullman, when these robbers got through with it. The sheets, blankets and mattresses were scattered everywhere, and disorder reigned supreme.

This robbery occupied about three quarters of an hour, and then the bandits vanished from the train; and having removed the obstructions, the train men got on board, and with all speed pulled out for Kansas City, which point was reached about 10 o'clock, the train being just half an hour late.

Of course there were the usual amounts of telegrams flying back and forth, and the usual exclamation of the "James boys," and the usual exaggeration of the amount captured.

A small posse started out from Kansas City and reached Glendale at midnight. At this point the Sheriff of Salina county with a band of armed men was met, and a diligent search prosecuted for two or three days; the search looking always toward the capture of the Jameses, rather than to the ascertaining first who were present, and next, what was the best mode of securing them.

This robbery settled the animosity of Jesse James, and Dick Little and Jim Cummings now felt that all chance of any future friendship between them was cut off. They, as well as the Fords, recognized the fact that they had not the nerve, sense nor judgment to play their part alone, and this led to the final disintegration of the band.

Dreading the anger of Jesse James on the one hand, though they were half a dozen against one; and seeing the determined efforts of the law on the other, they felt themselves in a predicament from which they could only be rescued by something little short of a miracle. What they determined on will be seen hereafter.

No matter in what light we consider this robbery, we are forced to conclude that it was neither planned nor carried out by the James brothers. In the first place they would not have selected a train bound west when they knew, as did every man of common sense, that the current of money was then flowing in the opposite direction. The train would have been held by not more than half the number of men Little drummed up, if Jesse or Frank James had been in charge. There would have been no attempt at unnecessary murder, as in this case. Trivial amounts would not have been taken from train men and needy laborers, as was done here. There would have been no tedious harangues such as the leader of these thieves favored his prisoners with. There would have been no boasting of having killed a man, as this could have been no novelty to men who had killed from eight to ten in a single hand to hand fight. There would have be no previous solicitation of raw recruits, to whom the fact that Jesse James was to lead them was held out as an inducement to enter into the scheme, if either of the Jameses were really concerned in it. This was done so that it was bound to leak out, and was a trick of the robbers to throw the pursuit on to the track of the Jameses, and transfer the hunt to Clay county, while they had a chance to slink quietly to their homes.

It was destined that, at Glendale, Jesse was to perform his last act of rapine and of crime. Death, that comes alike to the good and to the bad; death, that is no respecter of rank or person; death, the one thing inevitable to all that is mortal, was doomed to cut short all the plans of the noted outlaw, before he could again organize a band for the perpetration of other daring robberies. After Glendale he found a spirit of revolt rising against him, and this culminated at Winston, where he was not only defied, but absolutely ignored. Knowing that he would have all the blame of this affair to bear, he demanded from the others a full share of the spoil secured, and a promise that they would never again engage in any thing of the kind, unless he was first notified. Fearing that he would want the lion's share of the booty, and anxious to break away from his rule, Little and Cummings refused absolutely, and the others joined with them in their rebellion. This, *and nothing else, no matter what may now be said,* was the cause of the deadly enmity shared by Little and Cummings against Jesse James, which was known to every one to exist before and at the time of the death of the latter. Ford, finding that new developments were taking place daily, and not knowing how soon after Clarence Hite his time might come to serve the State, fled to James, and threw himself upon his mercy. He saw that there was only danger, without a chance of profit, under the lead of surly Cummings and vainglorious Little, and he fled to his old leader. The course of the others we will show in our next chapter.

CHAPTER XXXVIII.

BANDIT BICKERINGS.

The New Gang—Discordant Elements—Their Conduct at Glendale—Woot Hite—Dick Little—Thieves by Necessity—Thieves by Choice—Advantages of the Latter—Fear of the Law and Fear of Jesse James—The Coward's Course—Charlie Ford's Behaviour—Little's Proposal to Surrender—The Thieves' Emissary—The Governor—"The Veiled Lady"—Plot Filled—End of Act First—Curtain Falls.

AFTER the terrible depletion of his band at Northfield, Jesse James, as has been said before, set about the work of selecting new members, and while he well knew that he could never hope to replace such men as the Youngers, whom he had seen tested in the dangers of a warfare unequalled in civilized annals for its desperate character, and while he could not but doubt that he would not be able to supply again such men as Clell Miller, Chadwell and Pitts, all of whom had an established character for desperate and reckless courage and staunch fidelity, yet still it was a necessity of his very existence that he should gather together another band of freebooters to aid him in his plans.

The trial resulted in the selection of Dick Little, Jim Cummings, Ed. Miller, Woot and Clarence Hite and the Fords. The conduct of these men at Glendale satisfied him in every particular, except the brutality of Ford, and this he felt could be easily corrected. In speaking with his intimates, after that affair, he expressed himself as having got together a good band of men, but he soon had cause to think this declaration rather a premature one.

Woot Hite, like Dick Little, was a great admirer of himself, as
well as of the opposite sex, and, like the dandy robber, he was
greatly smitten with the charms of the widow Boulton, who seems
to have been rather promiscuous in the bestowal of her favors. Dick
Little had become *ennuied* with the charms of the piquant Miss
Mattie Collins, and was demeaning himself at this time as a devoted suitor of Mrs. Boulton. Woot Hite, too, found the time to
pass pleasantly while listening to the sweet voice of the syren, and
in the course of events, from the very nature of the two men, a
conflict between them was inevitable.

Jim Cummings required the petting of a baby to keep him in
good humor, and fancying himself a man of much importance,
sulked whenever the petting was not forthcoming.

Clarence Hite was too young to use the continual care necessary in this dangerous business; and Jesse soon found that the
task of holding these men together, and of conciliating these discordant elements, would be no light one. It was a continual bick-
ering whenever any two of them met, and it was plain to be seen
where it would end.

Jesse now bitterly realized the difference between men who
go into robbery from necessity, and those who do so from prefer-
ence. To the Youngers, as well as to Frank and himself, no other
path was left open; but to these other men, there was no barrier
to an honorable career, other than their own innate sloth and a
greedy desire for money. For himself and the Youngers there might
have been some excuse for rapine and violence; for the Littles,
Fords and men of their kind, there was none whatever. The first
had been forced to rob, because they were not allowed to stay
at home in peace and quiet; the last had volunteered to rob, because
it offered a way of making money more easily than honestly earning
it.

By a singular heresy of the law, not justice, these latter, the
willful thieves, might any day have their crimes condoned by betraying the enforced thieves; but this rule was a poor one, in that
it would not work both ways.

And this was what happened when these wilful thieves found

that they were unable to plan and carry out robberies with safety to themselves and friends, and when they realized that their revolt at Winston and at Blue Cut had placed them at deadly enmity with a man they feared, as well as hated; they immediately began to attempt to make terms for themselves with the authorities. They were, it is true, half a dozen to one, but still they feared that one so greatly that they did not dare to risk a combat that they knew must come whenever they met. It was no desire to perform an act of honesty, and to turn from the evil of their ways, and become peaceful, law abiding citizens; it was only that they saw on one side of them the pursuing anger of the law, which they knew that, without a leader, they could not hope to evade, and on the other, the anger of an estranged comrade, whom they feared to encounter.

In this dilemma they determine to avail themselves of any clemency the law may extend, and so they open communications, looking towards giving themselves up.

But just here we will state what we have omitted, and that is, that Charlie Ford, finding the officers of the law hot upon his track, had gone to Jesse James; owned up that he had not acted honorably, and avowing that he had bitterly regretted his course asked to be received again under his protection. This was accorded, and thus matters stood when the negotiations of Liddil for surrender began. Whether Ford's action at this time was a part of the scheme afterwards developed, or whether he was drawn into that later, each must judge for himself.

Ed. Miller had fled from the State, and Jim Cummings withdrew himself to some of his many hiding places, and so far has eluded pursuit.

The proper emissary from these thieves and murderers to the political trickster, who filled the highest office in the State, all felt must be a harlot, and so Mrs. Boulton was selected, and she soon makes her appearance on the scene as "the mysterious lady in the black vail." So the characters to the plot now stand, and the curtain falls upon the first act.

Governor Thomas T. Crittenden.

CHAPTER XXXIX.

DEATH OF JESSE JAMES.

Crittenden's Plot—Bob Ford—A Noble (?) Pair—An Assassination Planned —Four of a Kind—The Kansas City Conference—Plans and Promises— Crittenden's Character—Actions During the War—A Drum-Head Court Martial—His Braggadocio—Murder, Not Arrest, Contemplated—"Malice Domestic"—The Viper Warmed—A Quiet Home—The Assassin's Shot— Grief of the Wife—Telegrams—Crittenden's Exultation.

WHILE all right-minded men must execrate and condemn every act of robbery, violence and murder, no matter by whom committed, nor how great the provocation for their commission may have been, yet still the fair and honest man will always allow to those accused of these crimes the chance to be heard in his defense; and so the law, the very essence, as it were, of all honesty and fairness, makes it first necessary to give a man a patient hearing before he can be condemned and made to suffer for crimes charged against him. In order to bring about this trial and fairness of judgment, the man must submit himself to a jury of his peers for examination in regard to the crimes and offenses alleged to have been committed by him. In the absence of this voluntary submission, the law has a right to enforce the attendance of the supposed criminal by summon and arrest. Should this summon not be obeyed, officers may be deputized to arrest the person and bring him by force before the court; and if he is supposed to be a desperate person, a large force, called a posse, may be summoned to the aid of the regular officers, in order that the party summoned to appear in court shall be forced to attend. So great is the majesty and power of the law, that if the party, so sought to be arrested, either by the officer or his posse, or any member of it, shall offer resistance, and shall use, or attempt to use, deadly weapons in such resistance, then he may be shot down by the officer, posse or member thereof; but the attempt to arrest shall first be made. This is the extent of the law: it assumes to itself no further or greater power, and no lawyer will pretend that this is not the utmost limit of its power. It gives to no one, whether officer or private citizen, governor or renegade thief, the authority to sit in judgment on any criminal and compass his death. The law presumes that its officers have sufficient power to arrest any supposed criminal, and to enable them to do so, it delegates to them the privilege and power of summoning to their aid a posse of citizens. It nowhere contemplates giving to any of its officers the right to condemn to death any one, without allowing to him first a fair trial. The officer is not permitted to plead in justification of an official murder that he is afraid of the victim. The cowardice of the officer does not justify the murder of the criminal.

That society is in a terrible state of insecurity when men are elevated to high offices, who have so little knowledge of the letter and so little comprehension of the spirit of our laws, that they will bargain with thieves and murderers for the assassination of their comrades. That brain is too ill-balanced, and that soul is too perverted, that cannot comprehend the hideous evils of the infamous crime of assassination. To the noble soul, and the bold, free and honorable mind of the Anglo-Norman, assassination is as foreign and as far as hell is from heaven. If it is possible that there can be degrees in a crime so utterly damnable as assassination, that for hire must certainly be the worst; and if this be the case, how shall we speak of the crime of that man who will go into the house of his friend, eat of his bread, accept his shelter, be comforted by him in his troubles, and nursed by him in his sickness, and shall requite him by a dastardly shot in the back? What shall we think of an official, who standing at the head of affairs in his State; placed there by her people to keep pure her laws and preserve her skirts from stain and her name from reproach, and yet who, while occupying this position, proves himself such a moral leper as to hire this assassin to perpetrate this heretofore unheard of crime? Who is safe, if we may be tried before the bar of one man's judgment, and then the paid assassin may be set on to dog our steps, watch our outgoing and our incoming, and in our first unguarded moment, when our back is towards him, shall be permitted to shoot us down; a pardon for the crime being promised in advance? It may be said that this case was an exception. To this we say that law and justice have no exceptions. What applies to one applies to all.

The visit of the veiled woman to Governor Crittenden, gave to that worthy an opportunity that he was not slow in seizing. Ever preferring the violent method of brute force to the slower, though more legal and humane modes prescribed by law, he saw in the revelations made to him by Mrs. Boulton, an opportunity for notoriety such as he fancied would endear him to the populace, and insure him future political honors. He had long desired to succeed to the senatorial mantle of George Vest, which would, could he obtain it, hang about him like the robe of a giant upon the person of a pigmy, and now he saw opened up to him a pathway to the highest honors. His political dickering and unblushing mendacity had made him an object of ridicule and contempt to his political associates, but now he would retrieve all that. He would become the benefactor of his people. He would blot forever from this great commonwealth the title of the "robber State." Whether he has succeeded remains to be seen, but it is even now certain that the blot with which he obliterated the name of "robber state" leaves behind it a vastly greater stain; that of the "assassin state."

When Mrs. Boulton had obtained for her paramour, Little, permission to surrender himself, he was still red-handed from the murder of Woot Hite, a crime for which both he and Bob Ford seem to claim the notoriety. That both were equally guilty there seems to be but little doubt, and their ready made tale of a "free fight" is more than doubtful. It is safe to venture the assertion that Hite was murdered in his bed by these fiends, to whom assassination causes not a qualm of conscience. The state in which the body was found, and all the evidence that can be gathered, go to show that Hite was murdered while asleep. The hired man, who was unlucky enough to have heard the firing, has since disappeared. Where he has gone no one knows, though it is easy to conjecture. His evidence would prove embarrasing to these pets of our Governor; he could swear that instead of a heavy fusilade for two or three minutes, there were but two shots fired, these both at the same time, and neither of them by Hite. It is safe to predict that his evidence will never be heard.

Little had gone to Kansas City and given himself up to one Craig,[1] a creature of the Governor, and the plot was laid that was to end in the assassination of the bandit leader, Jesse James.

Bob Ford had also joined the detectives under Craig, and Charlie Ford was housed with Jesse James. Through Charlie Ford *the domicile and every move* of the great outlaw *were at all times known, not only to his brother, Bob, but also to Crittenden, Craig and Timberlake.*[2]

It was this knowledge, AND ONLY THIS, that enabled Crittenden to predict so confidently, a week or two before the outlaw's death, that he would "soon have Jesse James." His bargain, too, with Ford was—not for an attempt at arrest, but for assassination. When, and it was but for a single time suggested, it was mentioned that James might be taken alive, Bob Ford shrank back horrified at the mere mention of such a thing; and, although in the power of the Governor to do with as he chose, would not promise to make this attempt. From this time on, all bargains and promises looked to assassination as the method, and pardon for the crime as the reward.

Of the moneys offered for the capture of the bandit, the Fords were to get $2,500—or just one-fourth. There were but *three* other parties to the plot, Crittenden, Craig and Timberlake; where, then,

[1]The Craig mentioned here was Henry H. Craig, police commissioner of Kansas City, Mo. He should not be confused with Enos Craig, city marshal of St. Joseph, Mo.

[2]James H. Timberlake, sheriff of Clay County, Mo.

Captain Henry H. Craig, police commissioner of Kansas City, active
in the pursuit of Jesse James.

Bob Ford, who shot and killed Jesse James. He later opened a tent saloon in Creede, Colorado; it was here in 1892 that he was shot and killed by Edward O'Kelley.

Charlie Ford was in Jesse James' home as a guest when his brother
Bob shot Jesse. *Courtesy St. Joseph Museum.*

Mrs. Ford, mother of Robert and Charlie. *Courtesy St. Joseph Museum.*

were the other *three*-fourths to go? Why had it been divided into fourths at all? Is not the solution of this transparent riddle easy to one and all?

The "Craig Rifles" gave a ball in Kansas City, and of course Governor Crittenden was honored with an invitation. With this as his ostensible business he goes to Kansas City, and there, in one of the rooms of the "St. James Hotel," he meets his men; Craig, Bob Ford and probably Timberlake, and then and there was concocted the most diabolical plan ever conceived and adopted to rid the State of an outlaw since the world began. Even had Jesse James been guilty of all with which he was charged, and his dearest friends do not claim that he was innocent of all the crime laid to his door, yet would it have been better for him to have still run and rioted on his career, rather than that the fair name of the State should have been stained by so foul a deed, originated, sanctioned and perfected by her chief magistrate and his accomplices.

That an outlaw shall pillage is to be expected; that in his wild and crime-stained career even red-handed murder and cruel assassination may stalk companion-like beside him would cause surprise to no one; but that the Governor of the State, the conservator of the liberties of her people, and the preserver and executor of her laws, should league with harlots, thieves and murderers to procure assassination, is astounding almost beyond belief. What if the cry was raised that no man's life was safe while Jesse James lived, is his safety any more assured while such men as the Fords, licensed by Crittenden to assassinate, are at large? If they will murder a comrade; a man, who has befriended them; whose bread they have broken, and whose hospitality they have accepted, and this for $2,500; how much, or rather how little, will it take to cause them to assassinate you or me? What man, except Crittenden, Craig, Timberlake, or some of their other accomplices, is safe, while they are at liberty? Who would not rather have taken his chance in the lonely wood, or the night-darkened street, with Jesse James, than with the Fords or Littles? Who knows how many a sickening tragedy, how many a horrid murder, that den of infamy and debauchery near Richmond has witnessed? Are Woot Hite and the hired man, Gibson, the only victims whose untimely ends can be charged to these thieves, more deadly than East Indian thugs?

The whole State should rise in protest against the turning loose of these fiendish murderers upon society. Of course the Governor will pardon them, after their conviction—for their indictment must lead to conviction—because he has promised this, and *he is afraid to break this promise,* though heretofore promises have not been held as ultra sacred by this tricky schemer.

The plot engendered of a harlot, in conjunction with a few pimps, thieves and murderers, a governor of a state and some city and county officials, was about to bear fruit. The plan which this combination gave birth to was about what would most naturally have been expected. To the insincerity of the prostitute, it added the cunning of the paltry politician, the cowardice of the pimp, and the deadly brutality of the cold-blooded murderer; in fact it was treason domestic and foul assassination.

A thousand plans had been laid before to trap the Jameses, and each in turn had failed. The sheriff and his posse, brave men and true, had sought him earnestly, and failed to find him. The wary detective, half thief, half police officer, with all his love of gain and his trained cunning, had proved himself no match for this bold rider and still bolder fighter. Surrounded dozens of times, he either fought his way out of the toils of the hunters, or passed quietly through them in impenetrable disguises. His most untiring trailers were the officials of Jackson county; he goes to Kansas City, its rich metropolis, and lives in undisturbed security for weeks and weeks. St. Joseph guarded him well for many months —another inland city, lying beside that mighty stretch of river, the Missouri; that, taking its start from the melting snows of the far off summits of the Rocky Mountains, dashes on past hamlet, town and city, and mingles at last with the salt waters of the mighty ocean, almost under the tropics. Nashville, Tennessee, seated high amongst her bluffs and covered with roses and lilacs, had given him long and needed shelter. The far off vines and pines of California had known him well, and the mining camps of the cloudenvironed Sierras had witnessed both his peace and his prowess. The sun-kissed plains of mighty Texas, in herself an empire, had felt the hoof-beats of his gallant horses, and beyond the Rio Grande, in the vales and amidst the mountains of the summer lands of the of the Incas, where once roamed and reigned Montezuma, still loved and still expected—the lovely signorita and the gallant caballero had listened to his light words or felt his heavy hand.

Through all he seemed, although he bore it ever in his open palm, to carry a charmed life. No odds appalled him, nor did danger ever cool his fervent blood. But

> "Fate and the hour await the boldest man."

What courage and skill, twin demi-gods, cannot conquer, cold cowardice and base treachery yet may vanquish. All the blood-hound instinct, educated skill and readiness to resort to any means (even if criminal!) of Pinkerton's detectives failed to make headway against the cool judgment, iron nerve and ready wit of this man; but an agency no less infamous, but far more cruel and cowardly, did succeed.

Through Charlie Ford it was known just where Jesse James lived in St. Joseph. The communication of this fellow with his co-conspirators was frequent and complete. They knew that at any time, day or night, this house might be easily surrounded; by fifty men, if they felt that five would not answer; by five hundred, if fifty were not sufficient, and by five thousand or fifty thousand in case the last named number should not prove ample. In this way the outlaw could have been arrested; or, if he would not submit to arrest, having had this chance given him to surrender, he must take the consequences, and if killed while resisting, his blood would have been upon his own head.

Against this plan we have heard this argument submitted; if any number of men had gone against Jesse James to arrest him, he would have killed some of them. Granted, but what of that? When the soldier in "the forlorn hope" dashes on to the entrenchments of the enemy, does not he know that danger and death lurk ever in his pathway? What officer with any pretensions to manhood will let his sense of duty become so blinded by fears for his personal safety, that he will turn from the prosecution of a task because it is dangerous? Let any such rule as this once obtain, and the protection of the law becomes the merest farce. When honor and duty is cowed by desperate bravery of the criminal, then is the country indeed in a woeful strait. Thank heaven! it has not yet come to this, for it is, we know, safe to assert that there are in the State hundreds of officers, who would dare nobly to do their duty, even if the certainty, instead of the possibility of death lay before them.

But the policy of arrest, and the peaceful trial that would follow in the courts, did not suit our Governor. That would fall too flat; he must have a coup, something telling and sensational; not a tame, uneventful capture. He has had his wish. If he is satisfied, he is certainly entitled to all of the glory he can obtain from his brilliant achievement.

He was, in 1864, able to reconcile to his conscience the murder of Hamilton and Dr. Zimmermann; for his informal drum-head court martial conviction of these parties amounted to murder, and it is but natural to infer that his moral sense received no shock at his complicity in this last assassination. Of the so-called court martial, which assembled to try these men, we shall give a more detailed account further on. At present we will follow out the incidents of Crittenden's plot to its successful termination in assassination.

From day to day events had run on their usual course; the Fords were heard from regularly, the conspiracy was making headway, Bob Ford had been admitted to the family circle of the Jameses, and thus another link was added to the chain that Fate was rapidly drawing around her victim.

This Ford, like his brother, *"par nobile fratrum,"* ate of James' bread, played with his children, chatted with his wife, and plotted domestic treason, waiting for a chance to murder his host. The robber races of the desert, once they have eaten of your salt, would die sooner than harm you; they are the children of the sand and of the sun, their vices as well as their virtues are those of nature,

not cultivation. Born robbers, they continue so until the day of
their death, and bloodshed and violence are as natural to them
as the breath they draw, but the basest of their tribe has never
yet accepted hospitality and returned ingratitude. To widow wives,
to orphan children, and to return murder for hospitality is reserved
for the Crittendens, Craigs and Fords. Too base for the ignorant
children of the desert, it requires the peculiar attributes and moral
culture of such men as these to concoct, countenance and enact
such iniquities.

Crittenden, according to his own account, given with all the
vanity and bombastic self-assertion of the man to some newspaper
reporter, found great difficulty in getting the men to stick to their
work; they would get discouraged, want to withdraw, etc.; but
our brave Governor would morally pat them on the back, comfort
and console with them, and send them back to their work. He
says so himself, and no one who knows the man will for one
moment doubt it. It only proves, however, that even those debased
wretches, the brothers Ford, with their souls already steeped in
rapine and in blood, were men of finer natures than Governor
Crittenden. It only proved that they were ashamed of villainy that
he gloried in. It only proved that, seared as their consciences were
by long years of crime, they still retained at least a glimmering
sense of decency and humanity, while the moral nature of Governor
T. T. Crittenden, if he ever had one, had become utterly perverted,
and in the eyes of the Divine Ruler of the Universe he really stands,
to-day, the chief criminal in this infamy, and the Fords his almost
unwilling tools and accomplices.

At last, under this stimulus of Crittenden, and no one knows
the extent of that stimulus, the act is accomplished. The fatal
hand was moving slowly but surely to the destined time, and the
hours of the daring outlaw's life were numbered.

We may become great; we may attain to fame; we may ac-
cumulate wealth; all of the probabilities are ours, but we possess
only a single certainty: *We must die!* This fact seemed to have
been no more realized by Jesse James, whose every moment was
one of imminent peril, than by those of us, whose lives are most

quiet and orderly. The 3rd day of April, 1882, had dawned upon
the beautiful little city of St. Joseph with the warm, cheery beauty
of early spring, and it found the outlaw with spirits in unison with
its own brightness, though there seems to have been some slight
presentiment of impending evil; for visiting his mother at her home,
in Clay county, on Friday, two weeks before he was killed, he
said to her at parting: "I am not feeling well to-night; I am a little
low spirited—may be I'll never see you again." His mother tried
to cheer him, and with the prescience born of the true love of a
mother, she warned him against the Fords, saying: "I have noticed
Charlie since he has been here this last time; he has greatly changed;
he does not look at me as honestly as he used to; I fear he is
meditating treachery." To this Jesse replied: "Bob Ford I don't
trust; I think he is a sneak; but Charlie Ford is as true as steel."
When Bob Ford came a night or two later, she followed him to
the gate, and boldly asked him if he was still Jesse's friend. Taking
her hand in one of his, he raised the other one to heaven, and
swore, as he hoped for mercy hereafter, that he'd die sooner than
see her son harmed.

When next she saw them Jesse lay cold and still in death, and
the Fords were in the hands of the law as his slayers. On the
morning of April 3rd, 1882, Jesse James stood in a chair, brushing
some pictures with a feather duster. His coat was off, as the
weather was warm; the door was open to admit the breeze, and
he feared that suspicion might be attracted if he continued to
wear his belt containing one pistol, not two, as has been asserted.
Laying his belt aside, as he had often done before, all the assertions
of the Fords to the contrary notwithstanding, he got upon a chair
to use a feather duster, and here he committed the fatal mistake
of turning his back to the Fords. It was a chance they had waited
for four weeks. Time and again had they found him with his pistols
off, but he was wary and kept his eyes toward them. That very
morning he had gone with them to the stable with his coat off
and no pistol about him, as he had done for weeks, but he had
not turned his back, and they feared his spring even when unarmed.
Often and often, the Fords being by, would he take his re-

volvers, *empty out the cartridges* for fear of accidents, and belt one around his boy, and tie the other with a handkerchief around the waist of his little girl. The Fords' hearts misgave them, however, for they knew that the failure of their pistols to explode their cartridges would place them under the paws of the lion, unarmed it is true, but terrible. They would not risk it; he must not only be unarmed, but he must have his back to them, and they must be two to one.

Fate had upon this morning brought about this combination of circumstances. The breakfast was just over; Mrs. James was in the next room, busily engaged in clearing up the breakfast table, her two little children playing around her, when suddenly ominous sounds broke upon her ear—a shot, a fall, then dead silence.

Crazy with fear and grief, she springs to the connecting door, only to see her husband lying still in death, and the Fords flying in panic-stricken terror through the front door. Calling out in her grief: "He's dead, he's dead," they summon up courage to return, and try to explain to her that it was an accident, but she realizes, too late, the character of the men she has harbored. It is the old, old tale of the serpent taken in and warmed, only to turn and strike its benefactor.

The joy has died out of the hearts of his wife and children, and the song is silenced on their lips. Death has entered their home, and sorrow broods over all. Outside the sun shines on as brightly, and the birds still carol their matin songs. Though mortals may grieve at death, yet does not nature sympathize with them, for to her death is as common as life; for the countless myriads that fall, like the ripe fruit or the rotten tree, she has neither sigh nor sorrow, neither grief nor repining. Myriads on the morrow will replace the myriads of the yesterday, and still the vast sum of human misery and happiness is balanced in equal poise. Weep, care-worn, sorrow-stricken wife and lisping babes; you have but fallen heir to the common inheritance of mortality—the unavailing sorrow for the dead.

Throughout the length and breadth of the land the telegraph

The James home immediately after the shooting of Jesse James.

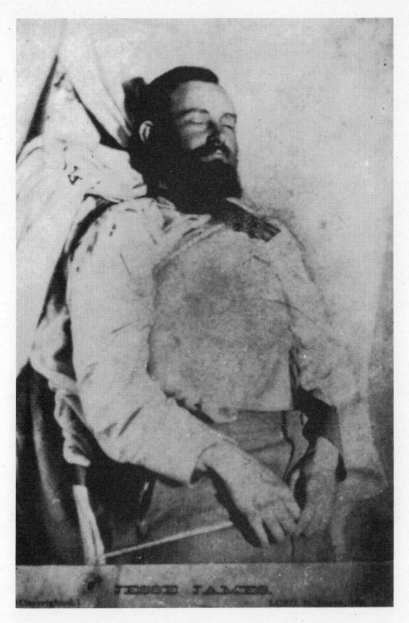

Jesse James. Photo taken about the time of the inquest.

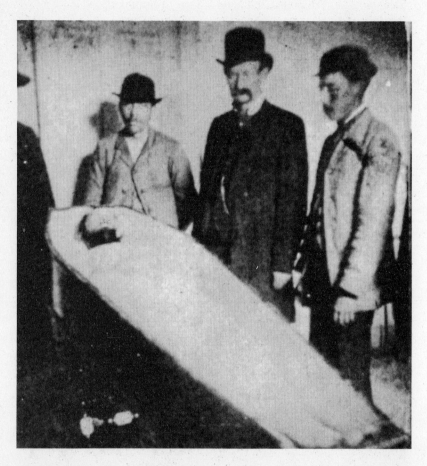

Body of Jesse James at Siden Faden's. Frank James second from right.

flashed, into city and town, village and hamlet, the intelligence that Jesse James, the great outlaw chief, lay dead in his house in Saint Joseph, Missouri, assassinated by a supposed friend. When the full particulars came out, the exclamation was on many a lip: "Better, nobler and braver the dead bandit, than those who assassinated him." This sentiment seemed universal amongst honorable, fair-minded men of all parties and of every shade of opinion.

The remains of the dead bandit were placed upon ice in the undertaker's establishment, and here they remained until removed to Kearney, where they lay, to be viewed by relatives and friends, before the burial in the yard of his boyhood's home.

In answer to telegrams sent the day before, Mrs. Samuel did not arrive from Kearney until 3 o'clock the next morning, and at once she was driven to the residence of her daughter-in-law, Mrs. Jesse James, where her son had been killed. Not until after she had asked many questions would she think it was Jesse who had been shot, and would not believe it until she had seen him.

Shortly after 9 o'clock she drove to the undertaker's establishment, with the widow of Jesse and the two children; and it being known who she was, every one was made to leave the building, and she entered and looked at the body. After a long look, she exclaimed:

"Oh, yes, it is my poor boy; would to God that it was not. Why was he killed? The traitors, to kill such a good man."

Mrs. James tried to quiet her, and for a time succeeded, but the mother broke out several times, and remained in the room with the body for about half an hour before she could be induced to leave for the court house, where she gave her testimony before the coroner's jury, in regard to the identity of the murdered man.

At an early hour on the morning of the day succeeding the assassination, hundreds of people; men, women and children, began to wend their way toward the undertaker's establishment, where the dead body of the outlaw had been placed on the ice, eager for a look at the noted train robber, and so dense was the throng at 9 o'clock that the doors had to be closed, and a special detail of police called in to keep the tide of humanity back.

About the establishment, the long watches of the night had been to many anything but wakeful ones, and for several hours the members of the Kansas City police force—Sergeant Ditsch and Policeman [Ben] Nugent—were the only officers on guard, and the suspicion entertained that an attempt might be made to steal the body of Jesse from the hands of the officers, was a false one. To be sure, there were many persons in St. Joseph who talked openly of such a move, but no sane man could have had a like idea in his head.

Sheriff Timberlake and Captain Craig, who really had all arrangements touching the future disposition of the body and of the Ford boys in their hands, did not retire to their quarters at the Pacific House until a very early hour, but at 8 o'clock were on the streets again, and the telegraph was brought into use in order to communicate with Governor Crittenden, who, it was known, had reached Kansas City.

For some unaccountable reason, the authorities at St. Joseph acted in the strangest possible manner regarding the body and effects of the dead outlaw, and from the very first had been at sixes and sevens with Sheriff Timberlake and Captain Craig, who were acting under direct orders from the Governor. Governor Crittenden had telegraphed for the body to be turned over to Mrs. James, and the effects found upon his body to the Kansas City officials. It was all right about the body, but about the effects, which consisted of two watches, some diamonds, two revolvers and other firearms, it was different; it being claimed that they should go into the charge of the probate judge, or the public administrator.

At last Mrs. James gave an order for all the articles to be turned over to Sheriff Timberlake, and the disgraceful scramble, which St. Joseph officers are much to blame for, ended.

In the meantime strangers had come into St. Joseph from all the surrounding county, called by the knowledge that the greatest outlaw of the age was on partial exhibition; and at the hotels, in the saloons and at the court house, the shooting and wonderful life of the deceased was commented upon in every possible way. Many persons condemned the killing as cowardly in the extreme, he being shot without a chance being given to defend himself; but this is the way the Ford boys knew it had to be done, as he had often boasted that he could kill three men after receiving his death wound, if only his trusty weapons were in his hand.

It was thought that Governor Crittenden would reach St. Joseph over the Missouri Pacific road, until the receipt of a telegram announcing his presence in Kansas City, and at 10 o'clock all interest again centered at the court house, where the inquest was being held. The court room was more crowded than on Monday, and every word of testimony eagerly listened to. The climax was reached however, at the close of Mrs. Samuel's examination, and rarely has a more sensational scene been witnessed in the criminal annals of any country.

As the coroner announced that a recess would be taken, Mrs. Samuel arose, her tall form towering above even the men about her, and cast her eyes over the crowd facing her. Her resolute face plainly showed that she was looking for some one, and turning to her daughter-in-law, she said:

"Show me the man who killed my boy."

Mrs. James whispered something to the old lady, and the two, preceded by City Marshal Craig, of St. Joseph, started to leave the court room. Not ten feet distant, at the end of the reporter's table, stood Dick Little, the former trusted friend of Jesse, and, as the two women reached the point where he stood, Mrs. James suddenly pulled her veil one side, exposing her face, and pushing close up to Little, said:

"Oh, Dick Little, you are the traitor, who, with Bob Ford, killed Jesse and made me a widow. How dare you stand there and look me in the face, you traitor? You did it, you did it, and before God, you traitor, punishment will come."

These words were uttered so that every one heard them, and Mrs. Samuel, who was close at hand, also spied Dick, and with her one arm raised above her head, hissed between her teeth:

"Oh, you coward, you did all this; you brought it all about. Look upon me, you traitor. Look upon me, the broken-down mother, and this poor wife and these children. Ah, you traitor, better for you that you were in the cooler where my boy is than here, looking at me."

All this time her actions became more excited, and her words more venomous, and with the words, "Coward, that you are, God will swear vengeance upon you," she was partially pulled and pushed by the point where Dick stood.

As she was leaving, he looked at her, and said;

"Mrs. Samuel, I did not hurt him; I thought you knew who did it."

By this time the infuriated woman was about ten feet from him, but her face was not turned away, and with denunciations upon the supposed betrayer of Jesse, she passed from sight.

The scene is one which will not soon be forgotten by those who witnessed it, and it was the real sensation of the day.

When Mrs. Samuel entered the room and passed by Little, he covered his face with a hat, and said:

"I don't know but she will slap me in the face."

To the few, who still doubted, the testimony and inconsolable grief of Mrs. Samuel at the coroner's inquest carried the belief that there was no longer room for doubt of the fact that the corpse was really that of Jesse James.

Additional identifiers were also on hand; they were Prosecuting Attorney [William H.] Wallace, Harrison Trow, one of Quantrell's men; James Wilkinson, J. Clay, Mattie Collins Little, wife or mistress of Dick Little; Mr. Mimms, brother-in-law of Jesse James; Mr. James, cousin of Jesse James; and C. D. Axman. About midnight the above named party were driven to the undertakers, and the body was positively identified as that of Jesse James, some of the men having known him for years. Mattie Collins was terribly excited as she viewed the remains, and in the strongest language denounced the parties who brought it all about. She cried and talked loud for awhile, but at last calmed down and was led away.

All now knew that Jesse James had raided his last bank; held up his last railroad train, and was calmly sleeping that slumber that at life's termination comes alike to all.

"The evil that men do lives after them;
The good is oft interred with their bones."

So says "the immortal bard," and its truth was never more clearly exemplified than in this case. Jesse James alive might deny his guilt of some of the evil with which he was charged; dead, the Fords, Little and others of his subordinates, make haste to saddle all of their outrages upon him in addition to the already heavy burden rightly charged upon him. He it was, according to them, who committed every bank robbery in the country; he it was that held up every stage coach and railway train; he it was who killed Westfall, Askew, and Whicher; in fact, he was prime instigator and perpetrator of every damnable action that had disgraced the country since his outlawry began. As they represent it, he was omni-present whenever there was a robbery, outrage or murder to be committed. Like all too ready witnesses, *they prove entirely too much,* and thus vitiate every particle of their testimony.

No sane person would claim that Jesse James was innocent of all with which he has been charged, and at the same time no reasonable person can believe that he is guilty of all with which he is accused. His enemies have declared him guilty of every crime requiring boldness to execute and judgment to plan; his friends do not pretend that he was innocent of *all* of these, but they point to the manifest absurdity of his having been engaged in all. For instance: two great crimes are perpetrated on the same day; one in Missouri, one in Mississippi. He cannot possibly be present at both, but some of his enemies show to their own satisfaction that he was certainly present at one; while others, inimical to him, show just as conclusively that he participated in the other.

The dead bandit finds, of course, no one to apologise for his career of crime and bloodshed, and but few who are even willing to allow him the scanty justice demanded by the jealous Othello:

"Speak of me as I am;
Nothing extenuate, nor aught set down in malice."

Marshal Enos Craig of St. Joseph was in charge of the funeral train which took Jesse James' body from St. Joseph to Cameron, Missouri. *Courtesy St. Joseph Museum.*

CHAPTER XL.

AFTER THE ASSASSINATION.

The Fords' Panic—Return to the House—Their Victim Dead—Telegraph Craig and Crittenden—Surrender to the Marshal of St. Joseph—Sent to Jail—The Coroner's Inquest—Examination of Charles Ford—Robert Ford —Henry Craig—Sheriff Timberlake—Dick Little—Charles Alderman Deputy-Marshal Finley—Mrs. Zerelda Samuel, Mother of Jesse James— Finding of the Jury.

WHEN the Ford brothers had fired the fatal shot, and had witnessed the fall of Jesse James, a panic seems to have taken possession of them; and without waiting to see if he were dead, they burst out of the house and leaped over the front fence, not taking time to open the gate, so abject was their terror. It was only the agonized cries of the heart-broken wife, that checked their head-long flight long enough for them to return, and see that they had thoroughly completed the revolting business they had been sent to perform. Finding their victim dead, they hastened to telegraph to the Governor and to Craig to inform them of this fact, and then hunted up the Marshal to deliver themselves up to him.

Going to his office, they ascertained that he was not there; they surmised that he had gone to the home of the bandit. This supposition proved correct, and returning there they surrendered to him, and were taken to the jail for safe keeping. Here they were locked up, and here they remained until the day of the holding of the

CORONER'S INQUEST.[1]

[1] The coroner's inquest was held at 4 p.m., April 3.

A jury having been duly empaneled and sworn, the examination was then proceeded with, and resulted as follows:

Charles Ford On The Stand.

When Charles Ford was called to the witness stand on Monday afternoon, he testified that he was about 24 years old, and had lived in Ray county, near Richmond, for about three years. He met and became acquainted with Jesse James soon after his residence began, and last November left the farm and went to Kansas City. While there he met Jesse James.

"Did he ask you to join him?"

"Jesse James asked me if I did not want to make a trip with him, and we would go and make a raise somewhere. He was living in Kansas City then. We left Kansas City on the 5th, and arrived in St. Joe on the 8th, and went to Twenty-first and Lafayette streets, where we lived until the day before Christmas, when we rented the house where he was killed, and we lived there ever since. He said he wanted to take a trip out through Kansas and see how the banks were situated, and said he would get the men, and wanted to know if I knew of any one we could get to help us. I told him I thought I could get my brother to help, if I could go down and see him. So we went down there, and we went to his mother's and stayed there until Friday night, and then went to my brother's and stayed until Saturday and started to St. Joe. On the way a storm came up and we stayed that night in a church. We stayed there until just before daylight, and then we came on to within two miles east of St. Joe, where he said for us to stay until night, and he went on in. He said there was going to be a murder trial in Plattsburg, and we would go up there, and if the bank was all right we would rob it. He said when they were making the speeches everybody would be up to the court-house and we could rob the bank."

"Well, now, explain how it was you came to kill him?"

A. "Well, we had come in from the barn, where we had been feeding and currying the horses, and Jesse complained of being warm and pulled off his coat and threw it on the bed and opened the door, and said that he guessed he would pull off his belt, as some person might see it. Then he went to brush off some pictures, and when he turned his back I gave my brother the wink, and we both pulled our pistols, but he, my brother, was the quickest and fired first. I had my finger on the trigger and was just going to fire, but I saw his shot was a death shot and did not fire. He heard us cock our pistols and turned his head. The ball struck him in the back of the head and he fell. Then I went out and got our hats, and we went and telegraphed to Captain Craig and Sheriff Timberlake what we had done. Then we went to the marshal's office and asked a policman that was there if he knew where the marshal was. He said that he did not, but that he would go with us to look him up. I asked a gentleman up town if he knew where the marshal was; he said he had just seen him get on a car going down in that direction. I said that that was probably where they were going, and that we might as well go down there; and I told them who it was in the house and who it was that killed him, and how it took place and where his pistols, gun and jewelry could be found, and from there we came up here."

"How did you know it was James when he came to you?"

"He came to my house two years ago last summer; he was a sporting man and so was I; gambled and drank a little, so did I. I was acquainted with Miller, and he came with him and introduced him as Mr. Johnston. He stayed until the next day and then left, and after that Ed. Miller told me it was Jesse James. I did not see him any more for some time, and when I did see him I asked him where Miller was, and he said that Miller was in bad health and he did not think that he could live long. Then he came back again in the fall; then I did not see any thing more of him until the next spring. He was there two or three times last summer. Then he came down last fall."

"He asked you to do what?"

"To help rob trains and banks. I have been with him ever since."

"Had you any intention of leaving St. Joe soon?"

"Jesse said he would like to rob a bank and look around a little beforehand, and I started out with him. We went first to Hiawatha, then to Pawnee City, from there to Forrest City, then to

White Cloud, Kansas, from there to Forrest City to see how the bank at that place was situated. He said that he liked the way the bank at Forrest City was situated, and said he wanted to take that bank, but I told him I did not want to go into that, as I was sick then. We came up to Oregon. He said that he wanted to look at that bank, and from there we came down here, and that is the only trip I ever made with him. He would go into a bank with a large bill or several small ones to get changed, and while the cashier was making the change he would take a look and see whether they were caged up, what sort of a looking safe it was, whether they had a time lock or not."

"How did you get your living?"

"I was not at any expense. I did not spend any money. He had a good deal of money. He had some $1,500 or $1,600."

"Where did he keep it."

"I don't know?"

"Where did he get it?"

"I have no idea where he got it. I guess he must have got it robbing."

"Did Bob, your brother, come here to assist in robbing a bank?"

"Jesse had looked at a bank at Platte City. He said they were going to have a murder trial there this week, and while everybody would be at the court house he would slip in and rob the bank. and if not, he would come back to Forrest City and get that."

"What was your idea in that?"

It was simply to get Bob here, where one of us could kill him if once he took his pistols off. To try and do this with his pistols on would be useless; as I knew Jesse had often said he would not surrender to a hundred men, and if three men should step out in front of him and shoot him, he could kill them before he fell.

ROBERT FORD, THE ASSASSIN, TESTIFIES:

Robert Ford, the young man who did the shooting, was then called, and as the individual who shot Jesse James walked forward he was the center of every eye in the room. He gave his evidence clearly, and stated that when he went to Ray county to live, he heard about the James boys, but did not meet Jesse until three

years afterward. He came with Ed. Miller. Witness had known
Miller, and he knew they were talking and planning a train robbery. Last January he went to Kansas City and had an interview
with Governor Crittenden, about capturing Jesse; at the St. James
Hotel.

"Did the Governor tell you any thing about a reward?"

"He said $10,000 had been offered for Jesse or Frank, dead
or alive.[2] I then entered into arrangements with Timberlake and
Craig. I afterward told Charlie of the conversation I had with the
officers, and told him I would like to go with him. He said if I
was willing to go, all right. We started that night, and went up to
Mrs. Samuel's and put the horses up.

"John Samuel (Jesse's half brother) was wounded, and they
were expecting him to die. There were some friends of the family
there, whom Jesse did not wish to see him, so we staid in the barn
all night until they left, and that was pretty nearly day-light, and
we staid in the house all next day, and that night we started away.
That was on Thursday night; Friday night we staid at his brother-
in-law's. We left Mrs. Samuel's and went about three miles into
the woods for fear the officers would surprise us at her house. We
started from the woods and came up to another of his brother-
in-law's and got supper there, and started from there here."

"This was last week?"

"Yes. We came at once to St. Joseph, and then talked over
the matter again, and how we could kill him."

"What have you been doing since you came here?"

"My brother and I go down town sometimes at night and
get the papers."

"What did you tell Jesse you were with him for?"

"I told him I was going in with him."

"Had you any plans made to rob any bank?"

"He had spoken of several, but had made no particular selection."

2Crittenden's reward notice offered $5,000 for the arrest of and an
additional $5,000 for the conviction of Frank and Jesse James.

PROCLAMATION

OF THE

GOVERNOR OF MISSOURI!

REWARDS

FOR THE ARREST OF

Express and Train Robbers.

STATE OF MISSOURI, }
EXECUTIVE DEPARTMENT.

WHEREAS, It has been made known to me, as the Governor of the State of Missouri, that certain parties, whose names are to me unknown, have confederated and banded themselves together for the purpose of committing robberies and other depredations within this State; and

WHEREAS, Said parties did, on or about the Eighth day of October, 1879, stop a train near Glendale, in the county of Jackson, in said State, and, with force and violence, take, steal and carry away the money and other express matter being carried thereon; and

WHEREAS, On the fifteenth day of July 1881, said parties and their confederates did stop a train upon the line of the Chicago, Rock Island and Pacific Railroad, near Winston, in the County of Daviess, in said State, and, with force and violence, take, steal, and carry away the money and other express matter being carried thereon; and, in perpetration of the robbery last aforesaid, the parties engaged therein did kill and murder one WILLIAM WESTFALL, the conductor of the train, together with one JOHN McCULLOCH, who was at the time in the employ of said company, then on said train; and

WHEREAS, FRANK JAMES and JESSE W. JAMES stand indicted in the Circuit Court of said Daviess County, for the murder of JOHN W. SHEETS, and the parties engaged in the robberies and murders aforesaid have fled from justice and have absconded and secreted themselves:

NOW, THEREFORE, in consideration of the premises, and in lieu of all other rewards heretofore offered for the arrest or conviction of the parties aforesaid, or either of them, by any person or corporation, I, THOMAS T. CRITTENDEN, Governor of the State of Missouri, do hereby offer a reward of five thousand dollars ($5,000.00) for the arrest and conviction of each person participating in either of the robberies or murders aforesaid, excepting the said FRANK JAMES and JESSE W. JAMES; and for the arrest and delivery of said

FRANK JAMES and JESSE W. JAMES,

and each or either of them, to the sheriff of said Daviess County, I hereby offer a reward of five thousand dollars, ($5,000.00,) and for the conviction of either of the parties last aforesaid of participation in either of the murders or robberies above mentioned, I hereby offer a further reward of five thousand dollars, ($5,000.00.)

IN TESTIMONY WHEREOF, I have hereunto set my hand and caused to be affixed the Great Seal of the State of Missouri. Done

[SEAL.]   at the City of Jefferson on this 28th day of July, A. D. 1881.

THOS. T. CRITTENDEN.

By the Governor:
MICH'L K. McGRATH, Sec'y of State.

"Well, now, will you give us the particulars of the killing and what time it occurred?"

"After breakfast, between 8 and 9 o'clock, this morning; he, my brother and myself were in the room. He pulled off his pistols and got up on a chair to dust off some picture frames, and I drew my pistol and shot him."

"How close were you to him?"

"About six feet away."

"How close was the hand to him, which held the pistol?"

"About four feet, I should think."

"Did he say any thing?"

"He started to turn his head, but didn't say a word."

"How often has Charley been at home since he first went to Jesse's house to live?"

"Once; during Christmas."

"Has he not been home since then?"

"No, sir; he came to my uncle's."

"How often has he been at your uncle's?"

"I saw him twice; once, when he was there, I was in Kansas City."

"Was Jesse James unarmed when you killed him?"

"Yes, sir."

"Do you remember ever hearing any of the Samuel's family calling him by name?"

"They always called him 'Dave;' that was the nick name. They never called him anything but Dave."

"Did any one speak to him and call him by name?"

"Yes; I heard his mother speak to him and call him Dave, and he called her mother."

"Do you know any one that can identify him?"

"Yes, sir; Sheriff Timberlake can when he comes; he was with him during the war."

This closed the testimony on Monday, and court adjourned to meet at 10 o'clock next morning, and at that hour an immense crowd filled the room. There was great excitement to see Little,

Mrs. Samuel and Mrs. James, all of whom entered the court after the testimony was about half over.

Mr. Henry Craig, police commissioner of Kansas City, was the first witness examined, as follows:

"I was not acquainted with Jesse James personally, but am positive the body of the dead man is the outlaw, as it corresponds with the descriptions I have heard. I know Robert Ford, and for two months he has assisted Sheriff Timberlake and myself in the endeavor to catch Jesse James. He was not employed regularly by us, but acted in good faith and according to our instructions, and assisted in every way he could aid us. Charlie Ford I had never seen until I came to St. Joe, but understand he and Robert had some understanding."

Sheriff Timberlake, of Clay county, was next called, and said he was sheriff, and was acquainted with Jesse James during life and recognized the body as that of Jesse. Had known him since 1864, and saw him the last time in 1870. Knew his face as well as any one. He had the second joint of his third finger shot off, by which I also recognize him. Ford was acting under my instructions, and said if he could see Charlie Ford we would accomplish our end the sooner, and he acted squarely to all agreements.

Dick Little was then called, and said: I have seen the body of the dead man and recognize it; I was with him a good deal last summer and know him perfectly; I also recognize him from wounds on hand and on the right side.

Charles Alderman, who keeps a livery stable in St. Joseph, testified that he was a trader; was not acquainted with Jesse James in life; had seen the body and recognized it as that of a man I traded horses with, but did not know who he was, and last Saturday I got it back from Charles Ford, who has been at my place several times. He said he wanted a horse for his uncle, who I now presume was Jesse James.

Deputy Marshal Finley, of St. Joseph, testified as follows:

I was not acquainted with Jesse James; went to the house where he was killed in answer to the telephone; found him on his back, and from Mrs. James got a description of the two men who killed the man, and started out in search of them. She said one was her nephew, and the other a young man, both named Johnson, but no relation. As we were going out, we met the boys coming back. Bob said: I am the man who killed the person in the house. He is the notorious outlaw, Jesse James, or I am mistaken, and I can identify him. He described the wounds on Jesse James' body. He told us there were two watches and some diamonds in the house. We could not find them at first, but did find a necktie and a gold ring with the name of Jessie on the inside. Afterwards we found two watches in the trunk. There was some small change in an old pocketbook, which I gave Mrs. James. On a $1 gold piece as a scarf pin were the initials J. W. J. Most of the property is now in the hands of the city marshal.

MRS. ZERELDA SAMUEL.

When the name of Mrs. Samuel was called, every man in the court room stood up for a good look at the mother of the dead bandit, and as she passed up the centre aisle, with the wife and the children of Jesse, and a Mrs. Turner, the crowd parted right and left, and the party passed the reporter's table, and took seats directly in front of the coroner. Her testimony was as follows:

"I live in Clay county, and am the mother of Jesse James." Here she broke down and moaned several times, "Oh, my poor boy. I have seen the body several times since my arrival, and have recognized it as that of my son, Jesse; the lady by my side is my daughter-in-law, and the children hers." (Mrs. Samuel again broke down at this point.) "He was a kind husband and son."

Mrs. Jesse James was here asked if any valuables were taken from the house at the time the officers arrived, and she detailed the articles found by the city marshal.

This concluded the testimony, and it was announced that a recess would be taken, and the court room began to empty.

Mrs. Samuel arose, as did Mrs. James, and as the former turned and faced the crowd, she spied Dick Little, and a most sensational scene occurred.

THE VERDICT.

The coroner's jury then retired for deliberation, and in about half an hour returned the following verdict:

"We, the jury, summoned to hear the testimony in the case before us, do hereby declare that the body of the deceased is that of Jesse W. James, and that he came to his death by a wound in the back of his head caused by a pistol shot fired intentionally by the hand of Robert Ford."

CHAPTER XLI.

INDICTED FOR MURDER.

The Grand Jury—Remanded to Jail—The Fords Express Their Opinions—Their Idea of Crittenden's Power—What They Anticipated—Grand Jury Finds A True Bill—Murder in The First Degree—Brought into Court—The Trial—They Plead Guilty—The Death Sentence—The Governor Telegraphed—A Hasty Pardon—The Special Messenger.

THE verdict of the Coroner's jury, and the admissions of the prisoners, pointed clearly to the duty of the Grand Jury of Buchanan county to indict the brothers for murder in the first degree, consequently they were remanded to the custody of the Marshal, and again placed in the jail at St. Joseph.

Holding as exaggerated an idea of the power of the Governor, as that functionary himself seemed to entertain of them, having to go back to jail seemed to the Fords a grievous wrong, and they did not hesitate to openly and bitterly express themselves in regard to it. They expected nothing less than being turned loose immediately after their examination; and they had calculated on getting their share of the reward immediately, and going off on a grand spree, consequently their indignation knew no bounds.

What had they done, they said, to merit such a foul imposition? Of what crime had they been guilty, that they should be locked up like common felons; they, the associates of Police Commissioner Craig and Governor Crittenden? True they had robbed trains, obstructed the United States mails, killed conductors, murdered a comrade and assassinated their leader, but what of that? These were mere, little peculiarities of theirs; idiosyncracies, that should be easily overlooked.

Commissioner Craig had known all this, and yet he felt it no disgrace to even sleep with them: Governor Crittenden knew all this, and yet he met them privately and sociably, and patted them on the back and encouraged them to persevere; telling them that he'd see them through!

It was, they said, the most damnable outrage ever committed upon two philanthropists since the world began. All this may have been so, still the authorities of Buchanan county held them, and on the 16th day of April, 1882, the Grand Jury found a true bill against them for murder in the first degree.

This being the case they were, on the 17th day of April, 1882, taken into the Circuit Court room by Sheriff Thomas, and after the indictment had been read sentence was passed.

The court room was crowded, but quiet and order prevailed. The boys were very respectably clad, and were quite cool and self-possessed. The indictment, which was in the usual form, was read to them by the County Attorney, O. M. Spencer, who read it to Robert first, after which the attorney asked him what plea he made, when he replied promptly and firmly "guilty." He then took his seat. The indictment of Charles Ford as aider and abetter was read to him, and in a firm and even tone Charlie plead guilty also to the charge of murder in the first degree.

The Judge then, after a few minutes' meditation, said that under the circumstances there was but one thing he could do, and that was to pronounce sentence upon the boys. He said as they had pleaded guilty there was no alternative for him but to pass sentence, and it would remain for others to say whether the sentence should be finally carried out.

He then asked Robert Fort to stand up. The latter rose promptly, and was asked if he had anything to say why the sentence of the Court should not be passed upon him. He replied, "Nothing," and Judge Shannon, in substance, said: "Robert Ford, you have pleaded guilty before me to the crime of murder in the first degree, and it becomes my duty to pass the sentence of death upon you. It is, therefore, the sentence of this Court that you be taken back to the jail, and on the 19th day of May be taken to some convenient place and there hanged by the neck until you are dead."

Robert then took his seat, and the Judge ordered Charles to stand up, and asked him if he had anything to say why the sentence of death should not be passed upon him. Charles replied, "Nothing," and the Judge passed the same sentence upon him as was passed upon Robert. After this there was no other action taken, and the boys were remanded to jail.

The Governor, it is understood, was opposed to trying them, because he considered that they have done the State a great service, and are entitled to a pardon at once.

The father of the Fords, a very respectable-looking old gentleman, occupied a seat by them while in court. Maj. William Warner, of Kansas City, acting as their attorney, in co-operation with Messrs. Doniphan & Read, and Marshall Craig, of Kansas City, were present in court. Cap Ford, brother of the boys, was present also.

THE PRISONERS PARDONED.

The Governor upon receipt of the news by telegraph from St. Joseph that the Ford boys had been indicted and arraigned for the killing of Jesse James, and after pleading guilty to murder in the first degree had been sentenced by the Court, granted them a full and unconditional pardon. A special messenger was dispatched with it to St. Joseph.

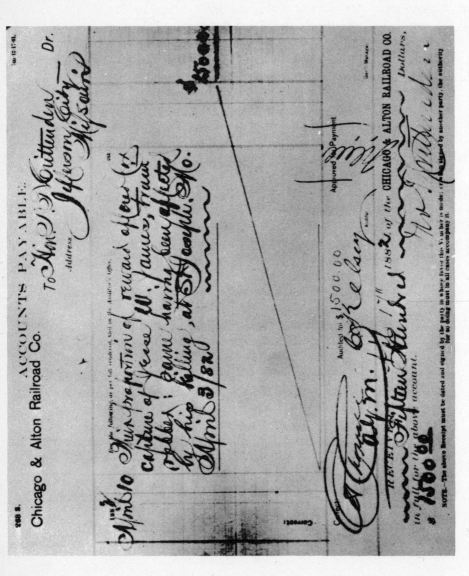

Receipt for $1,500 Jesse James reward money contributed by the Chicago & Alton Railroad.

CHAPTER XLII.

CRITTENDEN'S COURSE.

Is Crittenden Guilty of Murder?—His Conspiracy with the Fords, Craig and Others—What Crime Was Committed—Powers of the Legal Authorities Defined—What Constitutes Justifiable Homicide—Authorities on the Subject—Blackstone—Missouri Reports—Ford Guilty of Murder in the First Degree—Crittenden an Accomplice—His Boasting—Character of the Man —His Admissions—Newspaper Interviews—Ford's Threats Against Crittenden—Indecent Conduct of the Latter—Comments.

WE have not hesitated at any time to accuse Thomas T. Crittenden, Governor of the State of Missouri, of having conspired with Charles and Robert Ford for the commission of murder: we have not hesitated and do not hesitate to assert that we believe him guilty of bargaining with the Fords and others for the assassination of Jesse James in an absolute, tyrannical manner, contrary to all law and precedent. We should be sorry to make any such statements of our own belief, *did not all of the facts bear us out in them.* The proofs of his complicity and bargain are so overwhelming that no successful denial of, or apology for them can be given.

The fact stands proved by his own admissions; by the admissions of his accomplices; by his conduct as shown in his indecent haste to pardon his accomplices; by his not daring to risk the result of refusing so hasty an extension of executive clemency; by the threats, openly made, of the Fords that he didn't *dare* to "go back on them;" by unanswerable circumstantial evidence in addition to this positive proof.

We will now give, first: The legal authorities on the nature of the crime he and his accomplices committed;

And, second: The proof that they committed that crime.

AUTHORITIES ON THE SUBJECT, AND WHY THE FORDS AND CRITTENDEN SHOULD BE INDICTED.

BLACKSTONE ON JUSTIFIABLE HOMICIDE.—Justifiable homicide is of divers kinds. Such as is owing to some unavoidable necessity without any will, intention or desire, without any inadvertence or negligence in the party killing, and therefore without any shadow of blame. As, for instance, by virtue of such an office as obliges one, in the execution of public justice, to put a malefactor to death, who hath forfeited his life by the laws and verdict of his country. This is an act of necessity, and even of civil duty; and, therefore, not only justifiable but commendable where the law requires it. But the law must require it, otherwise it is not justifiable; *therefore, wantonly to kill the greatest of malefactors, a felon or a traitor, attainted or outlawed, deliberately uncompelled and extrajudicially, is* MURDER.

BLACKSTONE ON OUTLAWRY.—The outlaw's life is, however still under the protection of the law, as hath been formerly observed; so that though anciently an outlawed felon was said to have *caput lupinum,* and might have been knocked on the head like a wolf by any one that should meet him, because, having renounced all law, he was to be dealt with as in a state of nature, when every one that should find him might slay him; *yet, now, to avoid such inhumanity, it is holden that no man is entitled to kill him wantonly or willfully, but in so doing is guilty of* MURDER, unless it happens in the endeavor to lawfully apprehend him.

AN ACCESSORY DEFINED.—*An Accessory Before the Fact* is one who, being absent at the time of the crime committed, *yet procures, counsels or commands another to commit it.* Bouvier's Law Dictionary, 1 Hale 615, Wharton Criminal Law, §134. *An accessory before or after the fact* may be indicted, tried and punished, notwithstanding the principal felon may not have been arrested, tried and convicted. *Statutes of Missouri,* §1651.

The Constitution of Missouri, Bill of Rights, section 30, declares, that *"no person* shall be deprived of life, liberty or property without due process of law." The same declaration is announced in the Constitution of the United States in the Fifth Amendment. This is the corner-stone of American liberty.

By the Revised Statutes, page 218, section 1232, *any person* who shall deliberately kill another shall be guilty of murder; and section 1649, page 284, declares that an accessory to a crime shall be punished in the same manner as the principal criminal.

By the Bill of Rights, section 12, it is also declared that *"no person* shall for felony be proceeded against criminally otherwise than by indictment, except in cases arising in the land or naval forces, or in the militia when in actual service in time of war or public danger."

The "due process of law," by which a criminal may be deprived of life, is indictment by the grand jury of the county where the crime was committed, arrest, arraignment on the accusation in open court trial by a jury of the county in the presence of the prisoner, verdict of guilty, and sentence thereon of death by the court. This is the law of the land. This is order. This is civilization. Even then a sheriff dare not put a convict to death before the day named by the court in the sentence, or in any other manner than the sentence directs. If by any means the convict is not executed on that day, the sheriff cannot put him to death at all, until the court again pronounces a sentence of death and fixes the day of execution. (Revised statutes, page 325, section 1,955.)

No officer is authorized to kill an accused person, unless the accused is *resisting arrest* or *attempting to escape,* and then only as an absolute necessity.

Nowhere is there any authority given in the law to a Governor to decree a sentence of death upon any person, criminal or otherwise, or to hire assassins.

No monarch of a despotic government ever exercised more power over the lives of his subjects, than that assumed and usurped by Governor Crittenden in hiring murderers and thieves to assassinate James. The act is without example in American history.

He claims and has exercised the usurped power of secretly pronouncing sentence of death and hiring men to execute it. Juries and trials are ignored as useless to his administration. He at once sets aside the Constitution, disregards the statutes, assumes absolute power in himself, and, like Robespierre, issues his decrees of death upon whom he chooses, and for his instruments of execution hires confessed villains, robbers and assassins with promise of pay, pardon and glory. Such acts by the Governor of an American state are indeed monstrous.

The alleged excuse, that it was dangerous to attempt to arrest James, after it was known where he lived, and when the whole power of a great State was at the Governor's command, is so miserably base and pusillanimous as not to deserve notice.

An officer of the State, whether he is high or low, committing a crime, is punishable in the same manner as an ordinary citizen, and all persons instigated by him to commit crime are likewise punishable. If the next grand jury of Buchanan county does its duty, it will indict the two Fords and Governor Crittenden for murder, and have them brought to trial; and the next legislature should impeach Crittenden and remove him from office, according to article 7. section 2, of the Constitution of Missouri.

There is no such phrase in the civil libraries of civilized countries as "dead or alive." That belongs exclusively to barbarism. There was no legalized proclamation in this State offering a reward for Jesse James "dead or alive." What right has Gov. Crittenden to act as the agent of the railroad corporations and contract with and pay over to the Ford boys, who murdered James, the money which had been offered for his capture?

The power of the Governor of Missouri to suppress "Outlawry," as it is called, will be found in the Revised Statutes, chapter 135, section 6467. It is as follows:

Whenever the Governor shall become satisfied that there exists, anywhere within this State, any band of highway robbers, marauders, or other outlaws, and that it is beyond the power of ordinary officers and process of law to arrest and bring the members of such band to justice, he shall be authorized and empowered to organize and call into active service such a force of men, not to exceed twenty-five in number, as he may deem actually necessary for the purpose of arresting such band or any member thereof. All costs and expenses arising from the organization and service of such force shall be paid by the State, and it shall be the duty of the State Auditor to draw his warrant upon the State Treasurer for such sum or sums as may be approved by the Governor, which shall be paid by the State Treasurer, out of the fund created for that purpose. Such force, and each member thereof, shall have all the power and authority to make arrests anywhere within this State that is now possessed by sheriffs in their respective counties.

It will be observed that the Governor is not authorized, even indirectly, to employ anybody to kill a man who has set the laws of this State at defiance. When Lieut. Col. Thomas T. Crittenden, in 1864, caused Mr. Zimmerman and two other citizens of Johnson county to be shot as horse-thieves, he had the poor excuse of martial law on his side. It was afterwards shown in the Legislature that the courts of that county were open, and that Mr. Zimmerman was a reputable citizen, and a Legislative committee went so far as to publicly charge Mr. Crittenden with murder. Still, the war was in progress at the time Mr. Crittenden killed these men, and he was excused on the ground that passion and disorder stood in the way of the exercise of judicial functions. There was no such excuse for Crittenden, though, when he sat down and coolly hired the Fords to kill the bandit James for money. The State was at peace, and the laws were all open before the Governor. Will the Legislature again, through a committee, arraign Mr. Crittenden?

The Ford boys pleaded guilty to murder in the first degree. Governor Crittenden pleaded guilty to having knowingly employed them to perform the deed, by issuing a full and unconditional pardon, before he even received official notice of the court proceedings.

No sane man can now doubt any longer that the whole business was well understood and pre-arranged. At St. Joseph the grand jury presents the indictment. The Fords laugh and plead guilty. The Judge sentences them to death. The Fords laugh again. He fixes the date of execution. They roar. An hour after, or just as soon as a short telegram could reach the remarkable Chief Magistrate of this State, and the same could run from the Executive mansion to the Capitol, he issues a full pardon. He really knows nothing officially. Still he

issues an unconditional pardon, and sends it in hot haste by special
messenger on the next train. Was there ever greater promptness and
dispatch? Was there ever a plainer lack of all dignity? Was there
ever a clearer prostitution of the law, for the protection and reward
of assassins?

Never in the history of this State have the proverbially slow
wheels of justice moved with one thousandth part the rapidity to
vindicate the majesty of the law and punish criminals, with which
they were whirled around on purpose to pardon two assassins, and
let them loose upon a community in which, alas, both law and life
are already held in too little respect.

That Jesse James is dead is a matter of absolute rejoicing. That
he was killed by base treachery is a matter of comparative indiffer-
ence. That he was even killed by another murderer is a matter of no
great concern. But that he was assassinated by order of the Governor;
that his murderer was hired by our Chief Magistrate; that the assassination was a regular business contract between the Governor and these
paid assassins—that the Governor, not only by words, but deeds,
should openly confess, nay glory in his deed, is a question which
sensible people may well consider.

It is a dangerous innovation, this setting aside of all law, and
hiring of assassins by the highest law dignitary of the State. It is a
return to the barbarism of the middle ages.

The Fords sentenced to death one day are free men the next.
They are probably counting the greenbacks, which the Governor
may have sent by the same messenger who carried the pardon. In
one pocket the Governor's pardon, in another the greenbacks; in
their belt pistols with which they earned both, these fine specimens
of Western life will go forth as shining examples of the harm a vain,
weak, and ignorant Governor can do to the cause of law, justice and
progressive civilization.

AN EMINENT LEGAL AUTHORITY CHARACTERIZES THIS ASSASSINA-
TION AS ANOMALOUS AND MONSTROUS.

Mr. John Dos Passos, of New York, is one of the best known
lawyers in New York, his name having been connected with a number of *causes celebres,* especially with the Stokes case, as he managed

the defense with eminent skill and success. In fact, there are few men in the East more profoundly versed in the criminal law; there are few men better calculated to voice Eastern opinion upon the quasi-legal assassination, which has recently disgraced this State. He says: "The killing was unwarranted by law. You must understand that there is no such thing as outlawry in American jurisprudence. It is a relic of the common law which has not been heard of in this country. Under any circumstances outlawry did not begin until a man had been regularly indicted and convicted of crime and had then fled. As far as I can understand the killing of this man James, I can only describe it as an act fit for a barbarous state of society.

"What should have been done is this: It was the desire of the law to get him into custody for the purpose of ascertaining whether he was guilty of certain crimes or not. To hire a person to kill him when found, or to kill him under any circumstances, in which it could be done without harm to the one doing the killing, was certainly a monstrosity. I can find no other word to decribe the act.

"When a man is accused of crime he is either arrested upon warrant or by indictment of the grand jury. In either case the warrant of arrest is entrusted to the proper officer, who makes the arrest. If extraordinary resistance is expected, the officer can summon the whole power of the county to his assistance, and there is no officer in New York who would not be very unwilling to admit his inability to make an arrest. The case of a Governor of a State, who would make a bargain with one robber to kill another, is an anomaly in American jurisprudence. I would think it entirely illegal; and assuming the Governor to have authorized or prompted or commissioned a person to kill another accused of crime—and recollect that I cannot believe a Governor would do this—then the Governor is clearly guilty as an accessory before the fact. For this reason: the Governor, by virtue of his office, has no greater power in this respect than another citizen. He has no power to order a man killed, even though it be an individual of the most dangerous and desperate character. Such an act is usurpation of the rights, to which every man is entitled; it is assuming to try and convict him without a trial. And I will say this, if your Constitution authorizes your Governor to commission persons to shoot down those accused of crime, the sooner you repeal it the better. Not only is it inconsistent with every notion of Anglo-Saxon liberty, but is is directly antagonistic to the Constitution of the United States. As I understand it, when this bandit was killed he was engaged in the aesthetic occupation of hanging pictures, at which time, it seems to me, he could easily have been taken by determined officials. There is only one instance in which a man can be shot—when he is resisting the process of law. But to give carte blanche to a man to kill one accused of felony, without regard to whether he resists or not, is not only anomalous, but monstrous."

We will endeavor to give some idea as to whether the Governor really knew of Jesse James' whereabouts when he bargained with the Fords to assassinate him. The Fords having, on trial, been declared guilty of murder and sentenced to death, it is not surprising that Crittenden should now deny all complicity in their act. To a correspondent of the *Republican* at Jefferson City he emphatically declared that he did not know that the bandit was living in St. Joseph, and he affirms that he did not know that the Fords intended to kill their leader. When the crime was first committed, and the weak-minded Governor thought there was some personal glory in it for him, he was proud to say that he did it. To a reporter of the *Globe-Democrat* he said:

"People have no idea how much trouble I have had in getting my men to work together and keep at it. Some of them would work a while and get tired and want to quit, but I would encourage them to try a little longer. The result is I have succeeded in suppressing train robbing, and have broken up the gang of bandits. I tell you, my mysterious man 'Bob,' as I call him, did the work." To a newspaper representative in Columbus he said: "It is my work, and I assume all responsibility."

It is not chivalric for our Governor to crawfish now. Has the reaction in public sentiment frightened him?

We will here give the important points in an interview by a reporter of the Kansas City *Times*.[1] This happened immediately after

[1]This story appeared in the Kansas City *Times,* April 5, 1882.

the killing, and before the political weathercock had time to ascertain how the wind of public sentiment blew. The shameless bravado of the ex-Lieut.-Colonel is very characteristic of the man.

"GOVERNOR CRITTENDEN'S VIEWS.

"Governor Crittenden arrived in the city from the capital yesterday morning. He came in response to telegrams from Sheriff Timberlake and Police Commissioner Craig. He was met at Warrensburg by Major Henry Neill, and both gentlemen were interviewed by a *Times* representative at their rooms in the Blossom hotel yesterday afternoon.

"The Governor wore a self-satisfied look, which seemed to say: 'I've done it. Don't you think so?' He entered into conversation readily, and seemed less reserved than on former occasions, when asked for information concerning the James band of train robbers. One point he seems anxious to impress upon the press and public is that he has neither granted pardons to Dick Little (Liddil), the Ford brothers, nor any other members of the bandit crowd in advance of the action of the courts. He does not deny, however, that there is an understanding between those individuals and himself that they shall finally go free."

What is this but an admission of a bargain? But he goes on to orate further in answer to this question of the reporter:

"I wish to ask you, Governor, what were your instructions to the Ford brothers. Did you instruct them to capture Jesse James, if possible, before attempting to shoot him, or did you give them to understand that it was wholly discretionary with them whether they killed him or captured him alive?"

"I will answer you in this way: I am satisfied with the result of their action, and I feel confident it will meet with the sanction of every law abiding citizen, not only in this state, but throughout the United States, who has a proper understanding of the surroundings of the case, and a due appreciation of the enforcement of the law. Even if the instrumentalities bear not upon their face a true exhibit of justice, still time will develop that the end justifies the means.

"When your house is burning, you stand not upon the method of extinction.

"For sixteen years this state has been made the sufferer at home and abroad to the extent of millions of dollars, by the operations of Jesse James and his desperate gang. Thousands of quiet citizens in transitu from the east to the west and from the west to the east have avoided this state as they would a leper. After I became Governor I determined to overthrow this bold night rider and his gang, by any and all means known to human ingenuity; and within eight months from the time I inaugurated my policy, I am glad to say, despite much opposition which should not have existed, the lawless leader and his gang have been driven to the death, to the prison and to submission to the law and its officers. I give what glory there is in this to those brave officers, and to their instruments the credit of this victory.

"The criminal court of this county with its officers are entitled to a large share of the public gratitude. Now, in the face of events, should I complain of whatever indirect means have been used in the accomplishment of this great success? Jesse James showed no respect for the state of his nativity, the home of his people and its laws, showed no mercy to man, woman or child in the accomplishment of his ends. What right had he in life, or his friends now, to appeal to that law for the protection of others, and that rule of mercy which he never exercised toward others in his life. He who taketh the sword, by the sword shall he perish. I honor Missouri and its law abiding people more than I do Jesse James, and I have no fault to find with the boys who shot him down. They have done what many desired to have done, but had not the courage to do."

Never did he make any denial of his full knowledge and complicity until fully a week after the deed was done.

In his first bloviating interviews he claimed to have full knowledge of the designs of the Fords. He indorsed their performance to the fullest degree. At that time he thought the killing of the bandit was a big thing, and he wanted to appropriate the credit of it. This is the declaration that he made to a correspondent of the

St. Louis *Republican* immediately following the assassination:

I have no excuse to make, no apologies to render to any living man for the part I have played in this bloody drama, nor has Craig, nor has Timberlake. I am not regretful of his death, and have no censure for the boys who removed him. They deserve credit, is my candid, solemn opinion. Why should these Ford boys be so abused? If they are guilty of a heinous sin against society, others are also equally guilty" [meaning thereby the Chief Executive and his friends, Craig and Timberlake.]

On the heels of this declaration the Governor sat down and wrote to the various railroad companies to send him the money they had offered for the capture of James, in order that he might pay it over to the murderers. The Fords were promised immunity if they would kill the bandit. Now, who furnished that solemn pledge? Nobody but Thomas T. Crittenden.

For further proof of the bargain of Crittenden and the Fords, we give *the conduct, and threats,* of the Fords after sentence— *threats which their accomplice, Crittenden, didn't dare to disregard!*

An indictment for murder in the first degree was returned, April 17th, 1882, against Charles and Robert Ford by the grand jury of Buchanan county. The prisoners were brought into court at 1:30 o'clock, and when the indictment was read to them, they pleaded guilty, and were sentenced to be hanged on the 19th of May. The quick work of the court was a surprise to the large audience and spectators.

During the delivery of the sentence Judge Sherman was much moved, but *the Ford boys were perfectly nonchalant. Robert acted in a dare-devil manner and laughed,* while Charles, on the contrary, was very irritable, and showed unmistakable signs of anger.

After their return to the jail, the boys talked freely. *They are sure Crittenden will pardon them, and have no fears on that score.* They were indignant over the action of the St. Joseph authorities and very mad.

The whole proceedings occupied a brief period, and it was regarded by all concerned as a stupendous farce. There was little of the impressiveness of a court of justice, and the idea of being sentenced to be hanged seemed to cause much mirth to the Ford boys.

When the Fords had been taken back to jail, they were asked how they felt.

"Bully," they replied.

"Do you think you will hang?"

"Hang! Not worth a damn," said Bob.

"Hang h—l!" said Charlie. "We should smile. The Governor will attend to that part of the business; *that is in the contract.*"

"Contract—what contract?"

"Well, never mind that. *I tell you the Governor will pardon us.*"

"Yes," added Bob, "it is in black and white."

"Do you mean to say that you have a written agreement with the Governor about your pardon?"

"Now, don't you ask too much. I say we are all right. *Crittenden can't—daren't—go back on us.* WE KNOW WHAT WE KNOW."
WE KNOW WHAT WE KNOW."

At 3:45 p.m. of April 17th, 1882, just two hours and a quarter after they were sentenced, the Governor pardoned Charles Ford and Robert Ford, who, that day at St. Joseph, pleaded guilty to murder in the first degree on an indictment for said offense, thus proving that the threats and assertions of the Fords were true in every particular!

The St. Louis *Post-Dispatch* of the 19th of April contains the following special dispatch from Jefferson City, Missouri: "The Ford boys are to be held for the murder of Woot Hite and for the Blue Cut robbery. That I have positively. In conversation with them, in the St. Joe jail, Charlie Ford told me that a pardon had been guaranteed to them *for all previous crimes.* His exact language was that *they had it in black and white from the Governor.*"

"Do you mean," I asked, "that you have a contract to that effect with Crittenden?"

"It makes no difference what I mean. You will see that we get out of *all* these troubles all right. We know what we are about, and we would not go blindly into this thing if we were not sure of pardon."

"Was it understood by the Governor that Jesse James was to be killed?"

"I suppose so. We never had any understanding in our minds but that he was to be killed. In fact, nobody but a fool would undertake to do anything else. *They knew when they put us to work that we would kill Jesse,* and that is all there is about it. *We took the job on the chance that we would kill Jesse* before he would kill us."

This statement was made in answer to Sheriff Timberlake's assertion that the Fords were employed to locate Jesse, not to kill him.

Is it necessary to carry the proof of Crittenden's complicity and bargain any further. He, himself, at first glories in it, then moderates down to a tacit admission, and later still denies it; but those who are familiar with the character of the man, know just how much, or how little rather, the word of T. T. Crittenden is worth in any matter in which he happens to be himself interested.

If the Ford brothers were guilty of murder in the first degree, then was their employer, Crittenden, and his co-conspirators equally as guilty. That the Fords were guilty of cold-blooded, deliberate murder, no man of ordinary intelligence has the slightest doubt; and upon trial *they themselves pleaded guilty to it!* What more can be asked in the way of proof? Their confession settles all.

FRANK LESLIE'S ILLUSTRATED NEWSPAPER

No. 1,387—Vol. LIV.   NEW YORK—FOR THE WEEK ENDING APRIL 22, 1882.   Price 10 Cents

MISSOURI.—JESSE JAMES, THE NOTORIOUS DESPERADO, KILLED AT ST. JOSEPH, APRIL 3d.

The national notoriety of Jesse James is evidenced in the wide notice given his death.

CHAPTER XLIII.

Press and Other Opinions.

Crittenden's Course Condemned—What the Papers and People Say—New York Evening Post—Sedalia Democrat—Cincinnati Commercial—St. Louis Post-Dispatch—Globe-Democrat—Denver Tribune—New York Sun—Cincinnati Times—Star—Kansas City Times—New York World—Telegram—Tribune—Graphic—Cincinnati Enquirer—Louisville Courier-Journal—Chicago Inter-Ocean—News— Etc.—Lawyers, Legislators, and Others.

The New York *Evening Post* (Carl Schurz) made the following interesting observation about the ancient and peculiar manner in which we kill bandits in this State:

"All the great robbers of old times, and of other countries, lived in caves, or in mountain fastnesses, to which it was difficult for troops to pursue them, or in strong castles, or kept the sea in long, low, rakish black schooners. James, however, lived in a comfortable house, surrounded by a loving family, and went off on his expeditions apparently as a business man goes off to collect debts or to solicit orders. Moreover, although the State of Missouri had for long years been trying to arrest him, it was never able to do so, and in order to compass his death the Governer had to resort to the means by which the Venetian Council of Ten and other mediaeval powers occasionally tried to get rid of the obnoxious foreign sovereigns. He hired an assassin to go and kill him unawares, so that James really died what may be called a royal death. He fell as Henry IV, and William the Silent and Admiral Coligny fell, the victim of the hostility of a great community, who were unable to get the better of him in open fight, but felt that his taking off was necessary to their safety and prosperity. The Governor, in fact, justifies his own course in language which might have been used by Elizabeth after the defeat of the Armada. He describes the assassination of James as the relief of the State from a great hindrance to its prosperity, and as likely to give an important stimulus to real estate speculation, to railroad enterprise and foreign immigration."

The Cincinnati *Commercial* applauds and justifies Crittenden's course, but then it is easy to predict what the course of this paper will be in any given case, for while the editor of the Cincinnati *Commercial* is a very able he is also a very eccentric gentleman. In conducting his newspaper he always defers to what he conceives to be the popular will or frenzy. It is not an unusual thing for him to maintain mob law. He wanted Guiteau torn limb from limb after he assassinated the President, and he called on Marshal Henry several times during the trial to knock the assassin down in the court room and beat him into silence and deference. He wanted Bill Jones set free after he shot at Guiteau, and he maintained the right of Mason to assassinate the assassin. Last summer he busied himself by raising a subscription for a man, who had been held responsible to the law for committing an assault and battery. Now and then he advises somebody to drag a judge from the bench, and it is not an unusual thing for him to applaud a mob that has put a summary end to the existence of some despicable wretch. Mr. Halstead has some of the tastes and inclinations of a feudal despot. He would make a most excellent military satrap. It is to be hoped that he will never have occasion to regret his oft-expressed contempt for law and the forms established for the benefit of society; and yet, if he was in trouble to-day, he would be likely to insist most strenuously upon his rights as a citizen. He would want the protection and the usufruct of all the safeguards known to the judiciary. He should be careful not to teach bloody instructions or set bad examples.

TREAT THEM AS MURDERERS.

The St. Charles (Mo.) *Journal* says: "The taking off of Jesse James is a good riddance to the State, but we must protest against the manner of his death. It was dastardly, cowardly and criminal. The State has no right to procure the murder of any man in time of peace, no matter how enormous his crimes. The precedent is abominable, and if followed to its conclusions would overthrow all law. The justice may not be so apparent in the case of Jesse James, but it gives a privilege to the State and its tools dangerous to the safety of every man suspected of a crime. It strikes at the foundation of the right of trial, and places a premium on assassination. The murderer should be paid his reward, and then hung for his crime."

The Sedalia *Democrat* unhesitatingly condemns this infamous outrage upon all law and liberty.

CRITTENDEN'S CRIME — WHAT THE PRESS OF THE COUNTRY SAYS OF HIS LATE BLOODY EXPLOIT.

Under the above heading the Denver (Col.) *Tribune* says: "Governor Crittenden admits that he was in the conspiracy to murder Jesse James. Then why has he not been indicted along with the young man who did the killing?"

The New York *Sun* says: "Let any one read the account of the circumstances under which Robert Ford killed Jesse James, and then consider how enjoyable Mr. Ford's society would be, and how much safety could be insured to a train carrying treasure through any district which he may happen to haunt hereafter. To make a new murder, in the process of getting rid of an old one, is a practice which cannot be justified. The Governor of Missouri, however, undertakes to justify it. He feels 'confident that it will meet with the sanction of law-abiding citizens, not only of this State, but throughout the United States.' Time will show, he adds, that the end justifies the means. The end was doubtless important. The destruction of the notorious outlaw will naturally and properly give satisfaction everywhere. But the manner in which it was brought about can only excite regret among right-minded men. The crime of murder is detestable, irrespective of the victim; and those who condemn it when committed by Jesse James should not be heard to defend it when committed by Robert Ford. We share with the people of Missouri their contentment at the termination of so dangerous a life; but we dissent emphatically from their Governor's approval of the means by which that life was taken away."

Unpleasant comparison is made by the Cincinnati *Times-Star* of Gov. Crittenden's dealings with the James gang and Gov. Cameron's management of the oyster war between Virginia and Maryland. Instead of bribing scoundrels with princely rewards to steal upon the law-breakers and assassinate them in cold blood, says the *Times-Star,* Gov. Cameron boarded his ship and sailed down upon the piratical sloops, gave them a fair fight and gobbled them up. "The Missourian's plan is just as effectual, but it is not quite so chivalrous," adds the *Times-Star;* and further, "if Gov. Crittenden, of Missouri, reads the newspapers extensively, he has discovered that public opinion severely condemns assassination by law, even in the case of a notorious desperado and outlaw. Not a single reputable paper in the land justifies the part he played in the conspiracy to murder James."

"Frank James might find a safe asylum either in the *Herald* office at St. Joseph or the *Post-Dispatch* office at St. Louis. These papers mourn the loss of his brother Jesse as they have never mourned the loss of any of Missouri's great men."—*Kansas City Times.*

"It becomes our solemn and Christian duty to inform you that you utter a malicious and vicious and utterly indefensible lie, when you say that this paper has mourned the loss of Jesse James. We have never failed to express satisfaction with his death, and we congratulale the State now that he is no longer alive. We have severely criti-cised our asinine Governor for the lawless and uncivilized way in which he compassed the bandit's murder, and in this we have the indorsement of such journals as the New York *Sun, World, Tele-graph, Graphic,* and *Tribune,* Chicago *Inter Ocean* and *News,* Cin-cinnati *Enquirer,* Louisville *Courier-Journal,* and a host of other intelligent and influential representatives of public opinion. We do not see how our Kansas City contemporary hopes to help itself by lying about our position on this question."—*St. Louis Post-Dispatch.*

"The correspondent of the *Globe-Democrat* at Jefferson City has been at pains to ascertain the sentiments of the members of the Legislature touching the recent removal of J. James, bandit. He writes: 'The result is the stereotyped answer to the effect that the member is glad for the sake of Missouri that the bandit is dead, but he would have preferred that the killing had been done in some other manner.' That, we may remark, is the platform of the *Post-Dispatch*. We have never ceased to believe that Crittenden inflicted more disgrace on the State by the manner in which he brought about the murder of James, than the bandit could, if he had been left to continue his career. His death was a blessing, but the manner of his taking off a reproach upon our civilization."

Some of the friends of Gov. Crittenden affect to believe that "His Excellency" is in danger of assassination. Nothing of the kind. It would be well enough, however, for "His Excellency" to keep indoors when the foolkiller visits his town.

Gov. Crittenden never offered a prize for the carcass of Jesse James. His proclamation of last July offered $5,000 for his apprehension and delivery to the officers of the law, and $5,000 for his conviction. In conspiring with the Ford boys to murder the bandit, the wise Governor did not even have the sanction of his own proclamation.

The indecent haste of the Governor in pardoning his accomplices in the James murder has rather staggered the *Globe-Democrat*. It mildly suggests that the Fords should now be tried for the crimes they committed before they contracted to "remove" their leader for $10,000. Is this the proper way to treat the heroic young men who assisted our chivalric Governor?

It would be easy to go on and give an indefinite number of extracts from the press, and opinions of men high in station in this State and others as to the universal horror and detestation with which this action of Governor T. T. Crittenden is regarded. To the minds of all law-abiding men the employment of such infamous means makes the remedy far worse than the disease. All feel that there is neither safety for the State, nor the individual, when power is entrusted to the weak head and corrupt heart of such a creature as our Governor has proved himself. The remedy is first impeachment by the legislature, and then indictment by the grand jury of Buchanan county, and trial for murder in the first degree. In justice to the great State of Missouri and to her high minded and honorable people, the impeachment and removal from office of T. T. Crittenden and his indictment and trial in Buchanan county is imperatively called for. Will her representatives have the manly boldness to perform this act of justice?

CHAPTER XLIV.

The Drum Head Court-Martial.

Crittenden a Natural Tyrant—His Blood-Thirsty Nature—Dr. Zimmerman—
Hamilton—Their Murder—Gov. Chas. P. Johnson—Hon. W. S. Holland—
Dr. Jacob S. Merrill—Major Emory S. Foster—A Severe Rebuke—Capt.
A. R. Conklin—Letter of Wm. G. Howard—Crittenden's Ignorance of
Civil and Criminal Law—His Ignorance of Military Regulations—Ignor-
ance of Usages of War—His Tyrannical Conduct—His Brutal Declara-
tions—Legislative Censure—Authority for this Chapter.

THE extraordinary conduct of Gov. Thos. T. Crittenden in connection with the killing of Jesse James naturally recalls to public
recollection another incident in the history of the Governor's career,
illustrating his rashness and incapacity as a commanding officer even
more forcibly than the case of James betrays his lack of executive
ability. The execution of Dr. Zimmerman, a respectable citizen of
Henry county, Mo., by a drum-head court-marial, will not soon be
forgotten by the people of this State, and its details, as viewed to-day
in the light of all the surrounding circumstances and the legislative
action thereon, constitute a page in the Governor's history that carries its own deductions. Dr. Zimmerman was a regular practicing
physician, born in Pennsylvania, who emigrated to Missouri before
the war. He was an esteemed Union man, and when the war commenced he was particularly conspicuous in his declaration of ad-
herence to the Government. Yet it appears that in September, 1863,
he was arrested as a horse thief by Crittenden's militia, and, in com-

pany with a man named Hamilton, was taken out and shot—notwithstanding the civil courts of the county were in session at the time and alone empowered to try such cases. This flagrant violation of the articles of war, of general orders and all military custom, attracted the attention of the Union Legislature to such an extent that on December 4, 1863, a special committee of nine was appointed to "investigate the management and conduct of the Missouri State militia, the Missouri enrolled militia, and the provisional regiments," and was clothed with power to command the attendance of persons and papers. That committee consisted of the following gentlemen: Chas. P. Johnson, of St. Louis, afterwards Lieutenant-Governor, and at present a member of the House; Gert. Goebel, of Franklin county; Mr. Moore, of Mississippi county, an extreme democrat; R. B. Palmer, of Wright, a member of the Constitutional Convention of 1876, and of the Legislature of 1878; G. Smith, of Caldwell, afterwards Lieutenant-Governor; W. H. Follinsbee, of Daviess county; W. L. Lovelace, of Montgomery county, subsequently a judge of the Supreme Court, and Jo. Davis, of Howard county. The labors of the committee were thorough and exhaustive, closing with a scathing arraignment of Lieut.-Col. Crittenden.

Dr. Jacob S. Merrell, City Treas., speaking of Dr. Zimmermann to a press representative, said:

"I knew him well. He was a customer and friend of mine, and his execution was an outrage. He was a practicing physician of Henry county, and a man above reproach. He was a noble looking man, conspicuously and fearlessly in favor of the Union. Union men in Central Missouri were very scarce in those days, and Dr. Zimmermann became generally known to the Union men of St. Louis in that way.

"The guerrillas made frequent raids upon Dr. Zimmermann's stables, and took horse after horse, until none remained. Finally the Doctor obtained information that his horses were stabled at a farmhouse south of Henry county, and he made a desperate resolve to regain his property. So he proceeded south, found the stable in question, entered it, and in the darkness took the horse he presumed was his. On his return trip he was arrested by the Union militia. It afterwards transpired that the very next horse to the one he took from the stable was his own property. You must remember that those were turbulent days, and the Doctor thought a desperate case required desperate action."

In January, 1864, Hon. W. S. Holland, who was a member of the Constitutional Convention of 1865, wrote a letter to the Legislative committee, in which he said:

"Dr. Zimmermann was generally regarded by his neighbors as a very worthy, honest citizen.

"His loyalty has always been above suspicion, and for this reason alone he has been robbed and hunted from place to place, and even shot in his house by rebels and bushwackers. He carried in his flesh to the day of his death a bullet with which bushwackers shot him while he defended his own home. He was compelled to abandon his house, give up his profession, and, after being robbed of nearly all his valuable property, he abandoned this county, taking his family with him, for no other reason than that it was not safe to try to live there. * * * For one, I am willing to say that were Dr. Zimmermann alive to-day, after all that has been said against him, and were he known to be in this county, I do not know a Union man who would lock his stable door against him. The Union men of this county who knew the Doctor best deplore his death the most. I was going to characterize the killing of Zimmermann as a murder, but I will not call it by that name, though I will say that, so far as I have heard an expression from Union men who knew him well, they regard it as just about that."

Gov. Chas. P. Johnson, whose position, as chairman of the committee referred to, gave him knowledge of the circumstances of the case in question, says: "I remember the testimony brought before the committee, of which I was chairman.

"The circumstances as detailed to my committee were these: In September, 1863, Dr. Zimmermann and one Hamilton were arrested and carried to the post at Sedalia, at that time commanded by Lieutenant Colonel Crittenden. These men were charged with stealing two horses, one from a man named James, and one from a man by the name of Hazell. A drum-head court martial was called, or rather (as the evidence of Colonel Crittenden showed) came together to try these men; and the manner in which this improvised court undertook to pass upon the solemn question of life and death must remain a matter of painful interest to every lover of good government in this state. A few army officers of various grades assembled themselves together in a meeting that *they called* a drum-head court martial; tried, sentenced and ordered the persons executed, and in two days the sentence was carried into effect. How that court happened to meet is a mystery to this day. One of the officers said he was asked to attend by somebody else; that there were no written orders; and doubtless the same process was used to get together the other members of the court. It seemed that the *alleged* court was brought together by those who took an interest in having the prisoners tried, as men are invited to a corn-shucking; and the court seemed to be conducted with about as much regularity as is usual at a corn-shucking. No written charges were ever presented to the court, and not one word of record of the proceedings was ever preserved; but, organized as it was, it passed upon the momentous question of life and death with as little ceremony as the pedagogue would upon the case of an offending urchin. Waiving any doubt that might be entertained on the subject of their guilt, and assuming that they were guilty, the case will be no better for Crittenden. According to all the evidence these men were citizens at the time of the alleged larceny, and at the time of the arrest and trial. And what is more, the civil court in Moniteau county, the place where these scenes occurred, was in full operation and entirely unobstructed. But he alleged, as a justification of his course, that the civil process was too slow to protect the people. That argument, if true at all, is equally true at all times and in all places, for it is fair to presume that the civil process in Moniteau county is not more tardy than in other counties of the State.

"The result of the committee's investigations was that it administered the severest rebuke to Crittenden, and suggested that he was guilty of willful murder. The facts developed in the investigation produced the greatest indignation among the members, especially the German representatives. My friend, Dr. Pretorius, was a member of the House at the time, and his denunciations of Crittenden's conduct were most emphatic. My recollection is that Crittenden barely escaped being cashiered. The matter came up afterwards in the Senate, and a bitter and prolonged contest ensued."

Before the committee Lieutenant R. T. Berry testified: "I was ordered out with my company, as I supposed, by Lieutenant Colonel Crittenden; it was not a written order; this was on Friday, the latter part of September, about sunrise; the execution took place near Tipton; both prisoners were shot at the same time, and both fell from the same fire. The sergeant in command of the firing detail wished to be relieved from the duty, as he was unwilling to perform it. All I heard of Dr. Zimmermann was favorable."

Major Emory S. Foster testified: "Previous to the execution, Lieutenant Colonel Crittenden and I were standing in front of the Virginia Hotel in Jefferson City. Crittenden spoke of having caught some horse thieves, and said that he was going to have them shot; intended to call a drum-head court martial. About that time Lieutenant Governor W. P. Hall (then acting Governor) came up and asked, 'What is that you are going to do, Colonel?' Crittenden replied that he had caught some Union horse-thieves, and was going to drum-head and shoot them. This was about two or three days before they were shot."

Capt. A. R. Conklin testified as follows:

"On Wednesday or Thursday previous to the week in which Dr. Zimmermann was shot, Lieut.-Gov. Hall and myself were standing in front of the Virginia Hotel, talking, when Lieut.-Col. Crittenden came up. He was on his return then from Boonville. After the compliments of the day were passed, Lieut.-Gov. Hall inquired as to the state of the country up at Tipton. Crittenden remarked that there was some horse stealing going on there, and he said: "I understand they have got two of the thieves. By G—d, I'll shoot them before Sunday night, if I can get a board of officers to convict them?' Lieut-Gov. Hall remarked to him not to get too bloodthirsty, or words to that effect."

Maj. Henry Suess, of the Seventh Cavalry M. S. M., who presided over the alleged court, testified:

"Dr. Zimmermann and Hamilton were tried by a drum-head court martial which is a court summoned for meting out summary justice,

when the process of civil law is deemed insufficient. It was convened
by order of Lieut.-Col. Thos. T. Crittenden, of the Seventh M. S. M.
Col. Phillips told me at Sedalia that I had to proceed to Tipton upon
orders from Lieut. Col. Crittenden. I did not see the order. When I
arrived in Tipton, in company with other officers, Crittenden informed us that we were to sit on a drum-head court martial. The
members of the court were Capt. Hensley, Capt. O. B. Queen, Capt.
Bux, one other whom I do not recollect, and myself. Capt. Queen
and Capt. Hensley alternated as judge advocate. Zimmermann and
Hamilton were tried on the same charges. I do not know who preferred the charges. A drum-head court martial has in reality no judge
advocate, and the proceedings are informal. The sentence of the court
was that the prisoners should be shot to death by musketry, at such
time and place as the commanding officer may direct, all the members concurring therein. I believed at the time the civil courts in
Moniteau could not punish criminals speedily and safely, so as to
protect the interests of the community."

In reply to a letter of inquiry from Gov. Johnson, the following communication was received from Wm. G. Howard, then clerk
of the Moniteau County Circuit Court:

"In answer to your first question I state that the last term of our
Circuit Court was held in September, 1863, commencing on the
fourth Monday. Second: Our court has never been obstructed,
suspended or interfered with during the years 1862 or 1863, by
any one, except the March term, 1863, of said court, which was
suspended by an act of the Legislature. Third: There were fifty-one
indictments found at the last term of our court, to-wit: gaming, 19;
dramshops, 15; playing cards on Sunday, 4; gaming house, 4; grand
larceny, 4; horse racing on Sunday, 2; running horse on public
highway, 1; dealing with a slave, 1; taking up and not posting
stray, 1. Fourth: Cases tried and decided at the last term—One
for dealing with slaves, tried by jury, fined $20, and taken to
Supreme Court; one for grand larceny, tried by jury, sentenced to
penitentiary for three years; verdict confirmed by the court. Besides
this, there were a number of confessions for dramshops and gaming;

in each case of dramshops a fine of $20, and for gaming a fine of $10 was assessed by the court."

This letter proves conclusively that the civil courts were open and unobstructed.

In a lengthy communication, addressed to O. D. Greene, Assistant Adjutant-General, Crittenden reviews the Zimmermann and Hamilton matter, and concludes with this significant paragraph:

"Their punishment was bloody and summary, and required some fortitude to carry it into execution; but the times, the rapid accumulation of this species of crime in this part of the State, and the protection of the truly good and loyal men of this district (who, too, have an interest as dear as life) demanded it, and I think it has had a healthy influence already. Hundreds of honest men of all political parties have signified their indorsement of the act by letters and by messages. I am no lover of blood, and will never shed that which is innocent, but would feel no hesitancy, with all my respect for the law, in dealing with horse-thieves and bush-whackers with an unmerciful hand, if left to my own judgment."

The committee's arraignment of Col. Crittenden was put in the following legal form and designated: "A few points of law and order touching the case of Dr. Zimmerman." It was written by Governor Johnson and was always considered unanswerable:

I. Citizens cannot be tried by any kind of court-martial.

(Constitution of the United States, Amendments, article 5. 2. Constitution of Missouri, article 13, 8, 922. 3. Officers of the M. S. M. are sworn "to do their utmost to sustain the Constitution and laws of the United States and of this State." Gen. Ord. M. S. M. No. 2, November 29, 1861. 4. An act for enrolling and calling out the National forces and for other purposes, approved March 3, 1863, sections 24, 25, 30 and 38.)

II. Citizens may be tried by a military commission.

(1. When crimes or offenses committed by them affect military operations, such as giving information to the enemy, destruction of bridges, and other means of communication, murder of soldiers on duty, etc. Gen. Ord. No. 1, Department of the Mississippi, January, 1862; Gen. Ord. Department of Missouri No. 30,

April 22, 1863, section 8. 4. In districts occupied by our armies, where civil courts do not exist or are powerless; by custom of war: no laws on the subject; doubtful.)

III. Citizens cannot be tried by any military tribunal.

(1. *For civil offenses cognizable by civil courts,* whenever such loyal courts exist. Gen. Ord. Dept. of Mississipi, January 1, 1864. 2. And, in general, for offenses which do not affect military operations of the occupying army.)

IV. Citizens guilty of offenses cognizable by military tribunals must be tried by military commission.

(Drum-head courts martial are not recognized nor mentioned by law, orders, or usage of war. 2. Military commanders in this department are forbidden to impose any punishment of death, banishment, confiscation of property, or imprisonment exceeding the term of thirty days. *Such sentences can only be passed by a court-martial in cases of soldiers,* or a military commission in cases of citizens. General Order Department Missouri, No. 12, February 7, 1863.)

V. *A military commission for the trial of capital offenses can be called only by the General-in-chief, the Department Commanders, and District Commanders.* See Gen. Ord. No. 1, Jan., 1862, etc. A lieutenant-colonel in command of a sub-district cannot convene a military commission.

VI. A military commission is a court of record, and the record must be complete and accurate. Sec. 891, Army Regulations. *Informality or neglect in the specified points renders the proceedings and sentence illegal.*

VII. The record is to be forwarded without delay to the officer who appointed the commission. See 65th article of war, etc. "The proceedings are null and void if the commission was appointed by an officer not having competent authority. *All sentences of death and imprisonment in the penitentiary must be approved by the General commanding the department and confirmed by the President.*"

VIII. "If the punishment awarded be illegal or exorbitant, the reviewing authority has the right to disapprove the sentence. Horse-stealing is punished by imprisonment in the penitentiary not exceeding seven years. (Rev. Stat. of Mo., Laws of Mo., 1863, p. 16.)

"The officers participating in the drum-head court-martial are guilty of violations of articles of war, of general orders of Gens. Halleck, Curtis and Schofield, of the laws and customs of war, and guilty of interfering criminally with the functions of civil, loyal courts. Lieut.-Col. Crittenden is guilty of all that, and of summoning a tribunal for which he was not authorized. *His intentions previously declared render it difficult to decide where the dividing line is between his action and willful murder.*"

The complete report of the testimony taken by the committee can be found in the appendix to the House journal of 1863 and 1864, adjourned session.

Jesse James' children, Mary and Jesse Edwards. Jesse Edwards James later went into business and was always a very respected citizen. *Courtesy St. Joseph Museum.*

CHAPTER XLV.

FUNERAL OBSEQUIES.

The Funeral Train—Lying in State at Kearney—Appearance of the Corpse—
The Crowds at Kearney—His Old Comrades Present—The Mysterious
Pall-Bearer—The Church—The Procession—The Prayer—The Sermon—
Scenes at the Grave—His Burial Place—Reflections on His Character
—Names of Pall-Bearers—Relatives Present—His Wounded Brother.

WHEN the special train, tendered by the Hannibal & St. Joseph
railway, bearing all that was mortal of Jesse James, the most
daring outlaw of ancient or modern times, arrived at Kearney, the
metallic casket was removed to the "Kearney House," just opposite
the depot. The use of the house had been kindly tendered by Mr.
Woodruff, its gentlemanly host, and in its office, reposing calmly
in the sleep of death, and viewed by hundreds, lay what had in
life been a man "without fear;" would that we could add "and
without reproach." His appearance was perfectly natural.

"Life's fitful fever over, he slept well."

He looked as if, tired of the cares and toils of life, he had lain
down gladly to that dreamless sleep, that knows no waking, and
was at rest. The firm lines of his face had that quiet repose indicating that his death had been instantaneous and painless. The
bronzed hue of his complexion relieved the pallor usual in the
faces of the dead, and occasioned from many the remark: "How
lifelike; how perfectly natural."

The contused spot, almost over the left eye, and supposed by

some to have been caused by a stroke from Ford's pistol, after
he had fallen in death, had not received any additional discolora-
tion, and was consequently but a very slight disfigurement. It is
hardly probable that this contusion was caused by the pistol of
either Bob or Charlie Ford, but was more likely the result of his
striking upon this place, when he fell from the chair to the floor.

All through the fast flying hours of the 6th of April the crowds
of anxious visitors in Kearney increased. From far and near gathered
friends and strangers, curious to gaze upon the dead. His name
had become known throughout the length and breadth of his country for his daring bravery, his cool judgment, and alas! that we
must say it, for his wonderful career of crime and spoliation. Stranger
than fiction had proved his life of desperate deed and daring crime.
On the field of battle he strove gallantly and long; a boy hero, he
had won the admiration and commendation of desperate men, who
looked on the field of carnage as a carpet knight does upon the
face of his mistress, and shrank not from odds or dangers. He
had met his foe with the ardor of a Crusader, and fought him
fiercely to the bitter end. Forced by injustice and oppression into
evil courses, he had carried into crime the same impetuous daring,
cool judgment and clear insight, that had made him one of Quantrell's most trusted lieutenants. Amongst the outlaws, he was ever
their leader, and his skill and judgment, as well as his reckless
daring, had carried them safely through the longest and most
unchecked career of depredation ever run by any band of desperate
men.

To view him dead, had come for miles and miles the stranger,
the enemy and the friend. Criminal though he undoubtedly was,
yet all wanted to take one last look at the man whose like they
would never see again.

Amongst the motley throng, which in enfilading files passed
and repassed through the narrow halls into the spacious room in
which he lay, might be noticed many of his old guerrilla comrades;
men bronzed and tanned by sunshine and by storm; men who had
witnessed full often his terrible spring upon his foe in battle; who

had seen him court dangers innumerable, as through in love with
death. The hard lines in their bearded faces softened and their
eyes were moist, as they gazed long into his upturned face, as though
endeavoring to read there some of the mighty mysteries of the un-
knowable beyond. Had his troubled soul found now surcease of battle? was his storm-vexed spirit now at rest?

Useless pondering; idle speculation! no mortal eye may ever
pierce the sombre shadows of that dark veil, that shuts in the mysterious realm of the beyond. To all save the faithful follower of
"the lowly Nazarene," it is an infinite void filled with conjectures
and chimeras—only to the Christian is it pregnant with life
immortal, peace infinite and light and joy unquenchable.

Moving silently through the rooms in long lines, the crowd seemed
never to tire of gazing upon the placid features of the outlaw;
but now the time has come when it must be consigned to its mother
earth, and the plate of bronze is firmly screwed down over the
glass, shutting the face of the dead bandit from sight.

The coffin is next raised from its support by the pall bearers
and gently carried to the spring wagon which is to act as hearse,
and is drawn thence to the church in the older portion of the town,
the site of old Centerville. In this church had Jesse been converted
in 1866, and many a fervent prayer of his had gone up from before its humble altar.

The pall bearers were J. D. Ford, Charles Scott, James Hender-
son, J. T. Reed, and William Bond. The sixth was a man whom
no one had seen until just as the procession was about to start;
he then came forward, his countenance stern, his eye bright and
piercing. Moving to the head of the casket he directed the movements of the others quietly, dumbly, yet with a mien sad and commanding. His apparent age was about forty years, but his lithe,
muscular figure seemed to deny such age, while his face, stern,
sad and impenetrable as that of the sphynx, looked as though its
sadness might have abided with it for a century. None seemed to
know him; none questioned him, and he spoke to no one. Who
was he? Where was he from? Was it Frank James?

The relatives, consisting of Mrs. Samuel, Mrs. James and two children, Mr. and Mrs. Luther W. James, Mrs. Hall, Mrs. Mimms and Mrs. Kirkpatrick, were seated beside the coffin, placed in front of the altar. The services were opened by singing the hymn, "What a Friend We Have in Jesus." Rev. R. H. Jones, of Lathrop, read a passage of Scripture from Job, commencing, "Man born of woman is of few days, and full of trouble." Also the 4th and 5th verses of the 39th Psalm, beginning, "Lord make me to know mine end." He offered up a touching and pathetic prayer for the grief-stricken mother, wife and children, and asked the Lord to make their bereavement a blessing to them, by leading them to a true knowledge of himself.

THE FUNERAL SERMON.

Rev. J. M. P. Martin, pastor of the church, as an introduction to his discourse, said: "We all understand that we can not change the state of the dead. Again it would be useless for me to bring any new information before this congregation respecting the life and character of the deceased. The text which I have chosen today is the 24th chapter of Matthew, 44th verse: "Therefore be ready, for in such an hour as ye think not, the Son of Man cometh." First, I wish to call special attention to the certainty of the coming of Christ to each of us. There is the certainty of a grave before each of us. We can not jump over it, or pass it by. God's word is written on his tablets for our instruction and guidance. It takes it for granted that there is a certainty of death. It is constantly warning us of this solemn fact. We talk of death to others, and dwell upon its terrors, and are stricken down with grief when it lays its hand upon those we love, but seem unwilling to regard its certainty to ourselves. The truth I wish you to take home with you to-day is that Christ is sure to come to each of us. In the second place Christ is sure to come at such an hour as we think not. He comes like a thief in the night. As the thief comes when we are least expecting it, so Christ comes. Whatever the past has been, we all have our idle dreams of the future. We all in our imagination have fancy pictures, and are apt to forget the evils that are likely to befall us. If we could at all learn a lesson from the past, we would not expect the future as our fancy paints it. Though we are assured that others shall die and not live, we feel for ourselves we shall live and not die. Shall we not set about for a future which is as real as life is real? Our expectation then of the lengthening out of our lives will not keep away the coming of the Son of Man. Let us remember that he comes as a thief in the night, and not delay our preparations. But it seems idle to try to get men to make preparation for what seems imaginary. We will not entertain the fact as it is. It is necessary for us to prepare to meet our God. If men are so careful to prepare for things that pertain to this life, how much more important is it to prepare for the things that pertain to the life to come. If we accept Christ, our account will be acceptable to our Lord. How would we feel if God should come and we should be compelled to stand before him unprepared. As I said before, we can not change the past life or condition of the dead. I ask you to take your eyes off from that coffin; I ask you to take your eyes off from the open grave and look higher. Let us not forget our duties and responsibilities in life. A true prophet is not without honor save in his own land, and those who point the way to righteousness are often unheeded. Notwithstanding the many unheeded warnings, yet God is constantly reminding us and calling us to him. At the same time that he points us to the grave and tells us to look into it, he says to us it is not all of death to die, not all of life to live. But we need not die spiritually. All we need to do is to look and live. Yet we turn away, and turn away until our hearts become hard as stone. He asks us to turn to him and promises us everlasting life. What more could he say? Let us see that we make ready and stand ready when he calls us.

"Before the coffin is taken from the house I have been asked to make one or two requests. As John Samuel is very low on account of the shock caused by the death of his brother, and as the grave is very near the house, Mrs. Samuel asks that those who are here will not go out to the house. It is feared that the excitement of seeing so many persons present will injure him. It is therefore requested that none but the friends and relatives go to the grave."

Scene at the Grave.

During the services the women were all visibly affected. The mother moaned and groaned aloud. From the church the procession, composed of fifty or sixty persons in buggies, wagons, and horseback, moved out over the country to the Samuels farm, which lies about four miles nearly northeast of Kearney. It is a rough road, through vales, over hills, and across streams, and, in the neighborhood of the family residence, the country is heavily timbered and covered with a thick growth of "brush." Adjoining the Samuels farm is the farm owned by Askew, with whose untimely taking off the dead Jesse was charged. The "bush," as it is called, which consisted mostly of large growth trees, on the Kearney side of the fence, has within the past two years been mostly cut down.

Arrive at the house, the coffin was taken into the room where the wounded son, John Samuel, lay in bed. It was turned on edge, and he was raised up so that he could see the features of his dead brother. He wept bitterly and cried: "Oh, oh, God! Oh, Jesse, that ever I should see you brought home this way."

The mother approached the bedside and assuming a dramatic position, raised her only hand aloft and said in a loud tone of voice:

"Johnny, my boy, look upon your brother Jesse, your murdered brother Jesse! Look upon him and then look upon your poor, broken-hearted, shattered mother. He is dead; they have killed him— your poor brother Jesse. He has gone, and God will judge him. He is taken from me, and I have no one to lean upon now. Johnny, live for your mother, your poor, broken-hearted mother."

Johnny made no response, except to groan. The coffin was placed upon chairs in the yard, and the lid opened. Mrs. Samuel came out, sobbing: "My heart is broke, my heart is broke; broke! broke! broke!! Oh, my heart is broke! They have killed my son!" She was followed by Mrs. James, who, amid her sobs and with tears streaming down her cheeks, called on God to avenge the death of her good, kind husband, who was slain by a cowardly murderer for money. She clung to the coffin, bowing her head upon the glass, declaring that she would not let him go. She said: "God will condemn and punish all who had a hand in murdering him for money." Raising her voice and standing erect she exclaimed: "The Governor offered $50,000 to have them killed. He was killed for money, and may God punish them for it." She asked: "Why did they kill him? Why did they take him from me and my children? He would not harm them." Mrs. Samuel, standing at one end of the coffin, said: "Yes, they killed him for money—for gold and greenbacks; for money! for money! But let them take their money, their gold and their greenbacks. It will do them no good. The officers of the law have done this. They have hired murderers to do it. God will judge them for it. I have no money. I want no money. I shall not judge them. I will leave that to God. If he can forgive them I can. Last week," she continued, "he was at my house. He said to me when he was going away: 'Mother, you may never see me again, but I am not as bad as they would make me out to be.'" This was said sobbingly. By this time several women were weeping over the coffin, and not a few male eyes were moist. Becoming calm, both Mrs. Samuel and Mrs. James wanted the glass lid removed. At first Mrs. James pretended that she wanted a lock of Jesse's hair, but it was finally developed that she had come to the conclusion that his arms and legs had been taken off, and wax ones substituted for them. Sheriff Timberlake, having no screw driver large enough to turn the screws, offered to go to a farm house and borrow one, but the women were finally satisfied, and the body was committed to the grave in the yard, while they stood and watched the fresh earth thrown upon the board box, seemingly inconsolable.

Thus was consigned to its last resting place, in the door-yard where he had so often played in childish glee and innocence, the body of the great bandit. He whose whole life had been one of battle and of storm was at last quietly at rest. While, unlike noble old Paul, he had not "fought the good fight," nor "finished the faith," so far as our mortal eyes can see and our fallible minds judge, yet had he fulfilled the routine of mortality: he had lived and suffered and died. Of his loves and his hates; of his vices and

Jesse James' grave at the Samuel farm, Kearney, Missouri.

his virtues; of his good and his ill, we are forbidden to judge; therefore, let us leave him to his God for judgment, trusting in His infinite mercy, and let us say, paraphrasing gentle, tender, loving Tom Hood:

> "Cross his hands humbly,
> As if praying dumbly,
>   Over his breast;—
> Owning his weakness,
>   His evil behavior,
> And leaving, with meekness,
>   His sins to his Savior."

The Samuel farmhouse. Jesse James' mother, Zerelda Samuel, in foreground. *Courtesy Edward Knowles, Topeka.*

Sedalia, Mo., July 17th, 1882.
My dear Frank:
 I have just this
moment got back to find your
letter of June 28th, and your dispatch.
 Things are working as fast as they
can. There has been so much hell
lately all along the line about
the Governor that matters had to
wait. Be perfectly quiet. There is
nobody particularly anxious to
find you, although the sooner we
can settle this thing the better.
 You will hear from me again in
a couple of days—just so soon as
I can take my bearings.
 I write to your wife to-day for
the word that represents $100 in your
dispatch. I do not blame you in
the least for taking every imaginable

J. N. Edwards' letters to Frank James prior to Frank's trial.

~~You were to foolish~~
do otherwise.

enclose you a letter from your
wife, which explains itself. I ~~know~~
that they are anxious to ~~withdraw~~
the reward.

~~You, ~~yes~~, ~~I am ni~~~~ like~~ ~~to once was~~
~~with the ~~Governor~~ ~~that~~ ~~poor~~ ~~fool~~
~~was~~ murdered. ~~I denounced~~ ~~the~~
whole infamous piece of ~~business~~
in a ~~manner~~ that made a powerful
stir, and ~~I kept it up.~~ The ~~work~~
now going on in your behalf
is being done by others. They only
~~consult~~ me as your friend, and ~~as~~
one in whom ~~they~~ suppose you
~~have~~ perfect confidence, knowing that I do not understand the
meaning of the word betrayal.

You will hear again in a couple
of days.

         Your friend, as ever
           J. K. Edward

Sedalia, Mo., August 1st, 1882.

My Dear Frank:

I have just returned home from the Indian Territory to find your letters. Do not make a move until you hear from me again. I have been to the Governor myself, and things are working. Lie quiet and make no stir.

The word you wanted is <u>Eole</u>.

Your friend forever,

J. N. Edwards

Aug. 14th, 1885.

My dear Frank:

Just as I was getting on the train this morning for this place, your letter was brought me. I expect to answer it from St. Joseph, and so I do from here.

Go! if you want to, by all means. You have as much of a Confederate soldier as I was, and as good as the best. Only be dignified and circumspect, and avoid all display. Especially take no part at the fair in the matter of conspicuity at the races.

Remember me most truly to your mother and your wife.

Your friend ever,
J. N. Edwards

CHAPTER XLVI.

MISCELLANY.

The Post Mortem—Total Amount of Robberies—Ford's Anecdote—Massengale's Story—Jesse James' Horses—Hunting a Union Man.

THE POST MORTEM.

QUITE a sensation was caused in St. Joseph by the report that Dr. Catlett, superintendent of the lunatic asylum at St. Joseph, and Coroner Heddens had, during Monday night succeeding the killing, made a post mortem examination of the remains of the dead man, and ascertained much of interest. The fact had been kept a secret for some time, but Dr. Catlett admitted that the rumor was true, and that such an examination had been made.

In reply to various questions the doctor answered about as follows;

"In the first place we found that the reports about the shooting were all wrong. The bullet, which killed the man, did not go clear through the head.

"The boys must have clubbed the man with their revolvers, after the ball went into his head, for that cut on the side of his head was made with the trigger of a revolver and not by a bullet.

"All the officers thought the bullet must have gone clear through his head into the wall or ceiling of the room.

"It never went there at all, and they need not look for it. We have it all safe and sound, and took it out of his head. I will tell you now how it was. When Jesse James was shot, he was only partially turned away from the boys, and the ball went in sideways, at one side of the head, back of the right ear, and then lodged just under the skin behind the left, and that is where we found it.

"The skull was badly shattered: more so than any I have seen for years. It was all torn to pieces, the bullet passing through the brain.

"The brain was a most remarkable one, and showed the great will power, earnestness and determination of the man. It also showed thought and courage, and in most men would have accomplished wonderful things.

"It was once claimed by a man named Shepherd that he shot Jesse in the back of the head, and that when killed or captured the wound would show.

"There was not a wound of any kind on the back of the head, except that made by the bullet which killed the man; all reports to the contrary are false."

This confirms our statement in regard to the romance of that imaginative gentleman, Mr. George Shepherd, about the alleged shooting of Jesse in the back of the head. But hold up your head, George! "a harmless lie breaks no bones," say the Spaniards, and far worse men, than you, are toadied to and can write "Honorable" and "Governor" before their names. Your warm fancy and vivid imagination may have caused you to fancy myths and wondrous things, but your bitterest enemy can never call you assassin;—your foes, at least, have all been shot in front!

TOTAL AMOUNT OF ROBBERIES.

The amount of money obtained by the various railway, bank and stage robberies, as far as they can be ascertained. are as follows:

Liberty, Mo., Jan. 20, 1866	$ 72,000
Richmond, Mo., 1867	4,000
Russellville, Ky., March 20, 1868	14,000
Gallatin, Mo., December 7, 1869	700
Corydon, Iowa, June 3, 1871	4,000
Columbia, Ky., April 29, 1872	600
Kansas City Fair, Sept. 26, 1872	978

Ste. Genevieve, Mo., May 27, 1873.................. 3,500
Iowa Train Robbery, July 21, 1873.................. 2,500
Hot Springs Stage, Jan. 15, 1874...................... 2,000
Gads Hill, Mo., Jan. 31, 1874 5,000
Corinth, Miss. 10,000
Muncie, Kas. 30,000
Huntington, W. Va., September, 1875................ 10,000
Baxter Springs, Kas., April 18, 1876.................. 3,000
Otterville, Mo., July 7, 1876....................... 15,000
Northfield, Minn., Sept. 7, 1876...................... .....
Big Springs, Wy. T., Sept. 18, 1877.................... 60,000
Glendale, Mo., Oct. 8, 1879...................... 6,000
Winston, Mo., July 15, 1881...................... 4,000
Blue Cut, Sept. 7, 1881............................ 16,000
                    Total................................... $263,278

FORD'S ANECDOTE.

While in the St. Joe jail the Ford boys related several stories of Jesse James, for whose murder they were incarcerated.

Bob says when he was at Kansas City he slept with Marshal Craig, and that they got their drawers changed. On them were the initials "H. C." One day Jesse noticed them on the bed after having been washed, and his eyes were clapped upon the initials like a flash. "What does that mean?" he said in an awfully suspicious tone. Bob says he began to feel terribly anxious, for he thought Jesse had unmasked him and that there would be a dead man there soon. He gave Jesse some trivial answer and Jesse then dropped the drawers and said no more. The only thing that prevented a tragedy is the fact, Bob says, that Jesse did not know the initials of Marshal Craig, or had at least forgotten them. "Had he tumbled to the fact," Bob said, "it's doubtful whether I would be here now."

MASSENGALE'S STORY.

Mr. Geo. Massengale, of Massengale Bros., commission merchants, relates an interesting experience with Jesse James. Mr. Massengale was with the firm of O. F. Noel & Co., Edington, Tenn., and among others transacted business several times with a man known as J. D. Howard. Among other trades was a sale of 200 barrels of flour to Howard, who shipped it to Nashville on spec-

ulation. Mr. Massengale became quite well acquainted with Howard, who would occasionally come into Noel & Co.'s place of business on business or for a friendly talk. One day Howard happened
to be there when a farmer, known as a desperate character in that
country, came in to settle for some wheat he had sold. There was
some trouble in fixing the price, Mr. Massengale claiming that the
grain was not up to the grade he had bought it for, and the farmer
determined to accept only the price he had sold the wheat at on
his statement of its quality. The farmer acted in a rather suspicious
manner as the argument became warm, sidling up towards Mr. M.
and walking around in an excited manner, and finally Mr.
Massengale noticed Howard walk to the fireplace, pick up a heavy
poker standing in the corner and place himself near him. Finally the
farmer left; Howard then turned to Mr. M. and asked: "Did you
notice that fellow, what he was doing?" Upon Mr. Massengale
replying that he had not noticed anything except the fellow's anger,
Howard then stated that he saw the farmer draw a knife, open
the blade and conceal the weapon in his sleeve. "Then," said Howard, "I picked up that poker, and if he had made a move toward
you I would have broken his arm for him." Reading the interview
with Mrs. James in a morning paper, and noticing what she said
about a purchase of flour from Noel & Co., of Edginton, Tenn., it
immediately flashed upon Mr. Massengale that Jesse James and
Howard were one and the same individual, and one whom he had
always considered a friend, if not a preserver of his life, for there
is no doubt in Mr. Massengale's mind but that the farmer would
have used his knife upon him had not Jesse James been present.
This experience of Mr. Massengale's corroborates a part at least
of Mrs. James' statement as it appears in this morning's papers.

JESSE JAMES' HORSES.

The horses found in Jesse James' stable at the time of his death
were not his horses, but were horses stolen by the Fords and brought
there. Jesse's horses were in the stable of his mother in Clay county,
and they disappeared from there the night of the 4th of April, the

day succeeding the one on which Jesse was killed. They were removed by Frank James, for purposes that can readily be conceived.

HUNTING A UNION MAN.

A gentleman who formerly resided at Rocheport, Mo., gives the following incident. There is no doubt of its authenticity:

A neighbor boy of mine, Allen Bysfield, who had espoused the Union cause and who was stationed at Fayette, Howard county, paid a visit to his mother. By some means his presence in town was made known to the guerrillas and a search made for him. It was fruitless however, during the day, and I had gone to bed congratulating myself on Allen's escape. About midnight I was awakened, and on going to the door found Jesse James, John Hubbard and John Van Meter, who demanded of me the oars to a small boat I had, the oars being at home for safe-keeping. It at once flashed through my mind that young Bysfield had succeeded in crossing the river and that the party had determined to follow him to the death. I asked and received permission to go with them, and we were soon in Cooper county. The young man was found lying asleep in an old shanty and captured without difficulty. It was determined to kill him by cutting his throat and Jesse was chosen as executioner. If ever I pleaded for anything I did for that young man's life. For awhile I was without hope, but when I spoke of the boy's mother and his desire to see her, which had led him to brave all danger, Jesse laughed and said:

"D—n a man that wouldn't go through h—l to see his mother. Good bye, pard, you can go. If you can do this boy a good turn, do it; come on, let's go back." The river was crossed in silence, and as the good angel had possession of Jesse that night, he looked every inch a noble man, although but a boy in years himself.

CHAPTER XLVII.

MISCELLANY — CONTINUED.

Jesse's Boldness—George T. Hite's Anecdote—Daring Escapes—The Centralia Massacre—Oath of Allegiance—Dick Little's Anecdote—Cowardly Attack on a Steamer—Jesse's Musical Talent—The Escort—What Major Edwards Says—The Spoils Found—The Auction—John T. Samuel—An Error—Names for His Pets—Wild Bill Bluffed—Providential Interference —Jesse's Present to Ford—What Mrs. James Says—A Brother-in-Law— Cole Younger Talks—Was Frank James There?—The James Brothers Contrasted.

JESSE'S BOLDNESS.

THE same informant says:

The first I saw of Jesse James since the war was at Jefferson City, during the time the bill in his and Frank's behalf was trying to be put through the Legislature. I was at the Madison House one night when a prominent newspaper man of the State asked me to take a walk with him, and on going to a house, we were admitted to a room in which was Jesse James, a State Senator, two Representatives, and another prominent newspaper man. The amnesty bill had failed to pass, and I saw no more of Jesse until a few years ago, when I met him at the Laclede Hotel, St. Louis.

Last October I was walking up Twelfth street, Kansas City, and on the corner of Oak I met the redoubtable Jesse himself. He was not disguised at all. We walked together down Twelfth street to Main, passing on the corner of Grand avenue Officers Crabtree and Nichols. Hailing a hack, we entered it, and proceeded to take in the town.

"Let's go to George Gaston's."

"Do you know him?" I inquired.

"No, I do not; but I have heard he has expressed a desire to see me, and I want to gratify him."

I began to feel a little ticklish, and asked him if he intended to make himself known, and breathed easier when he said he did not. We stopped at Gaston's, but the Colonel wasn't there. Jesse took lemonade.

From Gaston's we went to the Coliseum, took a private box, and remained during the first part of the performance. As Jesse set up the beer pretty frequently, he was, for the time being, the favorite of the girls. Leaving the theatre, we went to a house on Third street. As we went in, Jesse's hat, a sombrero, attracted the attention of some young Hebrew bloods, one of whom was playing the piano.

"Gentlemen, this is Jesse James in disguise," said one of the girls.

He acknowledged the introduction, and the young man playing the piano struck up the following doggerel improvisation:

> "If Jesse James was here,
> And wouldn't treat to beer,
> He'd walk off on his ear—
>   Baby mine,"

Jesse's face flushed with anger, and I expected to see the house transformed into a hospital, but he good-humoredly set 'em up to the boys. Had the bloods known it was Jesse, they would have been running yet.

While in the carriage I alluded to the danger he ran in living in a city. His reply was that he had found that the safest place to hide was in a city.

"Why, these d—d detectives never catch a man unless he makes a bummer of himself, and it's devilish little that I drink. Besides, no man will ever get the drop on me unless he is a Missourian, for I don't trust any one else, and then they'll have to shoot from behind."

His words have proven prophetic.

We parted company at the corner of Sixteenth and Grand avenue, both taking cigars at the Topeka Exchange saloon. I saw no more of him until I saw him a corpse at St. Joseph, having gone there to satisfy myself of his identity. It was he beyond the question of a doubt.

There was nothing chivalrous in Jesse's nature. He lived for himself alone. Devoid of education, he had managed to become thoroughly posted on the affairs of the day. Licentious and cruel, yet there was something in his nature that led him to respect good women, and form liaisons with hundreds of others who were not pure. A natural child of his, a girl, about 16 years of age, is now living in Howard county, this State. She is the daughter of a fascinating grass-widow of Salt Creek bottom. Frank James has also an illegitimate boy, 16 years of age. The boy and his mother are now living in West Kansas. The country is well rid of Jesse, but having saved my life and spared a life for me, I was under eternal obligations to him, and am glad to say his trust was never betrayed. Dick Little and the Ford boys I do not know, and am not sorry. What I have written may or may not prove satisfactory, but it is the truth unembellished. Let those deny who can.

GEORGE T. HITE'S ANECDOTES.

Geor. T. Hite, a brother of Woot Hite, now lives at Adairville, Ky. An interviewer asked him:

"You knew Jesse James well?"

"Oh, yes; much better than I did Frank. He always stopped at my house until I moved over to father's, and then he came there, because he had no where else to go. He told very few about where he came from or where he was going. He used to tell me nearly everything."

"Are you positive he's dead?"

"At first I didn't believe it, but I got a letter from Kansas City that convinced me he was dead. I could hardly believe he would trust a boy like Ford and let him know where he lived. It was a cowardly act."

"Was Jesse a brave man?"

"He didn't fear anything. He has said to me often: 'If you hear they've captured me alive, say it's a lie; they may kill me, but they will never get me otherwise.'"

"When were any of the party at your father's house?"

"Jesse, Frank and Dick Little were there a year ago this month for about two weeks."

"When did they first commence coming there?"

"About 1865, and some of them have been here nearly every year since."

"Who robbed the stage coming from Mammoth Cave?"

"Why, Jesse and Bill Ryan did. They came and stopped at my house afterward. I don't know where they were before. Ryan told me that they made a negro preacher, who was on the stage, drink some whisky with them. They always talked about their robberies, and used to laugh considerable over them."

"I suppose Jesse and his gang were engaged in hundreds of robberies that they were never charged with?"

"I can't tell any names; but they were sure enough robbers, you know, and they did a good deal of devilment that they never got credit for. I wouldn't mind telling, but Jesse's wife is living and I wouldn't say anything to hurt her feelings."

"Jesse was a pretty honorable fellow, wasn't he?"

"Yes, he was. He wanted to quit the business, but he said he had to make a living, and as the whole world seemed to be pitted against him, and he couldn't do anything else, he kept on with it. He used to tell me if some fellow—I can't think of his name—was made Governor of Missouri, he'd pardon him out, and then he'd be happy. 'They wouldn't let me stay at home, and what else can I do?' He went to Chicago once to kill Allan Pinkerton, and staid there four months, but he never had a chance to do it like he wanted to. That was after the Pinkertons made a raid on his mother's home, blew her arm off, and killed his step-brother. He said he could have killed the younger one, but he didn't care to do it. 'I want him to know who did it,' he said; 'it would do me no good if I couldn't tell him about it before he died. I had a dozen chances to shoot him when he didn't know it. I wanted to give him a fair chance, but the opportunity never came.' He left Chicago without doing it, but I have heard him say often, 'I know God will some day deliver Allan Pinkerton into my hands.' "

"Will Frank settle down now?"

"I think he will. I believe Jim Cummings and Frank James are the only ones not dead or in prison. Frank is a fine business man and can make a living at anything."

In answer to a number of questions, Mr. Hite said: "I don't think Jesse was in the Russellville bank robbery; he was sick at the time at our house. I saw Frank last spring, the first time since 1868. Jesse's wife has been here only once since they were married. I think the rule was to kill any one who gave them away."

"Jesse has been in Adairville often?"

"Frequently at night. I remember one night he came here, and as we passed a store over there on the other side of the square one of those Nashville detectives was sitting inside, and Jesse saw him. He said, 'I could kill him now, and nobody would ever know who did it; but that ain't my business except they crowd me,' and he passed on without doing anything."

"Did Jesse love his wife?" asked the reporter, as a closing question.

"Yes, I believe he did."

DARING ESCAPES.

Stilson Hutchins, of Washington, D.C., formerly a St. Louis editor, is credited by some correspondent with the two following anecdotes. The last is certainly a mistake and most likely the first also:

In one of the last years of the war Jesse was captured at a Mississippi River town and put on board a steamer to be taken to Memphis. Even then he was known to be a desperate man, and to prevent any attempt at escape or suicide he was handcuffed to a Federal soldier — one of his guard — and confined to the lower deck. It was a desperate case and required heroic treatment. About midnight he struck his captive companion a stunning blow on the head, which killed him instantly, and without sound or alarm deliberately cut off the arm of the dead man to which he was hand-cuffed, jumped into the river and swam ashore. I am not sure about my dates, but this story and the one which follows I know to be in everything but mere detail, true.

Before his name had become the terror of the State of Missouri he was supposed, with his brother and the Younger gang, to have committed a daring bank robbery and murder at a small town in the northern part of the State, and Pinkerton put one of his shrewd-est and bravest detectives on his track. James was shadowed suc-cessfully, and was at last overhauled at Hannibal, a town ninety miles or more above St. Louis, on the river. The detective knew his man, and resolved to take no chances. He waited until he found him seated in a barber's chair, his face covered with lather, and his deadly hands folded in his lap. The pursuer pushed open the door of the shop, quietly drew his "navy" to a dead cover and announced that if he moved he would be shot dead. James attempt-ed to jump to his feet, but the handles of his heavy navy revolvers fell over on either side, and in coming in contact with the arms of the chair, fairly pinned him to it. As he rose the detective fired, and the ball went crashing through his mouth, taking two or three teeth along with it, and glancing, passed out of his neck. A faint conception of his splendid courage and presence of mind can be got from what he did. Disengaging both pistols from the chair, he drew one in less time than it requires to record it, and shot the detective dead, rushed from the room and made his way out of the town to a safe covert, with a wound, which would have de-prived ninety-nine men out of a hundred of their senses.

THE CENTRALIA MASSACRE.

The following anecdote is contributed by one who pretends, and probably justly, to have been there:

The history of the massacre at Centralia, of which I was an eye-witness (in which Jesse James made himself more notorious than ever) has been so often recounted that I will pass it by, merely correcting a few errors and relating an incident that closely followed. The soldiers taken from the train were not killed by Anderson

alone, but they were stood in line and shot down by a volley fired
by at least fifty men. The other soldiers under the command of
Major Johnson were scattered and the guerrillas rode them down;
shooting them down like dogs, Jesse James killing one man within
two miles of Sturgeon. Not a guerrilla was killed, and one only
wounded. The next day Anderson and his band were in Rocheport,
and Jesse James was at a private house visiting some young
ladies. A high spirited Southern girl now married to an ex-confed-
erate officer and living in Fayette, Howard county, was then the
object of Jesse's attention, and he, as usual, was boasting of his
prowess. Leaving the house for a few minutes, he returned with
the throat latch of his bridle, on which was strung seventeen gory
scalps. He exhibited them to the young ladies, thinking, no doubt,
to surprise them but he was the worst surprised of the party. Miss
K——, rising to her feet, said:

"Mr. James, I have two brothers in the confederate service, and
am a Southern woman. Captain Anderson or any of his men, who
are men, are always welcome to my house, but I will not entertain brutes. You can go!" When Jesse reached the sidewalk he
pulled off his hat, swung it around his head, threw it up in the air,
shot a couple of holes through it, and yelled: "Hurrah for Bill Anderson's horse thieves." This seemed to quiet his nerves, and mounting his horse he rode away. Jesse threw away his scalps, however, and was never known to scalp another man during the war.

OATH OF ALLEGIANCE.

As a reminiscence of the now far-away war times, we give here
the "oath of allegiance" that men, women and children were often
forced to take during those times that tried men's souls.

Twenty-one years ago Lieutenant-Colonel William R. Penick
captured Frank James in Clay county. Mrs. Samuel appealed to
him for the release of her son, which was granted on his taking
the oath of allegiance, which is still in possession of Colonel Penick.
It reads as follows:

"I, Franklin James, of Greenville, County of Clay, State of Missouri, do solemnly swear that I will support, protect and defend

the constitution and government of the United States against all enemies, whether domestic or foreign, that I will bear true faith, allegiance and loyalty to the same, any ordinance, resolution, or law of any state or legislature to the contrary notwithstanding; and, further, that I will faithfully perform all the duties which may be required of me by the laws of the United States. And I take this oath freely and voluntarily, without any mental reservation or evasion whatever, with a full and clear understanding that death or other punishment by the judgment of a military commission will be the penalty for the violation of this, my solemn oath and parole of honor.

FRANKLIN JAMES, [L. S.]

"Certificate: Subscribed and sworn to before me, April 26, 1862.

"W. R. PENICK,

"Lieutenant Colonel Ninth battalion cavalry M. S. M., Liberty, Missouri.

"Witness: L. W. Densmore, St. Joseph P. O., Buchanan county, Missouri."

Frank was then released, but the new colonel who succeeded Penick made it hot for the Jameses, and Frank and Jesse were both soon with Quantrell.

DICK LITTLE'S ANECDOTE.

Dick Little was asked by a reporter if Jesse James was a brave man.

"No," said this constitutional liar promptly, "he is not: why I saw a fellow take a little revolver and run him out of the road into the woods."

To Mattie Collins, Little told this tale in a different way when he first related it, before he and his leader had quarreled. He then said that they were riding along the road in Tennessee one day and overtook two finely mounted men. On passing them Jesse thought they must be detectives, and as he was riding in advance of Little he turned to him and gave him the wink to cover them with his revolver. The suspicious strangers drew their revolvers, noticing Jesse's sign, and began firing upon him and Little. The latter exhibiting a great deal of fear, Jesse shouted to him:

"Ride around me, ride around me."

This he did in order to get between Little and danger, and so that he could get a chance to use his revolver without the possibility of hurting Little, who was between him and the strangers. Little promptly spurred out of danger, and when Jesse drew his revolver the strangers turned and fled. Jesse then put up his pistol, but Dick Little pursued them, and it is said wounded one of them.

CAVALRY ATTACK ON A STEAMER.

A gentleman now residing in Kansas City, but who was a resident in 1864 of Rocheport, in Boone county, Missouri, vouches for the following anecdotes.

Rocheport was Bill Anderson's headquarters. One day when the band was in town a steamboat rounded the bend, going down the Missouri river, and was fired into by the guerrillas. A company of United States troops, armed with long range rifles, made it rather unpleasant for the long-haired gentlemen, who found it convenient to seek shelter behind buildings, with the exception of Jesse James and Hedge Reynolds, who, under a murderous fire from the troops on board, followed the boat for a mile down the river, and Jesse, with a carbine, succeeded in killing the captain of the troops, he having thoughtlessly exposed himself to his unerring aim. Shortly after the skirmish Anderson formed his men into line, and sitting on their horses in front of the Bailey House, they sang Quantrell's call, a favorite song of the freebooters, the first stanza of which is as follows:

> "Up, comrades, up, the moon's in the west,
>   And we must be gone ere the dawning of day;
> The hounds of old Penick will find out our nest,
>   But the Quantrell they seek shall be far, far away."

Hedge Reynolds, who is mentioned here, is an old and intimate friend of the writer. He is a brave, generous gentleman. I know not where he may now be, but no truer, gamer man ever lived than Hedge Reynolds.

JESSE'S MUSICAL TALENT.

The above song was an especial favorite of Jesse's, and as he was intensely emotional in his nature, he could sing it with as much gusto as he could cut a throat. Another favorite song of his was "Am I a Soldier of the Cross?" Strange as it may appear, Jesse believed in a God, and it is said he once put daylight through a companion's liver for doubting the existence of a hell. I will not vouch for the story.

To resume: Anderson had not been out of town more than an hour before Bill Stuart, Jim Carter and Jesse returned, and going into Harris & Hubbard's dry goods store, ordered the clerk to open the safe. About $30 was all that was secured. Stepping out of the door Jesse confronted a negro who was passing and ordered him to dance. The darkey's steps were accelerated somewhat by Stuart and Carter seeing how close they could shoot to his feet without hitting them.

When the dance was over, Jesse with characteristic generosity —with other people's money— presented the negro with the $30, cracked him over the head with his revolver as a gentle reminder of how good he had been to him, jumped on his horse and went yelling out of town.

THE ESCORT.

Jesse, among other accomplishments, could lay claim to being a good billiard player, and some of his evenings were spent in a saloon at South St. Joseph, where he could indulge his passion for the game with a number of young men whom he met. One dark night a young man said:

"Mr. Howard, I don't like the idea much of going home to-night. It is dark, and a man may be held up."

"Where do you live?" asked the pseudo Mr. Howard.

"On the hill," was the reply.

"I'll see you home," said Jesse, "and nobody shall lay a hand on you while I am with you."

He kept his word. They went home together. The bare recollection, though, always produces a cold sweat on the young man's person.

WHAT MAJOR EDWARDS SAYS.

Maj. Jno. N. Edwards, editor of the Sedalia *Democrat,* is a brave, noble gentleman, who hates anything low and mean. He says of this killing, under the heading, "The Murder of Jesse James:"

Not one among the hired cowards, hard on the hunt for blood money, dared face this wonderful outlaw until he had disarmed himself and turned his back to his assassins—that first and only time in his career, which has passed from the realms of an almost fabulous romance into that of history. We called him outlaw, and he was, but fate made him so. When the war closed Jesse James had no home. Proscribed, hunted, shot at, driven away from among his people, a price put upon his head, what else could the man do, with such a nature, except what he did do? He had to live. It was his country. The graves of his kindred were there. He refused to be banished from his birthright, and when he was hunted, he turned savagely about and hunted his hunters. Would to God he were alive to-day to make a righteous butchery of a few more of them. There never was a more cowardly and unnecessary murder committed in all American history, than this murder of Jesse James. It was done for money. It was done that a few men might get all the money. He had been living at St. Joseph for months. The Fords were with him. He was in the toils, for they meant to betray him. He was in the heart of a large city. One word would have summoned 500 men for his capture or extermination. Not a single one of the attacking party need to have been hurt. If, when his house had been surrounded, he refused to surrender, he could have been killed on the inside of it and at long range.

The chances for him to escape were as one to ten thousand, and not even that. But it was never intended that he should be captured. It was his blood that the bloody wretches were after—blood that would bring money in the official market of Missouri; and this great Commonwealth leagued itself with a lot of self-confessed robbers, highwaymen and prostitutes to have one of its citizens assassinated before it was positively known that he had ever committed a single crime worthy of death. Of course everything that can be said about the dead man to justify the manner of his killing will be said, but who is saying it? Those with the blood of Jesse James on their guilty souls. Those who wanted the reward and would invent any lie or concoct any diabolical story to get it. They have succeeded, but such a cry of horror and indignation at the infernal deed is even now thundering over the land, that if a single one of the miserable assassins had either manhood, conscience or courage, he would go as another Judas and hang himself. But so sure as God reigns, there never was a dollar of blood money obtained yet which did not bring with it perdition. Sooner or later there comes a day of vengeance. Some among the murderers are mere beasts of prey. These, of course, can only suffer through hunger, or cold, or thirst; but whatever they dread most, that thing will happen.

Others, again, among the murderers are sanctimonious devils, who plead the honor of the State, the value of law and order, the splendid courage required to shoot an unarmed man in the back of the head, and these will be stripped to their skin of all their pretensions and made to shiver and freeze, splotched as they are and spotted and piebald with blood, in the pitiless storm of public contempt and condemnation. This, to the leaders, will be worse than death.

Nor is the end yet. If Jesse James had been hunted down as any other criminal and killed while trying to escape, or in resisting arrest, not a word would have been said to the contrary. He had sinned and he had suffered. In his death the majesty of the law would have been vindicated, but here the law itself becomes a murderer. It leagues with murderers. It hires murderers. It aids and abets murderers. It borrows money to pay and reward murderers. It promises immunity and protection to murderers. It is itself a murder, the most abject, the most infamous and the most cowardly ever known to history; therefore, this so-called law is an outlaw; and these so-called executioners of the law are outlaws.

Therefore, let Jesse James' comrades, and he has a few remaining worth all the Fords and Littles that can be packed together between St. Louis and St. Joseph, do unto them as they did unto him. Yes, the end is not yet, nor should it be. The man had no trial. What right had any officer of this State to put a price upon his head and hire a band of cut-throats and highwaymen to murder him for money? Anything can be told of men. The whole land is filled with liars, robbers and assassins. Murder is easy. For $100 nothing is safe that is pure or unsuspecting or just, but it is not to be supposed that the law will become an ally and a co-worker in this sort of civilization. Jesse James has been murdered.

1. Because an immense price had been set upon his head, and there is not a low-lived scoundrel today in Missouri, who wouldn't kill his own father for money; and

2. Because he was made the scapegoat of every train-robber, footpad and highwayman between Iowa and Texas. Worse men a thousand times than the dead man have been hired to do this thing. The very character of the instruments chosen shows the infamous nature of the work required. The hand that slew him had to be a traitor's. Into all the warp and woof of this devil's work there were threads woven by the fingers of a harlot.

What a spectacle! Missouri, with splendid companies, regiments of militia; Missouri, with 117 sheriffs, as brave and as efficient on the average as any men on earth; Missouri, with a watchful and vigilant marshal in every one of her principal towns and cities; Missouri, with every screw and cog and crank and lever and wheel of her administrative machinery in perfect working order; Missouri, boasting of law, order, progress and development, had yet to surrender all of these in the face of a single man— a hunted, lied upon, proscribed and outlawed man—trapped and located in the midst of thirty-four thousand people, and ally with some five or six cut-throats and prostitutes, that the "majesty of the law might be vindicated and the good name of the State saved from all further reproach." "Saved!" Why, the whole State reeks to-day with a double orgie—that of lust and that of murder. What the men failed to do the women accomplished. Tear the two bears from the flag of Missouri; put thereon in place of them, as more appropriate, a thief blowing out the brains of an unarmed victim, and a brazen harlot naked to the waist and splashed to the brows in blood.

THE SPOILS FOUND.

The property found at the house of Jesse James after the assassination, still remains in possession of Marshal Craig. It consists of an 18 karat gold watch, stem-winder, with hunting case; made by Charles J. E. Jaeat; case No. 8289; movement No. 8389; a monogram on the case, "T. A. B."[1] a heavy 18 karat gold chain is attached. This watch is supposed to have been taken from the Governor of Arizona, at the Hot Springs stage robbery of seven years ago. The other watch was made by Apleton Tracy, Waltham, Massachusetts, movement No. 546895. The case is stamped William Kendrick, Louisville, Kentucky. It is an 18 karat gold hunting case, numbered 48006. It is supposed to have been taken from Lawyer Roundtree, of Lebanon, Kentucky, together with a diamond ring belonging to Mr. Roundtree's daughter. The other effects consist of a number of fire arms, which would bring fabulous prices at the present time as relics. The Marshal will hold them until the rights of property are determined, and then turn them over to their legal custodians.

THE AUCTION.

The personal effects of Jesse James, the dead outlaw, were sold on Monday afternoon at the old home in St. Joe. A very large crowd of people assembled on the grounds, and when the auctioneer began, the bidding was decidedly lively. About ten dollars worth of old rubbish brought nearly two hundred dollars. The chair on which he was standing and the duster he was using in brushing off the pictures at the moment he was shot brought five dollars each.

JOHN T. SAMUEL.

As a proof of how bitter a prejudice may become against all of the members of a family through the sins of a few, we need only take as an illustration the young man whose name appears at the

[1] Probably this was the watch which John A. Burbank, Richmond, Ind., claimed was stolen from him during the Hot Springs stage robbery of 1874.

head of this article. He is a man, or youth rather, just coming into his twenty-first year, and has been lying for nearly six months desperately wounded. Had he not belonged to the James family, the offense for which he lies wounded unto death would have been passed by unnoticed as the harmless escapade of a boy.

Last December he went with one or two companions to a dance or party at a house a few miles from his home. Here he, as did many other of the wild, thoughtless young fellows, who had gathered there, began to drink, and as a natural consequence all of them became noisy, but not boisterously so.

The owner of the house, a bitter enemy of the Jameses, was disposed to overlook the noise of all of the others, but insisted that young Samuel should go out of the house. At first he refused, but at last concluded to go, and in passing out of the door with some of his companions a chair was overturned. Not taking time to replace it, young Samuel had got outside of the yard and into the middle of the road. Stopping here, he said to his friends: "Well, boys, I guess we've got a right to stay out here and dance if we want to."

Hearing this, the party in the house ordered them to leave. Samuel said that he would not do so; that the road most certainly didn't belong to them, or any one else, and he'd stay there just as long as he wanted to.

Being unarmed, and not anticipating the least trouble, he and his friends were surprised to see two or three men rush to the fence and fire. Samuel fell to the ground, shot through and through, and when taken home was not expected to live twenty-four hours. The sole reason of his punishment was the fact that he was a half brother of the James boys.

Ever since early in December he has been lying in one room, and in all that time has been able to sit up but once, and that for but a few minutes. He bears his sufferings with a patience that challenges sympathy and pity. It would be a hard heart indeed that could look unmoved upon this poor boy expiating the sin of relationship to the dreaded bandit.

His face is one of the most remarkable that I have ever seen. His forehead is high and noble, his auburn hair lying about it in graceful waves. His complexion is as pure as any girl's; his eyes large, deep blue and liquid. His almost effeminate mouth is lightly shaded with a small moustache, and that and his beard are of the hue and growth that the old masters delight to give to their heads of the Savior of mankind.

Of all the faces of men that I have ever seen, whether real or ideal; whether human or on canvass, none other have ever had one half of the almost divine beauty of the face of the bandits' half brother. Transferred to canvass, with its patient, pleading look; its gentle sorrow and its almost girlish innocence of seeming, it would present a poet's ideal of the calm, benignant face of Him who died on Calvary nearly two thousand years ago; of Him who could forgive, even in his death agony, the wretches who had crucified him.

Wasted with his long suffering, it seems almost an impossibility that he can ever recover, and at best it can only be a short time until he must enter the dark valley of the shadow of death, and pass out into the dim realms of eternity. There he can hope to find a pity that opens to every bleeding heart, to every wounded soul, a balm beyond all price, if only it will be accepted ere it is too late.

To his murderer I could wish no more of agony or despair than to have him haunted by the sad, sorrowing look of those mournful eyes, and the knowledge that in his brutal rage he had inflicted upon the poor boy that wound that has chained him to a bed of suffering until death shall come to his relief. It will be many and many a day before the memory of that face with its wonderful eyes and its almost supernatural beauty will fade from my memory.

AN ERROR.

In the account of the hanging of Dr. Samuel at the first visit of the militia, Mrs. Samuel and the Doctor inform me that there is a slight error in the account, they having omitted to give the sequel to me on my first visit. The true account is this: After Mrs. Samuel had cut him down, taken him to the house and nursed him back to life, they returned from a search around the farm after Frank and took him with them towards the heavy timber between the house and the town. Here she heard them shouting and laughing, and in about half an hour one of them rode back and told her that they had hung the d—d old rebel sure this time, and that if she or any of the family dared to go near him that they would come back, burn the house, and kill every member of the family. With this he rode off in the direction of the timber again. For three days none of the family knew but that the Doctor was hanging in the woods, but at last a passing negro, who knew them, and who had been at Liberty, stopped at her house and told her he had seen the Doctor in prison at Liberty. Thus did these brutal fiends in human shape torture in body and in mind any who might fall into their power.

NAMES FOR HIS PETS.

Fronting this chapter is an engraving of the armory of Jesse James. It consisted, as will be seen, of four revolvers, a breech-loading double barrel gun, and a repeating rifle. The center-piece is one-half of the bomb-shell thrown into the Samuel's house by Pinkerton's detectives, and by which Mrs. Samuel lost her right arm and little Archie Samuel his life. This monument of detective barbarity, and of the most flagrant outrage of the century, is now in possession of J. H. Chambers, Publisher, of St. Louis, being sent to him by Mrs. Zerelda Samuel, mother of the James boys.

For each of his fire-arms Jesse James had pet names, and he would take them in his lap, so his wife informs us, and fondle them as a mother would her children. One of the revolvers he called "Pet;" another, "Baby;" another, "Daisy;" and the fourth, "Beauty."

The rifle he called "Old Faithful," and the double barrel gun was christened "Big Thunder."

The engraving gives a correct representation of these arms. On these pistols and guns he lavished a great deal of tender care, and seemed to regard them as if they were living beings. "Ah, old girl," he would say, "how often you've saved me." "Good little Baby, you sweet little thing you." "You are my best friend," etc., etc.

The piece of the shell represented here is of wrought steel; the other half was of cast iron, which blew to pieces. The whole shell was filled with scrap-iron, balls, etc., and it is a wonder that every one in the room was not instantly killed.

"WILD BILL" BLUFFED.

William Hickock, or, as he was more generally known, "Wild Bill," was in Texas once on some business connected with his government employment. While here Bill was for a time quite cautious. He recognized the fact that nearly every other man in this State was a "gun fighter," while up in Kansas he could bully almost any man he met. Bill was a "killer," but he was one of those cold blooded murderers, who gave his enemy no show, but "got the drop" and shot him without mercy. When his enemy was a quick, active, fighting man, not easily taken by surprise, Bill always "took water," as witness his encounter with Bill Thompson at Ellsworth, Kansas. As above stated Bill had been very quiet and orderly, and kept so until he was ready to leave the town. Having taken a few drinks, he thought he would risk a little bluster and bravado, and seeing a quiet looking man standing near him he drew his revolver, fired at a small tree about fifty yards off and put a bullet in the center of it.

"By G—!" he almost howled, "I could just cut a fellow's hair to-day without touching his head," and he looked significantly at the quiet man. The latter threw both hands to his sides, drew his pistols, straightened out both arms, his revolvers going off simultaneously, and two balls were planted, one above the other, below "Wild Bill's." As he replaced his pistols he quietly said: "Just open up your barber shop as soon as you like." Bill saw that he was no match for the quiet man, who was no other than Jesse James, so he very prudently delayed his tonsorial efforts until some more opportune time, and left the town.[2]

PROVIDENTIAL INTERFERENCE.

Mrs. Samuel being questioned by Marshal [James] Liggett of Kansas City as to the presence of her boys at Northfield, said

[2] Again Triplett is probably inventing events in the life of Hickok. See Chapter XXXIII, note 1.

that Frank had told her to tell every one, who enquired about the matter, to explain, if they had been there, how it was that they got away; was it by their own smartness, or by providential interference? She clearly attributed it to providence. An old Methodist sister in St. Louis has very similar ideas of providential interference. Her husband, having made over to her all his property, then failed, and at every meeting was fervent in his prayers that providence might spare to his poor wife a sufficiency of live upon. The courts decided that she was entitled to about $130,000 of the property that her husband had cunningly made over to her. This she often mentioned as an answer to prayer. To the prayers of some poor women, whom her husband had defrauded out of small sums, she was not so lenient as providence, always turning a deaf ear to them.

JESSE'S PRESENT TO FORD.

By a singular fatality Jesse James was killed with a pistol that had been his own. It was presented to Bob Ford by Jesse, but a few days before his death.[3] A repetition of Achilles' present to Paris.

WHAT MRS. JAMES SAYS.

Mrs. James said, in speaking of their residence in Kansas City: Jesse used to get the papers regularly. When that train robbery was committed in Arkansas, he read it the next morning. He was charged by the papers with being connected with it. When he read it, he said he hoped the real robbers would be caught, and then the people would see that he was not connected with every robbery. When that was committed, we were living on Troost avenue, in this city. We had previously lived on Ninth street and Woodland avenue, and I remained one week at the Daggert House. Jesse wasn't with me, there, however. Kansas City was the safest place we could get into, for people would not suspect us living here. St. Joseph was a safe place also. We lived there nearly a year, and Jesse went all over the town. When we were living in

---

3In an affidavit printed in the Kansas City Times, May 6, 1882, Bob Ford stated the murder weapon was a .45 calibre Colt's revolver, serial number 50432.

Kansas City no one knew of our presence except my brother, who clerks in the city. My sister didn't even know it. Jesse used to often visit his mother. He told me after his return on one trip that he had gotten on the train at the bridge depot. When the conductor came along, he noticed that he had one finger off. Upon his coming back the second time, Jesse said he stopped him, and asked if he was not Jesse James, telling him that Jesse was minus a finger. When making these trips he was very prudent, and always careful to avoid officers.

A BROTHER-IN-LAW.

Mr. Bowling Browder, who keeps a hotel at Adairville, was next seen. He is a brother-in-law of Jesse James, they having married sisters.

"Well, I see my famous brother-in-law is dead," was his first salutation. "I could give you matter enough to fill your paper about the James boys, but I'd rather not say anything. I think Frank is the head and brains of the whole gang. He speaks French, German and Spanish, and is as fine a comedian as I ever saw. I have heard him say it was as much fun as he wanted to go into the city dressed up as a German, go and drink beer with them and talk their language. Next day he would assume a French dress, speak French with anybody who wanted to, and finally wind up his stay by taking in the sights as a Spaniard. Yes, I believe Jesse is dead."

COLE YOUNGER TALKS.

Cole Younger, the friend and former comrade of Jesse James, said, in speaking of Jesse's identification:

"That there would be no trouble about identifying the body, if it was Jesse, for—pointing to his right breast—he has a bullet wound here that would tell. He was shot twice in the same place, and was attended by Dr. Wood, of Kansas City.

"For six or eight months he was lying at Kansas City, hovering between life and death, and continued under the doctor's care for four or five years, until he went to California. In 1868 he lost

Frank James in 1865, at age 22.

In 1898, when Frank James was about 54 years old, he was enjoying domesticity, having been acquitted of all the charges made against him. He was popular wherever he went.

John Philips, attorney for Frank James at Gallatin trial.

THE JURY THAT CLEARED FRANK JAMES.

AT GALLATIN, MO., SEPTEMBER, 1883.

J. Snyder.   R. F. Feurt.   C. B. Nace.   Jas. E. Smith.   B. H. Shellman.   Wm. H Merritt.   Jason Winburn.   Oscar Chamberlain.
W. F. Richardson.   L. W. Gilreath.   E. K. Hale.   J. W. Boggs.

Frank James in 1898, at age 55. *Courtesy Edward Knowles, Topeka.*

the use of that lung, and consequently has but one, which would be revealed by a post mortem."

WAS FRANK JAMES THERE ?

Sheriff Timberlake, of Clay county, Mo., denied that Frank James was present at Jesse's funeral, and he also said that he is sure that he has not been in St. Joseph since the killing. The sheriff gives as his reason for this belief that Frank did not dare to go into civilized communities at the present time from the fact that he knew the officers were on his track. He also said that Frank did not know half the arrangements that had been made to effect his capture.

Sheriff Timberlake ought to be well posted and undoubtedly thinks he knows what he is talking about, but when he says that Frank James has not been in St. Joseph since the killing of his brother he is contradicted by men who know the outlaw personally, and who are positive that they have seen and talked to him during the time. The probability is that Timberlake is mistaken, for if two months ago some one had told him that Jesse James was in St. Joseph, the sheriff would have laughed, and with the same incredulity would have exclaimed, "nonsense." The fact of the matter is, *the sheriff does not know Frank when he sees him,* and is inclined to regard every story of his whereabouts as a lie, manufactured by the newspapers.

THE JAMES BROTHERS CONTRASTED.

There is a great contrast between these two men, Frank and Jesse James. Both were equally brave and determined men, but here all the resemblance ended. Jesse was fond of show and notoriety, while Frank shuns publicity and is not at all given to boasting. Jesse was reckless in exposing himself to detection and danger, while Frank is just the reverse; there were fully one hundred persons who knew Jesse to every one who knew Frank. Of the two Frank had naturally the worst disposition, but he had more intellect than Jesse and obtained over himself much better control than the latter ever had over his actions.

Frank was a wild, reckless fellow in 1866, when Jesse was a

member of the Baptist Church at old Centerville, as Kearney used to
be called. Many and fervent were the prayers that used to ascend
from the young convert for his older and more reckless brother;
in later years the conditions seemed to be greatly reversed, for
Frank had become the more settled of the two.

It is very doubtful if Frank was present at the Glendale robbery, and it is certain that he was not at Winston, or Blue Cut.
He has endeavored of late years to settle down to a life of peace
and rest.

Probably nothing goes to show the great influence of woman
more strongly than this wonderful change in the two brothers.
Marrying about the same time, Frank took to wife a woman
who, in addition to goodness, aimability and true Christianity,
possessed a noble disposition, and a firm, strong will. Her impulses
being all for good, her influence over her husband was entirely
salutary, and in consequence he could not but become a better
man.[3] Jesse, however, married a woman, who while amiable,
good and true to him in every sense of the word, yet possessed no
will of her own, and whose mind, weak, plastic and yielding, took
form from, rather than shaped that of her husband. To such a
mind as this, no matter how good, no strong effort is a possibility,
and it will sooner drift into the channels of excuse and justification
than to make a bold, strong stand against wrong. Those people and
journals do her injustice, however, when they declare that she
boldly apologized for and justified Jesse's crimes, and that she
could not sympathize with any other sufferings than her own.
She most certainly had sympathy for the victims of her husband's
crimes, and realized to its fullest extent the criminality of his
career, but hers was not a mind and soul of that heroic mould,
that could nobly and bravely battle against sin and crime, and
hate the sin while mayhap she loved the sinner. Tamely submitting, she accepted ready-made her creed and her apologies, always
hoping for deliverance. The Fords did not hesitate to say of her

[3]Frank married Annie Ralston, daughter of Samuel Ralston, in June, 1874.
Kansas City *Times*, May 30, 1882.

that she joined heartily in Jesse's schemes and enjoyed the recitals of his brutality; but of what worth is the testimony of such base assassins? No! weak and fond and foolish she may have been—no doubt was—but criminal never. Her destiny was linked to that of a dark and desperate outlaw, but let us believe that, like the galley-slave to the bench, so her bonds were those of loathing, at least so far as the crimes of her husband were concerned.

CHAPTER XLVIII.

VENGEANCE.

DOES REVENGE PAY?

"Vengeance is mine, saith the Lord, I will repay." Thus is man warned that it is not his province, but that of the Ruler of the Universe, to repay injuries with the punishment that they may deserve, or rather that we mortals may think they deserve, and experience has abundantly proven that the usurpation of this prerogative of the Almighty has always resulted disastrously, and always will, to any mortal who attempts it. Like the Carthaginians, who inscribed upon their banners as a rallying cry, "Revenge!" the individual who adopts this passion as his guide and director is sure to come to ill.

True, for a time he may succeed, even as Hannibal in his wonderful career of blood and battle pushed his armies to the very gates of Rome, only to fall back at last in ruin and defeat, and the proud city from which his triumphal armies had once issued crumbled beneath the awakened anger and military genius of Rome. *"Delenda est Carthago!"* was not the edict of the haughty Roman, but it was the inevitable decree of the Ancient of Days. It has been written, and it will be written of every people and of every individual, who dares to defy and attempt to set at naught the laws of the Almighty.

The subject of this work affords one of the strongest examples of this truth, that man may not with impunity disobey the commands of God. True he had suffered indignities, and it was only obeying the dictates of our fallible and corrupt natures to revenge the outrage upon them who had offered it; still, the gentle Saviour of men, who abrogated the stern law of Moses: "An eye for an eye, a life for a life," taught that it was meet to "return good for evil," and that when smitten upon one cheek to turn also the other to the smiter. The accursed tree at Calvary witnessed the apotheosis of this doctrine, when Christ, racked with torture and subjected to every humiliation that a brutal mob could offer, said even in his final agony: "Father, forgive them, for they know not what they do."

What years of sin and shame and remorse would this man have escaped, could he but have restrained his heated passion and obeyed the Divine command. What untold agonies of grief and uncertainty would he not have spared to all of those who loved him; mother, wife and friends.

There is but one safe rule in life and death, the Bible. There is but one infallible guide, teacher and example, Christ. There is but one law immutable, wise and merciful, the law of God. In these lie life and hope and happiness—and in these only.

COMPILER'S EPILOGUE.

To those who may feel disposed to criticise the literary merits of this work, I can only plead in excuse the hurried manner in which it was written, as the time devoted to the composition of it was less than three weeks; and even had the compiler been capable of turning out a book whose composition would have been above cavil, it can be easily seen and must be admitted that, under the circumstances stated, it would have been an impossibility in this case.

For more than a week from thirty to sixty pages of manuscript (making from twenty to forty printed pages) were furnished daily to the compositors. In this haste no time was given for any attempt at fine writing.

A great deal of time, too, was lost, owing to the necessity that existed for making the notes from the dictation of parties, who had but little idea of literary composition, and who detailed the occurring events, not in regular chronological order, but as they happened to think of them. The Mosaic artist is said to use dozens of shades in his delicate art, but these shades are arranged in classes and in so orderly a manner that he knows just where to find any shade desired at any time. Let his gems, or the little bits of stones with which he works, be thrown together and thoroughly mixed, and then fancy him making a picture, with all its varying shades and delicate tintings, from that confused mass of colors, and some idea of the difficulty experienced in the arrangement of the materials of this book may be imagined. A train robbery, a war incident and a midnight attack of Pinkerton's detectives form a combination, when the incidents of one are dovetailed into the account of another, that it requires some little patience, if not skill, to unravel and present accurately.

By persistent questioning and by carefully placing all the notes under their appropriate heads, already prepared, and then arranging these heads in chronological succession, the task was finally accomplished. Thus was not only a regular succession of events secured, but a wider range of facts obtained than could, by any other method, have been secured. Had, for instance, any certain train robbery been brought up and the most exhaustive questions asked, some information or some details would have failed of being elicited; but, by this plan, say a bank robbery was under consideration, and any fact in regard to a stage or train robbery was called out, that head was turned to and the incident carefully noted down under it, and then the examination into the bank robbery continued.

In this way, as has been said above, fuller and more accurate details have been obtained, and more reliable information secured, than could have been done by confining the relators systematically to any given subject. It is true that this method is by far the most troublesome to the compiler, but it secures infinitely better results, and ends in the production of a book not only fuller in details, but also in facts, as the incidents of one occurrence often, by some mental association, refresh the memory, or call to mind similar incidents of some entirely different action.

In regard to any seeming bias towards the outlaws, that this work may exhibit, I have only this excuse to offer: that to those who will take the pains to candidly investigate the history of the Jameses and Youngers, and the occurrences immediately after the war, some slight shadow of an excuse at least may be found for the commencement of their course, which led on by easy degrees to the commission of terrible crimes. The old poet says:

"Facilis est decensus Averni,"

and once in the grooves of crime, it is natural and easy for men to sink lower and lower, until there is no possibility of return or reform. Truly the downward path is made easier by every descending footstep, therefore the greatest of care should be taken by the courts and the authorities that none should ever be forced to take the first footsteps in crime.

Having been intimately acquainted with Nat Teague, Andy Idson, Hedge Reynolds and many others of Anderson's and Quantrell's guerrillas, I have often been able to secure information that to strangers was in no way obtainable. By this means soon after the robbery of the bank at Liberty I came into possession of a knowledge of the names of the parties participating in that affair. Although almost universally accused of it at first, and although even now many believe them to have been present, yet neither of the Jameses was there. The planner of the affair and the leader in it, the lieutenant of Anderson's mentioned, was Arch. Clements. The other parties engaged in it, with the exception of three brothers, whose last robbery it was, are mentioned in the account of that robbery.

Some may feel disposed to hold the compiler responsible for any favorable expression of opinion regarding the criminal career of these noted brothers, but this is manifestly unjust, as this work is not an expression of the opinions of the compiler, but of the mother and wife of the outlaw, who have dictated it, and who could hardly be expected to pass as severe judgment upon the life and actions of those so near and dear to them, as were the subjects of this sketch. There is no mother alive, who has the true love of a mother in her breast, but will still find excuses for her boy, and who, in spite of his sin and his shame, his crime and his degradation,

"Will still fondly love on to the close."

And it is best that it is so, for to that mother the crime-stained outlaw, his hands red with blood and his soul blackened with outrage, is still her boy; the child over whose cradle she has hung, and whose childish troubles and sorrows she has lulled into forgetfulness. The son may cease to be good, may cease to be loving, may cease almost to be human; but the mother is always a mother, and in her breast the fountain of maternal love gushes forth ever pure and free and flowing, despite the baleful fires of sin and the fierce anguish of sorrow. Who would have it otherwise?

The wife, too, cannot be expected to adopt the hard opinions of the world regarding the man she has sworn to love, honor and obey. True, he may not be deserving of her love, her worship, or her obedience; but if she has ever truly loved him, she will give him all. Probably no man alive ever merited the true, earnest love; the beautiful faith, and the unselfish worship of a loving woman, but the Infinite Wisdom has so created her that she gives it all freely to the husband of her love, though he may be base, unworthy, brutal. It is the very necessity of her existence that she shall look up to some one stronger, if not better, than herself; it is the breath of her life that she must give love and trust and truth where it is often unworthily received; but shall we cavil against the laws of nature; the edicts of the Almighty? No! while the world stands, that cry of woman's heart, old as creation, yet ever new; free as God's charity, yet confined to one man, will ever ring out:

> "I know not, I ask not, if guilt's in thy heart;
> I but know that I love thee, whatever thou art."

It need surprise no one that this work, dictated as it is by Mrs. James and Mrs. Samuel, should express greater leniency towards the actions and lives of these outlaws than is felt by others; in fact, it is perfectly natural that, while they do not approve of the crimes they may have committed, yet they would as far as possible shield the perpetrators from blame and reproach. Everything has been viewed as from their stand-point, and while their crimes have not been concealed, yet every favorable circumstance has been adduced. This only makes the book the more valuable, as every story having two sides to it, it is best that each should have a presentation. This being the only work, the information for which has been obtained from those parties, is the one which presents their side of the case, and is the only one that can be relied on for accuracy, as the wife and mother of the outlaw most certainly were the persons most capable of giving the information for, and dictating a true history of, these bandit brothers.

A short synopsis of their deeds during the war was deemed almost indispensable to show the school in which they grew from childhood to man's estate, and in it may be found much palliation for their earlier crimes.

To all classes of society, even to those who took no part in the horrors of the civil war, a certain amount of demoralization was brought, and robbery and murder have, even to this day, run riot in consequence. The public plunderer carried on his career in an almost shameless manner, and the taint of thievish conspiracy and whole-sale robbery has besmirched the robes of those highest in office in the country. The cashier embezzling the funds of his bank; the merchant defrauding his creditors; the lawyer betraying his client, were at one time almost the rule, and even now these spectacles are too common.

In this general anarchy of society, and this almost general trampling down and disregard of the principles of public and private decency and honesty, it is not greatly surprising that men, who had led the wild, irresponsible lives of the guerrillas should have devised and executed schemes of violence and robbery, no matter how inexcusable they might be.

The strictures on Crittenden's course are not felt to be too severe, for they are directed, not at Crittenden, the man, but at Crittenden, the Governor and the Lieutenant-Colonel. His course, whenever he has been entrusted with power and authority, prove him a man ignorant of law, yet pretending to be a lawyer; ignorant of the customs and usages of war, yet wearing the epaulets of a Lieutenant-Colonel. In both situations he has proved himself to be a tyrant; assuming dictatorial power, and overriding the laws of his country.

If such usurpations as his are allowed to go on unchecked, with the already too great tendency to centralization of power and one-man-government, who can predict the end? If he can, without trial, decree the death of an outlaw and procure his assassination, what are the guarantees of our Constitution worth?

A man may be a Democrat, or he may be a Republican, but above all he should be a patriot, and should endeavor to see that the rights and traditions of our Constitution and liberties of the citizen are handed down to the next generation, as we have received them from our fathers, pure and unsullied. No infringements of these liberties should be tolerated, lest dangerous customs and innovations creep in and deadly precedents be established.

The first small leak, in the dykes of Holland, if taken in time, may be stopped with a handful of clay; neglected, hour by hour it grows until at last it admits a sea, breaking down all barriers and sweeping everything before it.

The first inroads of tyranny may well be likened to that tiny breach, and in its train may also follow all the horrors of the fatal flood. To a free people, who would remain free, there is ever danger in the slightest innovation on their privileges, and even the smallest irregularities should be checked. No man should be allowed to hold in his hand the lives even of outlaws and murderers; no officer should be allowed to countenance or procure assassination, a crime common to the Latin nations, but almost, thank God! unknown to those of Anglo-Norman blood.

Of Crittenden, the man, knowing nothing, we have nothing to say; but of Crittenden, the officer and Governor, we claim the right, that belongs to every free born citizen, to criticise his acts as they may deserve. So far they have proved him a tyrant, unscrupulous in the exercise of usurped powers, and a man dangerous to the liberties of the people. Such men should never be entrusted with power; but if it is thought that their ignorance of law should excuse their crimes, then they should speedily be relegated to a private station, where such crimes and outrages may not bring disgrace upon a whole people, but may be confined in their effects to the perpetrator solely.

THE END.

SELECTED BIBLIOGRAPHY

MANUSCRIPTS

Mary P. Clark Collection, manuscript division, Kansas State Historical Society.

"A True Narrative by Sergeant Thomas M. Goodman," manuscript division, Kansas State Historical Society.

"Governors Correspondence, Thomas A. Osborn," archives department, Kansas State Historical Society.

NEWSPAPERS

Gallatin (Mo.) *North Missourian.*
Hays City (Kans.) *Sentinel.*
Jefferson City (Mo.) *Peoples Tribune.*
Kansas City (Mo.) *Daily Journal.*
Kansas City (Mo.) *Times.*
Leavenworth (Kans.) *Times.*
Liberty (Mo.) *Tribune.*
Little Rock (Ark.) *Gazette.*
St. Joseph (Mo.) *Daily Gazette.*
St. Joseph (Mo.) *Weekly Gazette.*
Wyandotte (Kans.) *Herald.*

ARTICLES

Breihan, Carl W., "The Death of Jesse James," *The Denver Westerners Brand Book* (1956).

——, "What Brought About Jesse James' Death?" *Frontier Times,* v. 38, no. 1 (January, 1964).

Burton, Jeffrey, "Attributed to the James Gang," *The English Westerners' Brand Book,* v. 6, no. 4 (April, 1964).

Chilcote, Merrill, "Jesse James; a Scoundrel and Martyr," *Museum Graphic,* v. 2, no. 2 (Spring, 1950).

Croy, Homer, "I Knew Jesse James' Mother," *True West,* v. 6, no. 5 (May-June, 1959).

Ghent, W. J., "Jesse James," *Dictionary of American Biography* (New York, Charles Scribner's Sons, 1932).

Hughes, Albert Hilliard, "Outlaw with a Halo," *Montana, the Magazine of Western History,* v. 17, no. 4 (October, 1967).

"The James Brothers," *History of Clay and Platte Counties, Missouri* (St. Louis, National Historical Company, 1885).

"Jesse James," *American Heritage,* v. 11, no. 5 (August, 1960).

Jesse James special issue, *Museum Graphic,* v. 9, no. 2 (Spring, 1957).

"Jim Cummins, 1847-1929," Kansas City (Mo.) *Star,* September 22, 1929.

Love, Robertus, "Rise and Fall of Jesse James," Kansas City (Mo.) *Star,* July 19, 26; September 13, 20, 1925.

Russell, Don, "Jesse James—Postwar Bandit," *The Westerners Brand Book* (Chicago, 1944).

Shouse, T. R., "Origin of Plan Which Resulted in Jesse James' Death," *Missouri Historical Review,* v. 34, no. 1 (October, 1939).

Starnes, Lee, "The Legend of Jesse James," *Museum Graphic,* v. 4, no. 2 (Spring, 1952).

Thorp, Raymond W., "Mr. Howard of Tennessee," *The Graphic,* v. 6, no. 2 (February, 1925).

"Was Jesse James Shot With Own Gun?" *Great Guns,* v. 2, no. 4 (April, 1953).

BOOKS

Adams, Ramon, *Burs Under the Saddle* (Norman, University of Oklahoma Press, 1964).

Appler, Augustus C., *The Guerrillas of the West; or the Life, Character, and Daring Exploits of the Younger Brothers* (St. Louis, Eureka Publishing Co., 1877).

Black, Hugh Edwin, *History of the Descendants of John and Susanna Cole* (no place, no publisher, 1962).

Breihan, Carl W., *The Complete and Authentic Life of Jesse James* (New York, Frederick Fell, 1954, rev. ed. 1969).

―――――――, *The Day Jesse James Was Killed* (New York, Frederick Fell, 1961).

Buel, J. W., *The Border Outlaws, the Younger Brothers, Jesse and Frank James, and Their Comrades in Crime* (St. Louis Dan. Linahan & Co., 1882).

Castel, Albert, *A Frontier State at War: Kansas, 1861-1865* (Ithaca, Cornell University Press, 1958).

Connelley, William Elsey, *Quantrill and the Border Wars* (Cedar Rapids, Iowa, The Torch Press, 1910).

Croy, Homer, *Jesse James was My Neighbor* (New York, Duell, Sloan and Pearce, 1949).

Dacus, Joseph A., *Life and Adventures of Frank and Jesse James, the Noted Western Outlaws* (St. Louis, N. D. Thompson & Co., 1880)

Donald, Jay, *Outlaws of the Border. A Complete and Authentic History of the Lives of Frank and Jesse James, The Younger Brothers, and Their Robber Companions* . . . (Chicago, Coburn & Newman Publishing Co., 1882).

Edwards, John N., *Noted Guerillas or the Warfare of the Border* (St. Louis, Bryan, Brand & Co., 1877).

Hamersly, Thomas H. S., *Complete Army and Navy Register* . . . (New York, T. H. S. Hamersly, 1888).

Heitman, Francis B., *Historical Register and Dictionary of the United States Army* . . . (Washington, Government Printing Office, 1903).

Howes, Wright, *U. S. Iana* (New York, R. R. Bowker, 1962).

James, Jesse, Jr., *The Facsimilie Edition of Jesse James, My Father, the First and Only True Story of His Adventures Ever Written* (New York, Frederick Fell, c. 1957).

Jesse James: the Life and Daring Adventures of this Bold Highwayman and Bank Robber . . . (Philadelphia, Barclay & Co. 1882).

Martin, Charles L., *A Sketch of Sam Bass, the Bandit* (Norman, University of Oklahoma Press, 1956).

Miller, George, Jr., *Trial of Frank James for Murder* (Columbia, Missouri, E. W. Stephens Publ. Co., 1898).

Miller, Nyle H. and Joseph W. Snell, *Great Gunfighters of the Kansas Cowtowns, 1867-1886* (Lincoln, University of Nebraska Press, 1967).

Official Army Register for 1865 (Washington, Adjutant General's Office, 1865).

Rosa, Joseph G., *They Called Him Wild Bill* (Norman, University of Oklahoma Press, 1964).

Settle, William A., *Jesse James Was His Name; or, Fact and Fiction Concerning the Careers of the Notorious James Brothers of Missouri* (Columbia, University of Missouri Press, 1966).

Thorndike, Thaddeus, *Lives and Exploits of the Daring Frank and Jesse James* (Baltimore, I. & M. Ottoheimer, c. 1909).

Wallace, *George Selden, Cabell County Annals and Families* (Richmond, Garrett & Massie, 1935).

The War of the Rebellion: A Compilation of the Official Records of Union and Confederate Armies (Washington, Government Printing Office, 1880-1903).

INDEX

340

Chamberlain, Oscar, *321*
Chambers, J. H. & Co., xi, xiii, 314
Chicago, Ill., 160, 164
Chicago, Rock Island and Pacific, train robbery of, 73, 74
Chiles, William, 28, 31
Clay, J., 232
Cleary, Michael, 190, 191
Cleary, Thomas, 190
Clements, Archibald J., 20, 330
Cole, Zerelda (see Zerelda Samuel)
Collins, Bradley, 165
Collins, Jim (see Joel Collins)
Collins, Joel, 165, 168, 173
Collins, Mattie, 197, 208, 232, 305
Columbia, Mo., bank robbery at, 61, 62
Conklin, A. R., 273
Coons, Mr., 169, 170
Corinth, Miss., bank robbery at, 120*n*3
Corydon, Iowa, bank robbery at, 59
Cotts, William, 165*n*3
Cox, S. P., 39-41
Crabtree, Officer, 298
Craig, Enos, 214*n*1, *234*
Craig, Henry H., xvi, 214, *215*, 219, 223, 230, 231, 235, 237, 239, 247, 257, 259, 295, 311; testimony at inquest, 242, 245, 246
Craig rifles, 219
Crittenden, Thomas T., xii, xiv*n*6, xvi, *210*, 213, 214, 219, 220, 222, 223, 230, 231, 235, 239, 245-247, 249, 251-254, 256-261, 263-275, 277, 285, 332, 333
Crump, George, 68
Culver, Lieutenant, 4
Cummings brothers, 187
Cummings, James Robert, 174, 176, 178, 181, 189, 190, 191, 195, 199-201, 205-209, 302
Curley, Sam, 50, 51
Curtis, Samuel R., 277

Dacus, Joseph A., xi, 54*n*2
Daniels, Edward B., 81; death of, 82
Davis, Jack, 165, 168, 172

Davis, Jo, 270
Densmore, L. W., 305
Dillon, J. W., 123, 124
Ditsch, Sergeant, 230
Doniphan & Read, attorneys, 247
Dunning, Mr., 144
Duval, Claude, 67

Edmunson, Hal, 63
Edmunson, Hub, 63
Edmunson, J. F., 28, 31
Edwards, John N., ix, x, xvi, 308-310

Ferguson, Champ, 63
Feurt, B. F., *321*
Finley, Deputy Marshal, testimony at James inquest, 242, 243
Fitzgerald, Dr., 3
Follinsbee, W. H., 270
Ford brothers, 174, 176, 181, 187, 195, 197, 205, 207, 208, 214, 219, 222, 223, 225, 230, 231, 233, 235, 309
Ford, Cap, 176, 178, 247
Ford, Charles Wilson, 176, 177, 180, 181, 195, 199-201, 206, 207, 209, 214, *217*, 221, 224, 236-238, 241, 242, 245-247, 249, 252-254, 256, 258-261, 267, 280, 295, 296, 300; testimony at James inquest, 237, 238
Ford, J. D., 281
Ford, Mrs., *218*
Ford, Robert Newton, xi, xiv*n*6, 176-178, 213, 214, *216*, 219, 222, 224-231, 237, 238, 241-247, 249, 252-254, 256, 258-261, 265-267, 280, 295, 296, 300, 316; testimony at James inquest, 238, 239
Fort Scott, Kans., 131
Foster, Emory S., 273
Fox, Henry, 203, 204

Gad Hill, Mo., train robbery at, 77, 78
Gallatin, Mo., bank robbery at, x, 41
Garcia, Juan, 111-113
Garcia, Pedro, 111-113
Gaston, George, 299

344